MW01233440

# St. Paul's Epistle to the Romans

A. Maclaren

# EXPOSITIONS OF HOLY SCRIPTURE

# Expositions of Holy Scripture

A Commentary on the Entire Bible,
to be Completed in Thirty Volumes

## ALEXANDER MACLAREN, D.D., LIT.D.

To be published in series of six large
octavo volumes, magnificently bound in
red buckram cloth, printed in special
type of unique and beautiful face, and
on specially imported English feather-
weight paper.

**D**R. ALEXANDER MACLAREN's incomparable position as the prince of expositors has for more than a generation been recognized throughout the English-speaking world. He holds an unchallenged position, and it it is believed that this series, embodying as it does the treasure store of DR. MACLAREN's life-work, will be found of priceless value by preachers, teachers, and readers of the bible generally.

| What Ministers say of Dr. Maclaren | What the Press says of Dr. Maclaren |
|---|---|
| THEODORE L. CUYLER, D.D.: "Alexander Maclaren is the King of Preachers." | "These volumes are a treasury of thought for preachers, Sunday-school teachers and all who study the scriptures for a practical purpose."—*The Outlook*, New York. |
| W. ROBERTSON NICOLL, D.D., LL.D.: "He is the Prince of Expositors." | |
| DONALD SAGE MACKAY, D.D.: "The present idea of gathering the cream of Dr. Maclaren's expository genius from Genesis to Revelation is a fitting climax to his splendid contributions to scripture exposition." | "Unless we are very much mistaken 'Expositions of Holy Scripture' will have a permanent place in the library, of every thoughtful minister and layman."—*The British Weekly*, London, England. |
| MARCUS DODS, D.D.: "Dr. Maclaren is one of those exceptional men who can afford to print all they utter. Spiritual wisdom, sound and lucid exposition, apt and picturesque illustrations." | "Taken all in all 'Expositions of Holy Scripture' equal if not exceed in value for ministers any similar body of production —ancient or modern."—*The Observer*, New York. |

## SOLD ONLY IN SERIES OF SIX VOLUMES
### $7.50 net

FIRST SERIES, SIX VOLUMES

GENESIS    ISAIAH    JEREMIAH    ST. MATTHEW (3 vols.)

SECOND SERIES, SIX VOLUMES

EXODUS, LEVITICUS AND NUMBERS    DEUTERONOMY, JOSHUA
JUDGES AND RUTH    1ST AND 2D SAMUEL    1ST AND 2D KINGS
ST. MARK (2 vols.)    ACTS (1st vol.)

THIRD SERIES, SIX VOLUMES:

ACTS, VOL. 2    ST. JOHN, VOLS. 1, 2, 3
SECOND BOOK OF KINGS, from Chap. 7.    CHRONICLES, EZRA
NEHEMIAH    ESTHER    JOB    PROVERBS    ECCLESIASTES

FOURTH SERIES, SIX VOLUMES

PSALMS (2 vols.)    ST. LUKE (2 vols.)
EZEKIEL, DANIEL AND THE MINOR PROPHETS    ROMANS

# ST. PAUL'S EPISTLE TO THE

# ROMANS

BY

## ALEXANDER MACLAREN

D.D., Litt.D.

NEW YORK

## A. C. ARMSTRONG AND SON

3 & 5 WEST EIGHTEENTH STREET

LONDON: HODDER AND STOUGHTON

MCMIX

# CONTENTS

# CONTENTS

vii

# THE WITNESS OF THE RESURRECTION

'Declared to be the Son of God with power, . . . by the resurrection of the dead.'—ROMANS L 4 (R.V.).

IT is a great mistake to treat Paul's writings, and especially this Epistle, as mere theology. They are the transcript of his life's experience. As has been well said, the gospel of Paul is an interpretation of the significance of the life and work of Jesus based upon the revelation to him of Jesus as the risen Christ. He believed that he had seen Jesus on the road to Damascus, and it was that appearance which revolutionised his life, turned him from a persecutor into a disciple, and united him with the Apostles as ordained to be a witness with them of the Resurrection. To them all the Resurrection of Jesus was first of all a historical fact appreciated chiefly in its bearing on Him. By degrees they discerned that so transcendent a fact bore in itself a revelation of what would become the experience of all His followers beyond the grave, and a symbol of the present life possible for them. All three of these aspects are plainly declared in Paul's writings. In our text it is chiefly the first which is made prominent. All that distinguishes Christianity, and makes it worth believing, or mighty, is inseparably connected with the Resurrection.

I. The Resurrection of Christ declares His Sonship.

Resurrection and Ascension are inseparably connected. Jesus does not rise to share again in the ills and

A

weariness of humanity. Risen, 'He dieth no more; death hath no more dominion over Him.' 'He died unto sin once'; and His risen humanity had nothing in it on which physical death could lay hold. That He should from some secluded dimple on Olivet ascend before the gazing disciples until the bright cloud, which was the symbol of the Divine Presence, received Him out of their sight, was but the end of the process which began unseen in morning twilight. He laid aside the garments of the grave and passed out of the sepulchre which was made sure by the great stone rolled against its mouth. The grand avowal of faith in His Resurrection loses meaning, unless it is completed as Paul completed his 'yea rather that was raised from the dead,' with the triumphant 'who is at the right hand of God.' Both are supernatural, and the Virgin Birth corresponds at the beginning to the supernatural Resurrection and Ascension at the close. Both such an entrance into the world and such a departure from it, proclaim at once His true humanity, and that 'this is the Son of God.'

Still further, the Resurrection is God's solemn 'Amen' to the tremendous claims which Christ had made. The fact of His Resurrection, indeed, would not declare His divinity; but the Resurrection of One who had spoken such words does. If the Cross and a nameless grave had been the end, what a *reductio ad absurdum* that would have been to the claims of Jesus to have ever been with the Father and to be doing always the things that pleased Him. The Resurrection is God's last and loudest proclamation, 'This is My beloved Son: hear ye Him.' The Psalmist of old had learned to trust that his sonship and consecration to the Father made it impossible that that Father should leave his soul in

Sheol, or suffer one who was knit to Him by such sacred bonds to see corruption; and the unique Sonship and perfect self-consecration of Jesus went down into the grave in the assured confidence, as He Himself declared, that the third day He would rise again. The old alternative seems to retain all its sharp points: Either Christ rose again from the dead, or His claims are a series of blasphemous arrogances and His character irremediably stained.

But we may also remember that Scripture not only represents Christ's Resurrection as a divine act but also as the act of Christ's own power. In His earthly life He asserted that His relation both to physical death and to resurrection was an entirely unique one. 'I have power,' said He, 'to lay down my life, and I have power to take it again'; and yet, even in this tremendous instance of self-assertion, He remains the obedient Son, for He goes on to say, 'This commandment have I received of My Father.' If these claims are just, then it is vain to stumble at the miracles which Jesus did in His earthly life. If He could strip it off and resume it, then obviously it was not a life like other men's. The whole phenomenon is supernatural, and we shall not be in the true position to understand and appreciate it and Him until, like the doubting Thomas, we fall at the feet of the risen Son, and breathe out loyalty and worship in that rapturous exclamation, 'My Lord and my God.'

II. The Resurrection interprets Christ's Death.

There is no more striking contrast than that between the absolute non-receptivity of the disciples in regard to all Christ's plain teachings about His death and their clear perception after Pentecost of the mighty power that lay in it. The very fact that they continued

disciples at all, and that there continued to be such a
community as the Church, demands their belief in the
Resurrection as the only cause which can account for it.
If He did not rise from the dead, and if His followers
did not know that He did so by the plainest teachings of
common-sense, they ought to have scattered, and borne
in isolated hearts the bitter memories of disappointed
hopes; for if He lay in a nameless grave, and they were
not sure that He was risen from the dead, His death
would have been a conclusive showing up of the falsity
of His claims.   In it there would have been no atoning
power, no triumph over sin.   If the death of Christ
were not followed by His Resurrection and Ascension,
the whole fabric of Christianity falls to pieces.  As the
Apostle puts it in his great chapter on resurrection,
'Ye are yet in your sins.'  The forgiveness which the
Gospel holds forth to men does not depend on the
mercy of God or on the mere penitence of man, but
upon the offering of the one sacrifice for sins in His
death, which is justified by His Resurrection as being
accepted by God.   If we cannot triumphantly proclaim 'Christ is risen indeed,' we have nothing worth
preaching.

We are told now that the ethics of Christianity are
its vital centre, which will stand out more plainly
when purified from these mystical doctrines of a Death
as the sin-offering for the world, and a Resurrection as
the great token that that offering avails.   Paul did not
think so.   To him the morality of the Gospel was all
deduced from the life of Christ the Son of God as our
Example, and from His death for us which touches men's
hearts and makes obedience to Him our joyful answer
to what He has done for us.  Christianity is a new thing
in the world, not as moral teaching, but as moral power

to obey that teaching, and that depends on the Cross interpreted by the Resurrection.   If we have only a dead Christ, we have not a living Christianity.

III. Resurrection points onwards to Christ's coming again.

Paul at Athens declared in the hearing of supercilious Greek philosophers, that the Jesus, whom he proclaimed to them, was 'the Man whom God had ordained to judge the world in righteousness,' and that 'He had given assurance thereof unto all men, in that He raised Him from the dead.'   The Resurrection was the beginning of the process which, from the human point of view, culminated in the Ascension.   Beyond the Ascension stretches the supernatural life of the glorified Son of God.   Olivet cannot be the end, and the words of the two men in white apparel who stood amongst the little group of the upward gazing friends, remain as the hope of the Church: 'This same Jesus shall so come in like manner as ye have seen Him go into heaven.'   That great assurance implies a visible corporeal return locally defined, and having for its purpose to complete the work which Incarnation, Death, Resurrection, and Ascension, each advanced a stage. The Resurrection is the corner-stone of the whole Christian faith.   It seals the truths that Jesus is the Son of God with power, that He died for us, that He has ascended on high to prepare a place for us, that He will come again and take us to Himself.   If we, by faith in Him, take for ours the women's greeting on that Easter morning, 'The Lord hath risen indeed,' He will come to us with His own greeting, 'Peace be unto you.'

# PRIVILEGE AND OBLIGATION

'To all that be in Rome, beloved of God, called to be saints.'—ROMANS i. 7.

THIS is the address of the Epistle. The first thing to be noticed about it, by way of introduction, is the universality of this designation of Christians. Paul had never been in Rome, and knew very little about the religious stature of the converts there. But he has no hesitation in declaring that they are all 'beloved of God' and 'saints.' There were plenty of imperfect Christians amongst them; many things to rebuke; much deadness, coldness, inconsistency, and yet none of these in the slightest degree interfered with the application of these great designations to them. So, then, 'beloved of God' and 'saints' are not distinctions of classes within the pale of Christianity, but belong to the whole community, and to each member of the body.

The next thing to note, I think, is how these two great terms, 'beloved of God' and 'saints,' cover almost the whole ground of the Christian life. They are connected with each other very closely, as I shall have occasion to show presently, but in the meantime it may be sufficient to mark how the one carries us deep into the heart of God and the other extends over the whole ground of our relation to Him. The one is a statement of a universal prerogative, the other an enforcement of a universal obligation. Let us look, then, at these two points, the universal privilege and the universal obligation of the Christian life.

I. The universal privilege of the Christian life.

6

'Beloved of God.' Now we are so familiar with the juxtaposition of the two ideas, 'love' and 'God,' that we cease to feel the wonderfulness of their union. But until Jesus Christ had done His work no man believed that the two thoughts could be brought together.

Does God love any one? We think the question too plain to need to be put, and the answer instinctive. But it is not by any means instinctive, and the fact is that until Christ answered it for us, the world stood dumb before the question that its own heart raised, and when tortured spirits asked, 'Is there care in heaven, and is there love?' there was 'no voice, nor answer, nor any that regarded.' Think of the facts of life; think of the facts of nature. Think of sorrows and miseries and pains, and sins, and wasted lives and storms, and tempests, and diseases, and convulsions; and let us feel how true the grim saying is, that

> 'Nature, red in tooth and claw,
> With rapine, shrieks against the creed'

that God is love.

And think of what the world has worshipped, and of all the varieties of monstrosity, not the less monstrous because sometimes beautiful, before which men have bowed. Cruel, lustful, rapacious, capricious, selfish, indifferent deities they have adored. And then, 'God hath established,' proved, demonstrated 'His love to us in that while we were yet sinners Christ died for us.'

Oh, brethren, do not let us kick down the ladder by which we have climbed; or, in the name of a loving God, put away the Christian teaching which has begotten the conception in humanity of a God that loves. There are men to-day who would never have come within sight of that sunlight truth, even as a glimmering star, away down upon the horizon, if it had not been for the Gospel; and who now turn round upon that very Gospel which has given them the conception, and accuse it of narrow and hard thoughts of the love of God.

One of the. Scripture truths against which the assailant often turns his sharpest weapons is that which is involved in my text, the Scripture answer to the other question, 'Does not God love all?' Yes! yes! a thousand times, yes! But there is another question, Does the love of God, to all, make His special designation of Christian men as His beloved the least unlikely? Surely there is no kind of contradiction between the broadest proclamation of the universality of the love of God and Paul's decisive declaration that, in a very deep and real manner, they who are in Christ are the beloved of God. Surely special affection is not in its nature, inconsistent with universal beneficence and benevolence. Surely it is no exaltation, but rather a degradation of the conception of the divine love, if we proclaim its utter indifference to men's characters. Surely you are not honouring God when you say, 'It is all the same to Him whether a man loves Him and serves Him, or lifts himself up in rebellion against Him, and makes himself his own centre, and earth his aim and his all.' Surely to imagine a God who not only makes His sun to shine and His rains and dews to fall on the unthankful and the evil, that He may draw them to love Him, but who also is conceived as taking the sinful creature who yet cleaves to his sins to His heart, as He does the penitent soul that longs for His image to be produced in it, is to blaspheme, and not to honour the love, the universal love of God.

God forbid that any words that ever drop from my lips should seem to cast the smallest shadow of doubt on that great truth, 'God so loved the world that He gave His Son!' But God forbid, equally, that any words of mine should seem to favour the, to me, repellent idea that the infinite love of God disregards the character of the man on whom it falls. There are manifestations of that loving heart which any man can receive; and each man gets as much of the love of God as it is possible to pour upon him. But granite rock does not drink in the dew as a flower does; and the nature of the man on whom God's love falls determines how much, and what manner of its manifestations shall pass into his true possession, and what shall remain without.

So, on the whole, we have to answer the questions, 'Does God love any? Does not God love all? Does God specially love some?' with the one monosyllable, 'Yes.

And so, dear brethren, let us learn the path by which we can pass into that blessed community of those on whom the fullness and sweetness and tenderest tenderness of the Father's heart will fall. 'If a man love Me, he will keep My words; and My Father will love him.' Myths tell us that the light which, at the beginning, had been diffused through a nebulous mass, was next gathered into a sun. So the universal love of God is concentrated in Jesus Christ; and if we have Him we have it; and if we have faith we have Him, and can say, 'Neither life, nor death, nor things present, nor things to come, nor height, nor depth, nor any other creature shall be able to separate us from the love of God which is in Christ Jesus our Lord.'

II. Then, secondly, mark the universal obligation of the Christian life.

'Called to be saints,' says my text. Now you will
observe that the two little words 'to be' are inserted
here as a supplement. They may be correct enough, but
they are open to the possibility of misunderstanding,
as if the saintship, to which all Christian people are
'called,' was something future, and not realised at the
moment. Now, in the context, the Apostle employs the
same form of expression with regard to himself in a
clause which illuminates the meaning of my text.
'Paul, a servant of Jesus Christ,' says he, in the first
verse, 'called to be an Apostle,' or, more correctly, 'a
called Apostle.' The apostleship coincided in time with
the call, was contemporaneous with that which was its
cause. And if Paul was an Apostle since he was called,
saints are saints since *they* are called. 'The beloved of
God' are 'the called saints.'

I need only observe, further, that the word 'called'
here does not mean 'named,' or 'designated,' but
'summoned.' It describes not the name by which
Christian men are known, but the thing which they are
invited, summoned, 'called' by God to be. It is their
vocation, not their designation. Now, then, I need not,
I suppose, remind you that 'saint' and 'holy' convey
precisely the same idea: the one expressing it in a
word of Teutonic, and the other in one of classic
derivation.

We notice that the true idea of this universal holiness which, *ipso facto*, belongs to all Christian people,
is consecration to God. In the old days temple, altars,
sacrifices, sacrificial vessels, persons such as priests,
periods like Sabbaths and feasts, were called 'holy.'
The common idea running through all these uses of the
word is *belonging to God*, and that is the root notion
of the New Testament 'saint,' a man who is God's.

God has claimed us for Himself when He gave us Jesus Christ. We respond to the claim when we accept Christ. Henceforth we are not our own, but 'consecrated'—that is, 'saints.'

Now the next step is purity, which is the ordinary idea of sanctity. Purity will follow consecration, and would not be worth much without it, even if it was possible to be attained. Now, look what a far deeper and nobler idea of the service and conditions of moral goodness this derivation of it from surrender to God gives, than does a God-ignoring morality which talks and talks about acts and dispositions, and never goes down to the root of the whole matter; and how much nobler it is than a shallow religion which in like manner is ever straining after acts of righteousness, and forgets that in order to be right there must be prior surrender to God. Get a man to yield himself up to God and no fear about the righteousness. Virtue, goodness, purity, righteousness, all these synonyms express very noble things; but deep down below them all lies the New Testament idea of holiness, consecration of myself to God, which is the parent of them all.

And then the next thing to remind you of is that this consecration is to be applied all through a man's nature. Yielding yourselves to God is the talismanic secret of all righteousness, as I have said; and every part of our complex, manifold being is capable of such consecration. I hallow my heart if its love twines round His heart. I hallow my thoughts if I take His truth for my guide, and ever seek to be led thereby in practice and in belief. I hallow my will when it bows and says, 'Speak, Lord! Thy servant heareth!' I hallow my senses when I use them as from Him, with recognition of Him and for Him. In fact, there are

two ways of living in the world; and, narrow as it
sounds, I venture to say there are only two. Either
God is my centre, and that is holiness; or self is my
centre, in more or less subtle forms, and that is sin.

Then the next step is that this consecration, which
will issue in all purity, and will cover the whole ground
of a human life, is only possible when we have drunk
in the blessed thought 'beloved of God.' My yielding
of myself to Him can only be the echo of His giving of
Himself to me. He must be the first to love. You cannot
argue a man into loving God, any more than you can
hammer a rosebud open. If you do you spoil its petals.
But He can love us into loving Him, and the sunshine,
falling on the closed flower, will expand it, and it will
grow by its reception of the light, and grow sunlike
in its measure and according to its nature. So a God
who has only claims upon us will never be a God to
whom we yield ourselves. A God who has love for us
will be a God to whom it is blessed that we should be
consecrated, and so saints.

Then, still further, this consecration, thus built upon
the reception of the divine love, and influencing our
whole nature, and leading to all purity, is a universal
characteristic of Christians. There is no faith which
does not lead to surrender. There is no aristocracy in
the Christian Church which deserves to have the family
name given especially to it. 'Saint' this, and 'Saint'
that, and 'Saint' the other—these titles cannot be used
without darkening the truth that this honour and
obligation of being saints belong equally to all that
love Jesus Christ. All the men whom thus God has
drawn to Himself, by His love in His Son, they are all,
if I may so say, objectively holy; they belong to God.
But consecration may be cultivated, and must be culti-

vated and increased.  There is a solemn obligation laid upon every one of us who call ourselves Christians, to be·saints, in the sense that we have consciously yielded up our whole lives to Him ; and are' trying, body, soul, and spirit, 'to perfect holiness in the fear of the Lord.'

Paul's letter, addressed to the 'beloved in God,' the 'called saints' that are in Rome, found its way to the people for whom it was meant.  If a letter so addressed were dropped in our streets, do you think anybody would bring it to you, or to any Christian society as a whole, recognising that we were the people for whom it was meant ?  The world has taunted us often enough with the name of saints ; and laughed at the profession which they thought was included in the word.  Would that their taunts had been undeserved, and that it were not true that 'saints' in the Church sometimes means less than ' good men ' out of the Church!  'Seeing that we have these promises, dearly beloved, let us cleanse ourselves from all filthiness of flesh and spirit ; perfecting holiness in the fear of the Lord.'

## PAUL'S LONGING[1]

'I long to see you, that I may impart unto you some spiritual gift, to the end ye may be established ; 12. That is, that I may be comforted together with you, by the mutual faith both of you and me.'—ROMANS i. 11, 12.

I AM not wont to indulge in personal references in the pulpit, but I cannot but yield to the impulse to make an exception now, and to let our happy circumstances mould my remarks.  I speak mainly to mine own people, and I must trust that other friends who may hear or read my words will forgive my doing so.

[1] Preached after long absence on account of illness.

In taking such a text as this, I desire to shelter myself behind Paul, and in expounding his feelings to
express my own, and to draw such lessons as may be
helpful and profitable to us all. And so there are
three things in this text that I desire to note: the
manly expression of Christian affection; the lofty
consciousness of the purpose of their meeting; and
the lowly sense that there was much to be received
as well as much to be given. A word or two about
each of these things is all on which I can venture.

I. First, then, notice the manly expression of
Christian affection which the Apostle allows himself
here.

Very few Christian teachers could or should venture
to talk so much about themselves as Paul did. The
strong infusion of the personal element in all his
letters is so transparently simple, so obviously sincere,
so free from any jarring note of affectation or unc-
tuous sentiment that it attracts rather than repels.
If I might venture upon a paradox, his personal
references are instances of self-oblivion in the midst
of self-consciousness.

He had never been in Rome when he wrote these
words; he had no personal relations with the believers there; he had never looked them in the
face; there were no sympathy and confidence between
them, as the growth of years. But still his heart went
out towards them, and he was not ashamed to show
it. 'I *long* to see you,'—in the original the word
expresses a very intense amount of yearning blended
with something of regret that he had been so long
kept from them.

Now it is not a good thing for people to make many
professions of affection, and I think a public teacher

has something better to do than to parade such feelings before his audiences. But there are exceptions to all rules, and I suppose I may venture to let my heart speak, and to say how gladly I come back to the old place, dear to me by so many sacred memories and associations, and how gladly I reknit the bonds of an affection which has been unbroken, and deepening on both sides through thirty long years.

Dear friends! let us together thank God to-day if He has knit our hearts together in mutual affection; and if you and I can look each other, as I believe we can, in the eyes, with the assurance that I see only the faces of friends, and that you see the face of one who gladly resumes the old work and associations.

But now, dear brethren, let us draw one lesson. Unless there be this manly, honest, though oftenest silent, Christian affection, the sooner you and I part the better. Unless it be in my heart I can do you no good. No man ever touched another with the sweet constraining forces that lie in Christ's Gospel unless the heart of the speaker went out to grapple the hearts of the hearers. And no audience ever listen with any profit to a man when they come in the spirit of carping criticism, or of cold admiration, or of stolid indifference. There must be for this simple relationship which alone binds a Nonconformist preacher to his congregation, as a *sine qua non* of all higher things and of all spiritual good, a real, though oftenest it be a concealed, mutual affection and regard. We have to thank God for much of it; let us try to get more. That is all I want to say about the first point here.

II. Note the lofty consciousness of the purpose of their meeting.

'I long to see you, that I may impart unto you some spiritual gift.'  Paul knew that he had something which he could give to these people, and he calls it by a very comprehensive term, 'some spiritual gift'—a gift of some sort which, coming from the Divine Spirit, was to be received into the human spirit.

Now that expression—a spiritual gift—in the New Testament has a variety of applications.  Sometimes it refers to what we call miraculous endowments, sometimes it refers to what we may call official capacity; but here it is evidently neither the one nor the other of these more limited and special things, but the general idea of a divine operation upon the human spirit which fills it with Christian graces—knowledge, faith, love.   Or, in simpler words, what Paul wanted to give them was a firmer grasp and fuller possession of Jesus Christ, His love and power, which would secure a deepening and strengthening of their whole Christian life.   He was quite sure he had this to give, and that he could impart it, if they would listen to what he would say to them.   But whilst thus he rises into the lofty conception of the purpose and possible result of his meeting the Roman Christians, he is just as conscious of the limitations of his power in the matter as he is of the greatness of his function. These are indicated plainly.   The word which he employs here, 'gift,' is never used in the New Testament for a thing that one man can give to another, but is always employed for the concrete results of the grace of God bestowed upon men.  The very expression, then, shows that Paul thought of himself, not as the original giver, but simply as a channel through which was communicated what God had given.  In the same direction points the adjective which accompanies the

noun—a '*spiritual* gift'—which probably describes the
origin of the gift as being the Spirit of God, rather
than defines the seat of it when received as being the
spirit of the receiver. Notice, too, as bearing on the
limits of Paul's part in the gift, the propriety and
delicacy of the language in his statement of the
ultimate purpose of the gift. He does not say 'that
I may strengthen you,' which might have sounded
too egotistical, and would have assumed too much to
himself, but he says 'that ye may be strengthened,'
for the true strengthener is not Paul, but the Spirit of
God.

So, on the one hand, the Christian teacher is bound
to rise to the height of the consciousness of his lofty
vocation as having in possession a gift that he can
bestow; on the other hand, he is bound ever to
remember the limitations within which that is true—
viz. that the gift is not his, but God's, and that the
Spirit of the Lord is the true Giver of all the graces
which may blossom when His word, ministered by
human agents, is received into human hearts.

And, now, what are the lessons that I take from this?
Two very simple ones. First, no Christian teacher has
any business to open his mouth, unless he is sure that
he has received something to impart to men as a gift
from the Divine Spirit. To preach our doubts, to preach
our own opinions, to preach poor platitudes, to talk
about politics and morals and taste and literature and
the like in the pulpit, is profanation and blasphemy.
Let no man open his lips unless he can say: 'The Lord
hath showed me this; and this I bring to you as His
word.' Nor has a Christian organisation any right
to exist, unless it recognises the communication and
reception and further spreading of this spiritual gift

as its great function. Churches which have lost that
consciousness, and, instead of a divine gift, have little
more to offer than formal worship, or music, or
entertainments, or mere intellectual discourse, whether
orthodox or 'advanced,' have no right to be; and by
the law of the survival of the fittest will not long
be. The one thing that warrants such a relationship
as subsists between you and me is this, my consciousness that I have a message from God, and your belief
that you hear such from my lips. Unless that be our
bond the sooner these walls crumble, and this voice
ceases, and these pews are emptied, the better. 'I
have,' says, Paul, 'a gift to impart; and I long to
see you that I may impart it to you.' Oh! for more,
in all our pulpits, of that burdened consciousness of a
divine message which needs the relief of speech, and
longs with a longing caught from Christ to impart its
richest treasures.

That is the one lesson. And the other one is this.
Have you, dear friends, received the gift that I have,
under the limitations already spoken of, to bestow?
There are some of you who have listened to my voice
ever since you were children—some of you, though
not many, have heard it for well on to thirty years.
Have you taken the thing that all these years I have
been—God knows how poorly, but God knows how
honestly—trying to bring to you? That is, have you
taken Christ, and have you faith in Him? And, as
for those of you who say that you are Christians, many
blessings have passed between you and me through
all these years; but, dear friends, has the chief blessing
been attained? Are you being strengthened day by
day for the burdens and the annoyances and the
sorrows of life by your coming here? Do I do you

any good in that way; are you better men than when we first met together? Is Christ dearer, and more real and nearer to you; and are your lives more transparently consecrated, more manifestly the result of a hidden union with Him? Do you walk in the world like the Master, because you are members of this congregation? If so, its purpose has been accomplished. If not, it has miserably failed.

I have said that I have to thank God for the unbroken affection that has knit us together. But what is the use of such love if it does not lead onwards to this? I have had enough, and more than enough, of what you call popularity and appreciation, undeserved enough, but rendered unstintedly by you. I do not care the snap of a finger for it by comparison with this other thing. And oh, dear brethren! if all that comes of our meeting here Sunday after Sunday is either praise or criticism of my poor words and ways, our relationship is a curse, and not a blessing, and we come together for the worse and not for the better. The purpose of the Church, and the purpose of the ministry, and the meaning of our assembling are, that spiritual gifts may be imparted, not by me alone, but by you, too, and by me in my place and measure, and if that purpose be not accomplished, all other purposes, that are accomplished, are of no account, and worse than nothing.

III. And now, lastly, note the lowly consciousness that much was to be received as well as much to be given.

The Apostle corrects himself after he has said 'that I may impart unto you some spiritual gift,' by adding, 'that is, that I may be comforted (or rather, encouraged) together with you by the mutual faith both

of you and me.' If his language were not so transparently sincere, and springing from deep interest in
the relationship between himself and these people, we
should say that it was exquisite courtesy and beautiful
delicacy. But it moves in a region far more real than
the region of courtesy, and it speaks the inmost truth
about the conditions on which the Roman Christians
should receive—viz. that they should also give. There
is only one Giver who is only a Giver, and that is
God. All other givers are also receivers. Paul desired
to see his Roman brethren that he might be encouraged; and when he did see them, as he marched
along the Appian Way, a shipwrecked prisoner, the
Acts of the Apostles tells us, 'He thanked God and
took courage.' The sight of them strengthened him
and prepared him for what lay before him.

Paul's was a richly complicated nature—firm as a
rock in its will, tremulously sensitive in its sympathies; like some strongly-rooted tree with its stable
stem and a green cloud of fluttering foliage that
moves in the lightest air. So his spirit rose and fell
according to the reception that he met from his
brethren, and the manifestation of their faith quickened and strengthened his.

And he is but one instance of a universal law. All
teachers, the more genuine they are, the more sympathetic they are, are the more sensitive of their environment. The very oratorical temperament places a
man at the mercy of surroundings. All earnest work
has ever travelling with it as its shadow seasons of
deep depression; and the Christian teacher does not
escape these. I am not going to speak about myself,
but this is unquestionably true, that every Elijah, after
the mightiest effort of prophecy, is apt to cover his

head in his mantle and to say, 'Take me away; I am
not better than my fathers.' And when a man for thirty
years, amidst all the changes incident to a great city
congregation in that time, has to stand up Sunday after
Sunday before the same people, and mark how some
of them are stolidly indifferent, and note how others
are dropping away from their faithfulness, and see
empty places where loving forms used to sit—no
wonder that the mood comes ever and anon, 'Then,
said I, surely I have laboured in vain and spent my
strength for nought.' The hearer reacts on the speaker
quite as much as the speaker does on the hearer. If
you have ice in the pews, that brings down the temperature up here. It is hard to be fervid amidst
people that are all but dead. It is difficult to keep
a fire alight when it is kindled on the top of an iceberg. And the unbelief and low-toned religion of a
congregation are always pulling down the faith and the
fervour of their minister, if he be better and holier,
as they expect him to be, than they are.

'He did not many works because of their unbelief.'
Christ knew the hampering and the restrictions of
His power which came from being surrounded by a
chill, unsympathetic environment. My strength and
my weakness are largely due to you. And if you
want your minister to preach better, and in all ways
to do his work more joyfully and faithfully, the means
lie largely in your own hands. Icy indifference, ill-
natured interpretations, carping criticisms, swift forgetfulness of one's words, all these things kill the
fervour of the pulpit.

On the other hand, the true encouragement to give
a man when he is trying to do God's will, to preach
Christ's Gospel, is not to pat him on the back and say,

'What a remarkable sermon that was of yours! what a genius! what an orator!' not to go about praising it, but to come and say, 'Thy words have led me to Christ, and from thee I have taken the gift of gifts.'

Dear brethren, the encouragement of the minister is in the conversion and the growth of the hearers. And I pray that in this new lease of united fellowship which we have taken out, be it longer or shorter—and advancing years tell me that at the longest it must be comparatively short—I may come to you ever more and more with the lofty and humbling consciousness that I have a message which Christ has given to me, and that you may come more and more receptive—not of *my* words, God forbid—but of Christ's truth; and that so we may be helpers one of another, and encourage each other in the warfare and work to which we all are called and consecrated.

## DEBTORS TO ALL MEN

'I am a debtor both to the Greeks and to the Barbarians, both to the wise and to the unwise.'—ROMANS i. 14.

No doubt Paul is here referring to the special obligation laid upon him by his divine call to be the Apostle to the Gentiles. He was entrusted with the Gospel as a steward, and was therefore bound to carry it to all sorts and conditions of men. But the principle underlying the statement applies to all Christians. The indebtedness referred to is no peculiarity of the Apostolic order, but attaches to every believer. Every servant of Jesus Christ, who has received the truth for himself, has received it as a steward, and is, as such, indebted to God, from whom he got the trust, and to the men for whom he got it. The only limit to the obligation is, as Paul says in the context, 'as much as in me is.' Capacity, determined by faculties, opportunities, and circumstances, prescribes the kind and the degree of the work to be done in discharge of the obligation; but the obligation is universal. We are not at liberty to choose whether we shall do our part in spreading the name of Jesus Christ. It is a debt that we owe to God and to men. Is that the view of duty which the average Christian man takes? I am afraid it is not. If it were, our treasuries would be full, and great would be the multitude of them that preached the Word.

It is no very exalted degree of virtue to pay our debts. We do not expect to be praised for that; and we do not consider that we are at liberty to choose whether we shall do it or not. We are dishonest if we do not. It is no merit in us to be honest. Would that all Christian people applied that principle to their religion. The world would be different, and the Church would be different, if they did.

Let me try, then, to enforce this thought of indebtedness and of common honesty in discharging the indebtedness, which underlies these words. Paul thought that he went a long way to pay his debts to humanity by carrying to everybody whom he could reach the 'Name that is above every name.'

I. Now, first, let me say that we Christians are debtors to all men by our common manhood.

It is not the least of the gifts which Christianity has brought to the world, that it has introduced the new thought of the brotherhood of mankind. The very

word 'humanity' is a Christian coinage, and it was
coined to express the new thought that began to throb
in men's hearts, as soon as they accepted the message
that Jesus Christ came to give, the message of the
Fatherhood of God. For it is on that belief of God's
Fatherhood that the belief of man's brotherhood rests,
and on it alone can it be secured and permanently
based.

Here is a Jew writing to Latins in the Greek language.
The phenomenon itself is a sign of a new order of things,
of the rising of a flood that had surged over, and in
the course of ages would sap away and dissolve, the
barriers between men. The Apostle points to two of
the widest gulfs that separated men, in the words of
my text. 'Greeks and Barbarians' divides mankind,
according to race and language. 'Wise and unwise'
divides them according to culture and intellectual capacity. Both gulfs exist still, though they have been
wonderfully filled up by the influence, direct and indirect, of the Gospel of Jesus Christ. The fiercest
antagonisms of race which still subsist are felt to
belong to a decaying order, and to be sure, sooner or
later, to pass away. I suppose that the gulf made by
the increased culture of modern society between civilised and the savage peoples, and, within the limits of
our own land, the gulf made by education between the
higher and the lower layers of our community—I
speak not of higher and lower in regard to wealth or
station, but in regard to intellectual acquirement and
capacity—are greater than, perhaps, they ever were in
the past. But yet over the gulf a bridge is thrown,
and the gulf itself is being filled up. High above all
the superficial distinctions which separate Jew and
Gentile, Greek and Barbarian, educated and illiterate,

scientific and unscientific, wise and unwise, there stretches the great rainbow of the truth that all are one in Christ Jesus. Fraternity without Fatherhood is a ghastly mockery that ended a hundred years ago in the guillotine, and to-day will end in disappointment; and it is little more than cant. But when Christianity comes and tells us that we have one Father and one Redeemer, then the unity of the race is secured.

And that oneness which makes us debtors to all men is shown to be real by the fact that, beneath all superficial distinctions of culture, race, age, or station, there are the primal necessities and yearnings and possibilities that lie in every human soul. All men, savage or cultivated, breathe the same air, see by the same light, are fed by the same food and drink, have the same yearning hearts, the same lofty aspirations that unfulfilled are torture; the same experience of the same guilt, and, blessed be God! the same Saviour and the same salvation.

Because, then, we are all members of the one family, every man is bound to regard all that he possesses, and is, and can do, as committed to him in stewardship to be imparted to his fellows. We are not sponges to absorb, but we are pipes placed in the spring, that we may give forth the precious water of life.

Cain is not a very good model, but his question is the world's question, and it implies the expectation of a negative answer—'Am I my brother's keeper?' Surely, the very language answers itself, and, although Cain thinks that the only answer is 'No,' wisdom sees that the only answer is 'Yes.' For if I am my brother's brother, then surely I am my brother's keeper. We have a better example. There is another Elder Brother who has come to give to His brethren all that Himself possessed, and we but poorly follow our Master's pattern unless we feel that the mystic tie which binds us in brotherhood to every man makes us every man's debtor to the extent of our possessions. That is the Christian truth that underlies the modern Socialistic idea, and, whatever the form in which it is ultimately brought into practice as the rule of mankind, the principle will triumph one day; and we are bound, as Christian men, to hasten the coming of its victory. We are debtors by reason of our common humanity.

II. We are debtors by our possession of the universal salvation.

The principle which I have already been laying down applies all round, to everything that we have, are, or can do. But its most stringent obligation, and the noblest field for its operations, are found in reference to the Christian man's possession of the Gospel for the joy of his own heart, and to the duties that are therein involved. Christ draws men to Himself for their own sakes, blessed be His name! but not for their own sakes only. He draws them to Himself, that they, in their turn, may draw others with whose hands theirs are linked, and so may swell the numbers of the flock that gathers round the one Shepherd. He puts the dew of His blessing into the chalice of the tiniest flower, that it may 'share its dewdrop with another near.' Just as every particle of inert dough as it is leavened becomes in its turn leaven, and the medium for leavening the particle contiguous to it, so every Christian is bound, or, to use the metaphor of my text, is a debtor to God and man, to impart the Gospel of Jesus Christ. 'Greek and Barbarian,' says Paul, 'wise or unwise'; all distinctions vanish. If I can get at a man, no matter what colour, his race, his language, his capacity, his acquire-

ments, he is my creditor, and I am defrauding him of
what he has a right to expect from me if I do not do
my best to bring him to Jesus Christ.

This obligation receives additional weight from the
proved adaptation of the Gospel to all sorts and conditions of men. Alone of all religions has Christianity
proved itself capable of dominating every type of character, of influencing every stage of civilisation, of assuming the speech of every tongue, and of wearing the
garb of every race. There are other religions which
are evidently destined only to a narrow field of operations, and are rigidly limited by geographical conditions,
or by stages of civilisation. There are wines that are
ruined by a sea voyage, and can only be drunk in the
land where the vintage was gathered; and that is the
condition of all the ethnic religions. Christianity alone
passes through the whole earth, and influences all men.
The history of missions shows us that. There has yet
to be found the race that is incapable of receiving, or is
beyond the need of possessing, or cannot be elevated
by the operation of, the Gospel of Jesus Christ.

So to all men we are bound, as much as in us is, to
carry the Gospel. The distinction that is drawn so often
by the people who never move a finger to help the
heathen either at home or abroad, between the home
and the foreign field of work, vanishes altogether when
we stand at the true Christian standpoint. Here is a
man who wants the Gospel; I have it; I can give it to
him. That constitutes a summons as imperative as if
we were called by name from Heaven, and bade to go,
and as much as in us is to preach the Gospel. Brethren!
we do not obey the command, 'Owe no man anything,'
unless, to the extent of our ability, or over the whole
field which we can influence at home or abroad, we

seek to spread the name of Christ and the salvation
that is in Him.

III. We are debtors by benefits received.

I am speaking to men and women a very large proportion of whom get their living, and some of whom
amass their wealth, by trade with lands that need the
Gospel. It is not for nothing that England has won
the great empire that she possesses—won it, alas! far
too often by deeds that will not bear investigation in
the light of Christian principle, but won it.

What do we owe to the lands that we call 'heathen'?
The very speech by which we communicate with one
another; the beginning of our civilisation; wide fields
for expanding population and emigration; treasures of
wisdom of many kinds; an empire about which we are
too fond of crowing and too reluctant to recognise its
responsibilities—and Manchester its commerce and prosperity! Did God put us where we are as a nation
only in order that we might carry the gifts of our
literature, great as that is; of our science, great as
that is; of our law, blessed as that is; of our manu-
factures, to those distant lands? The best thing that
we can give is the thing that all of us can help to give
—the Gospel of Jesus Christ. 'Who knoweth whether
thou art come to the kingdom for such a time as this?'

IV. Lastly, we are debtors by injuries inflicted.

Many subject-races seem destined to fade away by
contact with our race; and if we think of the nameless
cruelties, and the iliad of woes which England's possession of this great Colonial Empire has had accompany-
ing it, we may feel that the harm in many aspects
outweighs the good, and that it had been better for
these men to be left suckled in creeds outworn, and
ignorant of our civilisation, than to receive from us the

fatal gifts that they often have received. I do not wish
to exaggerate, but if you will take the facts of the case
as brought out by people that have no Christian prejudices to serve, I think you will acknowledge that we
as a nation owe a debt of reparation to the barbarians
and the unwise.

What about killing African tribes by the thousand
with the vile stuff that we call rum, and send to them
in exchange for their poor commodities? What about
introducing new diseases, the offspring of vice, into the
South Sea Islands, decimating and all but destroying
the population? Is it not true that, as the prophet
wailed of old about a degenerate Israel, we may wail
about the beach-combers and other loafers that go
amongst savage lands from England—'Through you
the name of God is blasphemed among the Gentiles.'
A Hindoo once said to a missionary, 'Your Book is very
good. If you were as good as your Book you would
conquer India in five years.' That may be true or it
may not, but it gives us the impression that is produced
by godless Englishmen on heathen peoples. We are
taking away their religion from them, necessarily, as the
result of education and contact with European thought.
And if we do not substitute for it the one faith that
elevates and saves, the last state of that man will be
worse than the first.

We can almost hear the rattle of the guns on the
north-west frontier of India to-day. There is another
specimen of the injuries inflicted. This is not the place
to talk politics, but I feel that this is the place to ask
this question, 'Are Christian principles to have anything to do in determining national actions?' Is it
Christian to impose our yoke on unwilling tribes who
have as deep a love for independence as the proudest

Englishmen of us all, and as good a right to it? Are punitive expeditions and Maxim guns instalments of our debt to all men? I wonder what Jesus Christ, who died for Afridis and Orakzais and all the rest of them, thinks about such conduct?

Brethren, we are debtors to all men. Let us do our best to influence national action in accordance with the brotherhood which has been revealed to us by the Elder Brother of us all; and let us, at least for our own parts, recognise, and, as much as in us is, discharge the debt which, by our common humanity, and by our possession of the universal Gospel we owe to all men, and which is made more weighty by the benefits we receive from many, and by the injuries which England has inflicted on not a few. Else shall we hear rise above all the voices that palliate crime, on the plea of 'State necessity,' the stern words of the Master, 'In thy skirts is found the blood of the souls of poor innocents.' We are debtors; let us pay our debts.


## THE GOSPEL THE POWER OF GOD[1]

'I am not ashamed of the Gospel of Christ: for it is the power of God unto salvation to every one that believeth.'—ROMANS i. 16.

To preach the Gospel in Rome had long been the goal of Paul's hopes. He wished to do in the centre of power what he had done in Athens, the home of wisdom; and with superb confidence, not in himself, but in his message, to try conclusions with the strongest thing in the world. He knew its power well, and was not appalled. The danger was an attraction to his chivalrous spirit. He believed in flying at

[1] Preached before Baptist Union.

the head when you are fighting with a serpent, and
he knew that influence exerted in Rome would thrill
through the Empire. If we would understand the
magnificent audacity of these words of my text we
must try to listen to them with the ears of a Roman.
Here was a poor little insignificant Jew, like hundreds
of his countrymen down in the Ghetto, one who had
his head full of some fantastic nonsense about a young
visionary whom the procurator of Syria had very
wisely put an end to a while ago in order to quiet
down the turbulent province; and he was going into
Rome with the notion that his word would shake the
throne of the Cæsars. What proud contempt would
have curled their lips if they had been told that the
travel - stained prisoner, trudging wearily up the
Appian Way, had the mightiest thing in the world
entrusted to his care! Romans did not believe much
in ideas. Their notion of power was sharp swords and
iron yokes on the necks of subject peoples. But the
history of Christianity, whatever else it has been, has
been the history of the supremacy and the revolutionary
force of ideas. Thought is mightier than all visible
forces. Thought dissolves and reconstructs. Empires
and institutions melt before it like the carbon rods in
an electric lamp; and the little hillock of Calvary is
higher than the Palatine with its regal homes and the
Capitoline with its temples: 'I am not ashamed of the
Gospel of Christ, for it is the power of God unto salvation.'

Now, dear friends, I have ventured to take these
great words for my text, though I know, better than
any of you can tell me, how sure my treatment of
them is to enfeeble rather than enforce them, because
I, for my poor part, feel that there are few things

which we, all of us, people and ministers, need more
than to catch some of the infection of this courageous
confidence, and to be fired with some spark of
Paul's enthusiasm for, and glorying in, the Gospel
of Jesus Christ.

I ask you, then, to consider three things: (1) what
Paul thought was the Gospel? (2) what Paul thought
the Gospel was? and (3) what he felt about the
Gospel?

I. What Paul thought was the Gospel?

He has given to us in his own rapid way a summary
statement, abbreviated to the very bone, and reduced
to the barest elements, of what he meant by the
Gospel. What was the irreducible minimum? The
facts of the Death and Resurrection of Jesus Christ, as
you will find written in the fifteenth chapter of the
First Epistle to the Corinthians. So, then, to begin
with, the Gospel is not a statement of principles, but
a record of facts, things that have happened in this
world of ours. But the least part of a fact is the
visible part of it, and it is of no significance unless it
has explanation, and so Paul goes on to bind up with
the facts an explanation of them. The mere fact that
Jesus, a young Nazarene, was executed is no more a
gospel than the other one, that two brigands were
crucified beside Him. But the fact that could be seen,
plus the explanation which underlies and interprets it,
turns the chronicle into a gospel, and the explanation
begins with the name of the Sufferer; for if you want
to understand His death you must understand who it
was that died. His death is a thought pathetic in all
aspects, and very precious in many. But when we hear
'Christ died according to the Scriptures,' the whole
symbolism of the ancient ritual and all the glowing

anticipations of the prophets rise up before us, and that death assumes an altogether different aspect. If we stop with 'Jesus died,' then that death may be a beautiful example of heroism, a sweet, pathetic instance of innocent suffering, a conspicuous example of the world's wages to the world's teachers, but it is little more. If, however, we take Paul's words upon our lips, 'Brethren, I declare unto you the Gospel which I preached . . , how that Christ died . . . according to the Scriptures,' the fact flashes up into solid beauty, and becomes the Gospel of our salvation. And the explanation goes on, 'How that Christ died for our sins.' Now, I may be very blind, but I venture to say that I, for my part, cannot see in what intelligible sense the Death of Christ can be held to have been for, or on behalf of, our sins—that is, that they may be swept away and we delivered from them—unless you admit the atoning nature of His sacrifice for sins. I cannot stop to enlarge, but I venture to say that any narrower interpretation evacuates Paul's words of their deepest significance. The explanation goes on, 'And that He was buried.' Why that trivial detail? Partly because it guarantees the fact of His Death, partly because of its bearing on the evidences of His Resurrection. 'And that He rose from the dead according to the Scriptures.' Great fact, without which Christ is a shattered prop, and 'ye are yet in your sins.'

But, further, notice that my text is also Paul's text for this Epistle, and that it differs from the condensed summary of which I have been speaking only as a bud with its petals closed differs from one with them expanded in their beauty. And now, if you will take the words of my text as being the keynote of this letter, and read over its first eight chapters, what is the Apostle

c

talking about when he in them fulfils his purpose and
preaches 'the Gospel' to them that are at Rome also?
Here is, in the briefest possible words, his summary—
the universality of sin, the awful burden of guilt, the
tremendous outlook of penalty, the impossibility of man
rescuing himself or living righteously, the Incarnation,
and Life, and Death of Jesus Christ as a sacrifice for the
sins of the world, the hand of faith grasping the offered
blessing, the indwelling in believing souls of the Divine
Spirit, and the consequent admission of man into a life
of sonship, power, peace, victory, glory, the child's place
in the love of the Father from which nothing can separate. These are the teachings which make the staple of
this Epistle. These are the explanations of the weighty
phrases of my text. These are at least the essential
elements of the Gospel according to Paul.

But he was not alone in this construction of his message. We hear a great deal to-day about Pauline Christianity, with the implication, and sometimes with the
assertion, that he was the inventor of what, for the sake
of using a brief and easily intelligible term, I may call
Evangelical Christianity. Now, it is a very illuminating
thought for the reading of the New Testament that
there are the three sets of teaching, roughly, the
Pauline, Petrine, and Johannine, and you cannot find
the distinctions between these three in any difference
as to the fundamental contents of the Gospel; for if
Paul rings out, 'God commendeth His love toward us
in that while we were yet sinners Christ died for us,'
Peter declares, 'Who His own self bare our sins in His
own body on the tree,' and John, from his island
solitude, sends across the waters the hymn of praise,
'Unto Him that loved us and washed us from our sins
in His own blood.' And so the proud declaration of

the Apostle, which he dared not have ventured upon
in the face of the acrid criticism he had to front unless
he had known he was perfectly sure of his ground, is
natural and warranted—' Therefore, whether it were I
or they, so we preach.'

We are told that we must go back to the Christ of
the Gospels, the historical Christ, and that He spoke
nothing concerning all these important points that
I have mentioned as being Paul's conception of the
Gospel.  Back to the Christ of the Gospels by all
means, if you will go to the Christ of all the Gospels
and of the whole of each Gospel.  And if you do,
you will go back to the Christ who said, 'The Son of
Man came not to be ministered unto, but to minister,
and to give His life a ransom for many.'  You will go
back to the Christ who said, 'And I, if I be lifted up
from the earth, will draw all men unto Me.'  You will
go back to the Christ who said, 'The bread that I will
give is My flesh, which I will give for the life of the
world.'  You will go back to the Christ who bade His
followers hold in everlasting memory, not the tranquil
beauty of His life, not the persuasive sweetness of His
gracious words, not the might of His miracles of blessing, but the mysterious agonies of His last hours, by
which He would have us learn that there lie the
secret of His power, the foundation of our hopes, the
stimulus of our service.

Now, brethren, I have ventured to dwell so long
upon this matter, because it is no use talking about
the Gospel unless we understand what we mean by it,
and I, for my part, venture to say that that is what
Paul meant by it, and that is what I mean by it.
I plead for no narrow interpretation of the phrases
of my text.  I would not that they should be used to

check in the smallest degree the diversities of representation which, according to the differences of individual character, must ever prevail in the conceptions which we form and which we preach of this Gospel of Jesus Christ. I want no parrot-like repetition of a certain set of phrases embodied, however great may be their meanings, in every sermon. And I would that the people to whom those truths are true would make more allowance than they sometimes do for the differences to which I have referred, and would show a great deal more sympathy than they often do to those, especially those young men, who, with their faces toward Christ, have not yet grown to the full acceptance of all that is implied in those gracious words. There is room for a whole world of thought in the Gospel of Christ as Paul conceived it, with all the deep foundations of implication and presupposition on which it rests, and with all the, as yet, undiscovered range of conclusions to which it may lead. Remember that the Cross of Christ is the key to the universe, and sends its influence into every region of human thought.

II. What Paul thought the Gospel was.

'The power of God unto salvation.' There was in the background of the Apostle's mind a kind of tacit reference to the antithetical power that he was going up to meet, the power of Rome, and we may trace that in the words of my text. Rome, as I have said, was the embodiment of physical force, with no great faith in ideas. And over against this carnal might Paul lifts the undissembled weakness of the Cross, and declares that it is stronger than man, 'the power of God unto salvation.' Rome is high in force; Athens is higher; the Cross is highest of all, and it comes shrouded in weakness having a poor Man hanging dying there. That is a strange embodiment of divine power. Yes, and because so strange, it is so touching, and so conquering. The power that is draped in weakness is power indeed. Though Rome's power did make for righteousness sometimes, yet its stream of tendency was on the whole a power to destruction and grasped the nations of the earth as some rude hand might do rich clusters of grapes and squeeze them into a formless mass. The tramp of the legionary meant death, and it was true in many respects of them what was afterwards said of later invaders of Europe, that where their horses' hoofs had once stamped no grass ever grew. Over against this terrific engine of destruction Paul lifts up the meek forces of love which have for their sole object the salvation of man.

Then we come to another of the keywords about which it is very needful that people should have deeper and wider notions than they often seem to cherish. What is salvation? Negatively, the removal and sweeping away of all evil, physical and moral, as the schools speak. Positively, the inclusion of all good for every part of the composite nature of a man which the man can receive and which God can bestow. And that is the task that the Gospel sets to itself. Now, I need not remind you how, for the execution of such a purpose, it is plain that something else than man's power is absolutely essential. It is only God who can alter my relation to His government. It is only God who can trammel up the inward consequences of my sins and prevent them from scourging me. It is only God who can bestow upon my death a new life, which shall grow up into righteousness and beauty,

caught of, and kindred to, His own. But if this be the
aim of the Gospel, then its diagnosis of man's sickness
is a very much graver one than that which finds
favour amongst so many of us now. Salvation is a
bigger word than any of the little gospels that we hear
clamouring round about us are able to utter. It means
something a great deal more than either social or
intellectual, or still more, material or political better-
ment of man's condition. The disease lies so deep, and
so great are the destruction and loss partly experienced,
and still more awfully impending over every soul of
us, that something else than tinkering at the outsides,
or dealing, as self-culture does, with man's understanding or, as social gospels do, with man's economical and
civic condition, should be brought to bear. Dear
brethren, especially you Christian ministers, preach a
social Christianity by all means, an applied Christianity,
for there does lie in the Gospel of Jesus Christ a key
to all the problems that afflict our social condition.
But be sure first that there is a Christianity before you
talk about applying it. And remember that the process of salvation begins in the deep heart of the
individual and transforms him first and foremost.
The power is 'to every one that believeth.' It is
power in its most universal sweep. Rome's Empire
was wellnigh ubiquitous, but, blessed be God, the
dove of Christ flies farther than the Roman eagle
with beak and claw ready for rapine, and wherever
there are men here is a Gospel for them. The limitation is no limitation of its universality. It is no limitation of the claim of a medicine to be a panacea that
it will only do good to the man who swallows it. And
that is the only limitation of which the Gospel is
susceptible, for we have all the same deep needs. The

same longings; we are fed by the same bread, we are
nourished by the same draughts of water, we breathe
the same air, we have the same sins, and, thanks be to
God, we have the same Saviour. 'The power of God
unto salvation to every one that believeth.'

Now before I pass from this part of my subject there
is only one thing more that I want to say, and that is,
that you cannot apply that glowing language about
'the power of God unto salvation' to anything but the
Gospel that Paul preached. Forms of Christianity
which have lost the significance of the Incarnation and
Death of Jesus Christ, and which have struck out or
obscured the central facts with which I have been
dealing, are not, never were, and, I may presumptu-
ously venture to say, never will be, forces of large
account in this world. Here is a clock, beautiful,
chased on the back, with a very artistic dial-plate, and
works modelled according to the most approved fashion,
but, somehow or other, the thing won't go. Perhaps
the mainspring is broken. And so it is only the Gospel,
as Paul expounds it and expands it in this Epistle, that
is 'the power of God unto salvation.' Dear brethren,
in the course of a sermon like this, of course, one must
lay himself open to the charge of dogmatising. That
cannot be helped under the conditions of my space. But
let me say as my own solemn conviction—I know that
that is not worth much to you, but it is my justification for speaking in such a fashion—let me say as my
solemn conviction that you may as well take the key-
stone out of an arch, with nothing to hold the other
stones together or keep them from toppling in hideous
ruin on your unfortunate head, as take the doctrine
that Paul summed up in that one word out of your
conception of Christianity and expect it to work. And

be sure of this, that there is only one Name that lords
it over the demons of afflicted humanity, and that if a
man goes and tries to eject them with any less potent
charm than Paul's Gospel, they will turn upon him
with 'Jesus I know, and Paul I know, but who are
you?'

III. What Paul felt about this Gospel.

His restrained expression, 'I am not ashamed,' is the
stronger for its very moderation.  It witnesses to the
fixed purpose of his heart and attitude of his mind,
whilst it suggests that he was well aware of all the
temptations in Rome to being ashamed of it there.
Think of what was arrayed against him—venerable
religion, systematised philosophies, bitter hatred and
prejudice, material power and wealth.  These were the
brazen armour of Goliath, and this little David went
cheerily down into the valley with five pebble stones
in a leathern wallet, and was quite sure how it was
going to end.  And it ended as he expected.  His
Gospel shook the kingdom of the Roman, and cast it
in another mould.

And there are temptations, plenty of them, for us,
dear friends, to-day, to bate our confidence.  The
drift of what calls itself influential opinion is anti-
supernatural, and we all are conscious of the presence of that element all round about us.  It tells with
special force upon our younger men, but it affects
us all.  In this day, when a large portion of the
periodical press, which does the thinking for most of
us, looks askance at these truths, and when, on the
principle that in the kingdom of the blind the one-
eyed man is the king, popular novelists become our
theological tutors, and when every new publishing
season brings out a new conclusive destruction of

Christianity, which supersedes last season's equally complete destruction, it is hard for some of us to keep our flags flying. The ice round about us will either bring down the temperature, or, if it stimulates us to put more fuel on the fire, perhaps the fire may melt it. And so the more we feel ourselves encompassed by these temptations, the louder is the call to Christian men to cast themselves back on the central verities, and to draw at first hand from them the inspiration which shall be their safety. And how is that to be done? Well, there are many ways by which thoughtful, and cultivated, students may do it. But may I venture to deal here rather with ways which all Christian people have open before them? And I am bold to say that the way to be sure of 'the power of God unto salvation' is to submit ourselves continually to its cleansing and renewing influence. This certitude, brethren, may be contributed to by books of apologetics, and by other sources of investigation and study which I should be sorry indeed to be supposed in any degree to depreciate. But the true way to get it is, by deep communion with the living God, to realise the personality of Jesus Christ as present with us, our Friend, our Saviour, our Sanctifier by His Holy Spirit. Why, Paul's Gospel was, I was going to say, altogether—that would be an exaggeration—but it was to a very large extent simply the generalisation of his own experience. That is what all of us will find to be the Gospel that we have to preach. 'We speak that we do know and testify that we have seen.' And it was because this man could say so assuredly—because the depths of his own conscience and the witness within him bore testimony to it—'He loved me and gave Himself for me,' that he could also say, 'The power of God unto salvation to every one that believeth.' Go down into the depths, brother and friend; cry to Him out of the depths. Then you will feel His strong, gentle grip lifting you to the heights, and that will give power that nothing else will, and you will be able to say, 'I have heard Him myself, and I know that this is the Christ, the Saviour of the world.'

But there is yet another source of certitude open to us all, and that is the history of the centuries. Our modern sceptics, attacking the truth of Christianity mostly from the physical side, are strangely blind to the worth of history. It is a limitation of faculty that besets them in a good many directions, but it does not work anywhere more fatally than it does in their attitude towards the Gospel. After all, Jesus Christ spoke the ultimate word when He said, 'By their fruits ye shall know them.' And it is so, because just as what is morally wrong cannot be politically right, so what is intellectually false cannot be morally good. Truth, goodness, beauty, they are but three names for various aspects of one thing, and if it be that the difference between B.C. and A.D. has come from a Gospel which is not the truth of God, then all I can say is, that the richest vintage that ever the world saw, and the noblest wine of which it ever drank, did grow upon a thorn. I know that the Christian Church has sinfully and tragically failed to present Christ adequately to the world. But for all that, 'Ye are My witnesses, saith the Lord'; and nobler manners and purer laws have come in the wake of this Gospel of Jesus Christ. And as I look round about upon what Christianity has done in the world, I venture to say, 'Show us any system of religion or of no religion that has done that or anything the least like it, and then we will discuss with you the other evidences of the Gospel.'

In closing these words, may I venture relying on the melancholy privilege of seniority, to drop for a minute or two into a tone of advice?  I would say, do not be frightened out of your confidence either by the premature pæan of victory from the opposite camp, or by timid voices in our own ranks.  And that you may not be so frightened, be sure to keep clear in your mind the distinction between the things that can be shaken and the kingdom that cannot be moved.  It is bad strategy to defend an elongated line.  It is cowardice to treat the capture of an outpost as involving the evacuation of the key of the position. It is a mistake, to which many good Christian people are sorely tempted in this day, to assert such a connec- tion between the eternal Gospel and our deductions from the principles of that Gospel as that the refuta- tion of the one must be the overthrow of the other. And if it turns out to be so in any case, a large part of the blame lies upon those good and mistaken people who insist that everything must be held or all must be abandoned.  The burning questions of this day about the genuineness of the books of Scripture, inspiration, inerrancy, and the like, are not so associated with this word, 'God so loved the world . . . that whosoever believeth in Him should not perish, but have everlast- ing life,' as that the discovery of errors in the Second Book of Chronicles shakes the foundations of the Christian certitude.  In a day like this truth must change its vesture.  Who believes that the Dissenting Churches of England are the highest, perfect embodi- ment of the Kingdom of God?  And who believes that any creed of man's making has in it all and has in it only the everlasting Gospel?  So do not be frightened, and do not think that when the things that can be shaken are removed, the things that cannot be shaken are at all less likely to remain. Depend upon it, the Gospel, whose outline I have imperfectly tried to set before you now, will last as long as men on earth know they are sinners and need a Saviour. Did you ever see some mean buildings that have by degrees been gathered round the sides of some majestic cathedral, and do you suppose that the sweeping away of those shanties would touch the solemn majesty of the mediæval glories of the building that rises above them? Take them away if need be, and it, in its proportion, beauty, strength, and heavenward aspiration, will stand more glorious for the sweeping away. Preach positive truth. Do not preach doubts. You remember Mr. Kingsley's book *Yeast*. Its title was its condemnation. Yeast is not meant to be drunk; it is meant to be kept in the dark till the process of fermentation goes on and it works itself clear, and then you may bring it out. Do not be always arguing with the enemy. It is a great deal better to preach the truth. Remember what Jesus said: 'Let them alone, they are blind leaders of the blind, they will fall into the ditch.' It is not given to every one of us to conduct controversial arguments in the pulpit. There are some much wiser and abler brethren amongst us than you or I who can do it. Let us be contented with, not the humbler but the more glorious, office of telling what we have known, leaving it, as it will do, to prove itself. You remember what the old woman, who had been favoured by her pastor with an elaborate sermon to demonstrate the existence of God, said when he had finished; 'Well, I believe there is a God, for all the gentleman says.'

As one who sees the lengthening shadows falling

over the darkening field, may I say one word to my
junior brethren, with all whose struggles and doubts
and difficulties I, for one, do most tenderly sympathise?
I beseech them—though, alas! the advice condemns the
giver of it as he looks back over long years of his
ministry—to be faithful to the Gospel how that 'Jesus
Christ died for our sins according to the Scriptures.'
Dear young friends, if you only go where Paul went,
and catch the inspiration that he caught there, your
path will be clear.. It was in contact with Christ,
whose passion for soul-winning brought Him from
heaven, that Paul learned his passion for soul-winning.
And if you and I are touched with the divine enthusiasm, and have that aim clear before us, we shall
soon find out that there is only one power, one name
given under heaven among men whereby we can ac-
complish what we desire—the name of 'Jesus Christ
that died, yea, rather, that is risen again, who is even
at the right hand of God, and also maketh intercession
for us.' If our aim is clear before us it will prescribe
our methods, and if the inspiration of our ministry is,
'I determine not to know anything among you save
Jesus Christ and Him crucified,' then, whether men
will hear or whether they will forbear, they shall
know that there hath been a Prophet among them.

# WORLD-WIDE SIN AND WORLD-WIDE REDEMPTION

'Now we know, that what things soever the law saith, it saith to them who are under the law; that every mouth may be stopped, and all the world may become guilty before God. 20. Therefore by the deeds of the law there shall no flesh be justified in His sight: for by the law is the knowledge of sin. 21. But now the righteousness of God without the law is manifested, being witnessed by the law and the prophets;. 22. Even the righteousness of God which is by faith of Jesus Christ unto all and upon all them that believe; for there is no difference: 23. For all have sinned, and come short of the glory of God: 24. Being justified freely by His grace, through the redemption that is in Christ Jesus; 25. Whom God hath set forth to be a propitiation through faith in His blood, to declare His righteousness for the remission of sins that are past, through the forbearance of God; 26. To declare, I say, at this time His righteousness; that He might be just, and the justifier of him which believeth in Jesus.'—ROMANS iii. 19-26.

LET us note in general terms the large truths which this passage contains. We may mass these under four heads:

I. Paul's view of the purpose of the law.

He has been quoting a mosaic of Old Testament passages from the Psalms and Isaiah. He regards these as part of 'the law,' which term, therefore, in his view, here includes the whole previous revelation, considered as making known God's will as to man's conduct. Every word of God, whether promise, or doctrine, or specific command, has in it some element bearing on conduct. God reveals nothing only in order that we may know, but all that, knowing, we may do and be what is pleasing in His sight. All His words are law.

But Paul sets forth another view of its purpose here; namely, to drive home to men's consciences the conviction of sin. That is not the only purpose, for God reveals duty primarily in order that men may do it, and His law is meant to be obeyed. But, failing obedience, this second purpose comes into action, and His law is a swift witness against sin. The more

46

clearly we know our duty, the more poignant will be
our consciousness of failure. The light which shines
to show the path of right, shines to show our deviations
from it. And that conviction of sin, which it was the
very purpose of all the previous Revelation to produce,
is a merciful gift; for, as the Apostle implies, it is the
prerequisite to the faith which saves.

As a matter of fact, there was a far profounder and
more inward conviction of sin among the Jews than in
any heathen nation. Contrast the wailings of many a
psalm with the tone in Greek or Roman literature. No
doubt there is a law written on men's hearts which
evokes a lower measure of the same consciousness of
sin. There are prayers among the Assyrian and
Babylonian tablets which might almost stand beside
the Fifty-first Psalm; but, on the whole, the deep sense
of sin was the product of the revealed law. The best
use of our consciousness of what we ought to be, is
when it rouses conscience to feel the discordance with
it of what we are, and so drives us to Christ. Law,
whether in the Old Testament, or as written in our
hearts by their very make, is the slave whose task is
to bring us to Christ, who will give us power to keep
God's commandments.

Another purpose of the law is stated in verse 21, as
being to bear witness, in conjunction with the prophets,
to a future more perfect revelation of God's righteousness. Much of the law was symbolic and prophetic.
The ideal it set forth could not always remain unfulfilled. The whole attitude of that system was one of
forward-looking expectancy. There is much danger
lest, in modern investigations as to the authorship,
date, and genesis of the Old Testament revelation, its
central characteristic should be lost sight of; namely,

its pointing onwards to a more perfect revelation which should supersede it.

II. Paul's view of universal sinfulness.

He states that twice in this passage (vs. 20 to 24), and it underlies his view of the purpose of law. In verse 20 he asserts that 'by the works of the law shall no flesh be justified,' and in verses 23 and 24 he advances from that negative statement to the positive assertion that all have sinned. The impossibility of justification by the works of the law may be shown from two considerations: one, that, as a matter of fact, no flesh has ever done them all with absolute completeness and purity; and, second, that, even if they had ever been so done, they would not have availed to secure acquittal at a tribunal where motive counts for more than deed. The former is the main point with Paul.

In verse 23 the same fact of universal experience is contemplated as both positive sin and negative falling short of the 'glory' (which here seems to mean, as in John v. 44, xii. 43, approbation from God). 'There is no distinction,' but all varieties of condition, character, attainment, are alike in this, that the fatal taint is upon them all. 'We have, all of us, one human heart.' We are alike in physical necessities, in primal instincts, and, most tragically of all, in the common experience of sinfulness.

Paul does not mean to bring all varieties of character down to one dead level, but he does mean to assert that none is free from the taint. A man need only be honest in self-examination to endorse the statement, so far as he himself is concerned. The Gospel would be better understood if the fact of universal sinfulness were more deeply felt. Its superiority to all schemes for making everybody happy by rearrangements of

property, or increase of culture, would be seen through;
and the only cure for human misery would be discerned to be what cures universal sinfulness.

III. So we have next Paul's view of the remedy for
man's sin. That is stated in general terms in verses 21,
22. Into a world of sinful men comes streaming the
light of a 'righteousness of God.' That expression is
here used to mean a moral state of conformity with
God's will, imparted by God. The great, joyful message, which Paul felt himself sent to proclaim, is that
the true way to reach the state of conformity which
law requires, and which the unsophisticated, universal
conscience acknowledges not to have been reached, is
the way of faith.

The message is so familiar to us that we may easily
fail to realise its essential greatness and wonderfulness
when first proclaimed. That God should give righteousness, that it should be 'of God,' not only as coming
from Him, but as, in some real way, being kindred
with His own perfection; that it should be brought to
men by Jesus Christ, as ancient legends told that a
beneficent Titan brought from heaven, in a hollow
cane, the gift of fire; and that it should become ours
by the simple process of trusting in Jesus Christ, are
truths which custom has largely robbed of their
wonderfulness. Let us meditate more on them till
they regain, by our own experience of their power,
some of the celestial light which belongs to them.

Observe that in verse 22 the universality of the
redemption which is in Christ is deduced from the
universality of sin. The remedy must reach as far as
the disease. If there is no difference in regard to sin,
there can be none in regard to the sweep of redemption. The doleful universality of the covering spread

over all nations, has corresponding to it the blessed
universality of the light which is sent forth to flood
them all. Sin's empire cannot stretch farther than
Christ's kingdom.

IV. Paul's view of what makes the Gospel the
remedy.

In verses 21 and 22 it was stated generally that
Christ was the channel, and faith the condition, of
righteousness. The personal object of faith was declared, but not the special thing in Christ which was
to be trusted in. That is fully set forth in verses 24-26.
We cannot attempt to discuss the great words in these
verses, each of which would want a volume. But we
may note that 'justified' here means to be accounted
or declared righteous, as a judicial act; and that
justification is traced in its ultimate source to God's
'grace,'—His own loving disposition—which bends to
unworthy and lowly creatures, and is regarded as
having for the medium of its bestowal the 'redemption'
that is in Christ Jesus. That is the channel through
which grace comes from God.

'Redemption' implies captivity, liberation, and a
price paid. The metaphor of slaves set free by ransom
is exchanged in verse 25 for a sacrificial reference. A
propitiatory sacrifice averts punishment from the
offerer. The death of the victim procures the life of
the worshipper. So, a propitiatory or atoning sacrifice
is offered by Christ's blood, or death. That sacrifice is
the ransom-price through which our captivity is ended,
and our liberty assured. As His redemption is the
channel 'through' which God's grace comes to men, so
faith is the condition 'through' which (ver. 25) we make
that grace ours.

Note, then, that Paul does not merely point to Jesus

Christ as Saviour, but to His death as the saving power. We are to have faith in Jesus Christ (ver. 22). But that is not a complete statement. It must be faith in His propitiation, if it is to bring us into living contact with His redemption. A gospel which says much of Christ, but little of His Cross, or which dilates on the beauty of His life, but stammers when it begins to speak of the sacrifice in His death, is not Paul's Gospel, and it will have little power to deal with the universal sickness of sin.

The last verses of the passage set forth another purpose attained by Christ's sacrifice; namely, the vindication of God's righteousness in forbearing to inflict punishment on sins committed before the advent of Jesus. That Cross rayed out its power in all directions—to the heights of the heavens; to the depths of Hades (Col. i. 20); to the ages that were to come, and to those that were past. The suspension of punishment through all generations, from the beginning till that day when the Cross was reared on Calvary, was due to that Cross having been present to the divine mind from the beginning. 'The judge is condemned when the guilty is acquitted,' or left unpunished. There would be a blot on God's government, not because it was so severe, but because it was so forbearing, unless His justice was vindicated, and the fatal consequences of sin shown in the sacrifice of Christ. God could not have shown Himself just, in view either of age-long forbearance, or of now justifying the sinner, unless the Cross had shown that He was not immorally indulgent toward sin.

# NO DIFFERENCE

'There is no difference.'—ROMANS iii. 22.

THE things in which all men are alike are far more important than those in which they differ. The diversities are superficial, the identities are deep as life. Physical processes and wants are the same for everybody. All men, be they kings or beggars, civilised or savage, rich or poor, wise or foolish, cultured or illiterate, breathe the same breath, hunger and thirst, eat and drink, sleep, are smitten by the same diseases, and die at last the same death. We have all of us one human heart. Tears and grief, gladness and smiles, move us all. Hope, fear, love, play the same music upon all heart-strings. The same great law of duty over-arches every man, and the same heaven of God bends above him.

Religion has to do with the deep-seated identities and not with the superficial differences. And though there have been many aristocratic religions in the world, it is the great glory of Christianity that it goes straight to the central similarities, and brushes aside, as of altogether secondary importance, all the subordinate diversities, grappling with the great facts which are common to humanity, and with the large hopes which all may inherit.

Paul here, in his grand way, triumphs and rises above all these small differences between man and man, more pure or less pure, Jew or Gentile, wise or foolish, and avers that, in regard of the deepest and most important things, 'there is no difference,' and so his Gospel is a Gospel for the world, because it deals with all men on the same level. Now I wish to work out this great

52

glory and characteristic of the Gospel system in a few
remarks, and to point out to you the more important
of these things in which all men, be they what or who
they may, stand in one category and have identical
experiences and interests.

I. First, there is no difference in the fact of sin.

Now let us understand that the Gospel does not assert
that there is no difference in the degrees of sin.  Christianity does not teach, howsoever some of its apostles
may seem to have taught, or unconsciously lent themselves to representations which imply the view that
there was no difference between a man who 'did by
nature the things contained in the law,' as Paul says,
and the man who set himself to violate law.   There is
no such monstrous teaching in the New Testament as
that all blacks are the same shade, all sin of the same
gravity, no such teaching as that a man that tries
according to his light to do what is right stands on
exactly the same level as the man who flouts all such
obligations, and has driven the chariots of his lusts and
passions through every law that may stand in his way.

But even whilst we have to insist upon that, that the
teaching of my text is not of an absolute identity of
criminality, but only an universal participation in
criminality, do not let us forget that, if you take the
two extremes, and suppose it possible that there were
a best man in all the world, and a worst man in all the
world, the difference between these two is not perhaps
so great as at first sight it looks.  For we have to
remember that motives make actions, and that you
cannot judge of these by considering those, that 'as a
man thinketh in his heart,' and not as a man does with
his hands, ' so is he.'  We have to remember, also, that
there may be lives, sedulously and immaculately respect-

able and pure, which are white rather with the unwholesome leprosy of disease than with the wholesome purity of health.

In Queen Elizabeth's time, the way in which they cleaned the hall of a castle, the floor of which might be covered with remnants of food and all manner of abominations, was to strew another layer of rushes over the top of the filth, and then they thought themselves quite neat and respectable. And that is what a great many of you do, cover the filth well up with a sweet smelling layer of conventional proprieties, and think yourselves clean, and the pinks of perfection. God forbid that I should say one word that would seem to cast any kind of slur upon the effort that any man makes to do what he knows to be right, but this I proclaim, or rather my text proclaims for me, that, giving full weight and value to all that, and admitting the existence of variations in degree, the identity is deeper than the diversity; and there is 'not a just man upon earth that doeth good and sinneth not.'

Oh, dear friends! it is not a question of degree, but of direction; not how far the ship has gone on her voyage, but how she heads. Good and evil are the same in essence, whatever be their intensity and whatever be their magnitude. Arsenic is arsenic, whether you have a ton of it or a grain; and a very small dose will be enough to poison. The Gospel starts with the assertion that there is no difference in the fact of sin. The assertion is abundantly confirmed. Does not conscience assent? We all admit 'faults,' do we not? We all acknowledge 'imperfections.' It is that little word 'sin' which seems to bring in another order of considerations, and to command the assent of conscience less readily. But sin is nothing except fault considered in reference to God's law. Bring the notion of God into the life, and 'faults' and 'slips' and 'weaknesses,' and all the other names by which we try to smooth down the ugliness of the ugly thing, start up at once into their tone, magnitude, and importance, and stand avowed as *sins*.

Well now, if there be, therefore, this universal consciousness of imperfection, and if that consciousness of imperfection has only need to be brought into contact with God, as it were, to flame thus, let me remind you, too, that this fact of universal sinfulness puts us all in one class, no matter what may be the superficial difference. Shakespeare and the Australian savage, the biggest brain and the smallest, the loftiest and the lowest of us, the purest and the foulest of us, we all come into the same order. It is a question of classification. 'The Scripture hath concluded all under sin,' that is to say, has shut all men up as in a prison. You remember in the French Revolution, all manner of people were huddled indiscriminately into the same dungeon of the Paris prisons. You would find a princess and some daughter of shame from the gutters; a boor from the country and a landlord, a count, a marquis, a *savant*, a philosopher and an illiterate workman, all together in the dungeons. They kept up the distinctions of society and of class with a ghastly mockery, even to the very moment when the tumbrils came for them. And so here are we all, in some sense inclosed within the solemn cells of this great prison-house, and whether we be wise or foolish, we are prisoners, whether we have titles or not, we are prisoners. You may be a student, but you are a sinner: you may be a rich Manchester merchant, but you are a sinner; you may be a man of rank, but you are a sinner.

Naaman went to Elisha and was very much offended because Elisha treated him as a leper who happened to be a nobleman. He wanted to be treated as a nobleman who happened to be a leper. And that is the way with a great many of us; we do not like to be driven into one class with all the crowd of evildoers. But, my friend, 'there is no difference.' 'All have sinned and come short of the glory of God.'

II. Again, there is no difference in the fact of God's love to us.

God does not love men because of what they are, therefore He does not cease to love them because of what they are. His love to the sons of men is not drawn out by their goodness, their morality, their obedience, but it wells up from the depths of His own heart, because 'it is His nature and property,' and if I may so say, He cannot help loving. You do not need to pump up that great affection by any machinery of obedience and of merits; it rises like the water in an Artesian well, of its own impulse, with ebullient power from the central heat, and spreads its great streams everywhere. And therefore, though our sin may awfully disturb our relations with God, and may hurt and harm us in a hundred ways, there is one thing it cannot do, it cannot stop Him from loving us. It cannot dam back His great love, which flows out for ever towards all His creatures, and laves them all in its gentle, strong flood, from which nothing can draw them away. 'In Him we live, and move, and have our being,' and to live in Him, whatever else it may mean—and it means a great deal more—is most certainly to live in His love. A man can as soon pass out of the atmosphere in which he breathes as he can pass out of the love of God. We can no more travel beyond that great over-arching firmament of everlasting love which spans all the universe than a star set in the blue heavens can transcend the liquid arch and get beyond its range. 'There is no difference' in the fact that all men, unthankful and evil as they are, are grasped and held in the love of God.

But there *is* a difference. Sin cannot dam God's love back, but sin has a terrible power in reference to the love of God. Two things it can do. It can make us incapable of receiving the highest blessings of that love. There are many mercies which God pours 'upon the unthankful and the evil.' These are His least gifts; His highest and best cannot be given to the unthankful and the evil. They would if they could, but they cannot, because they cannot be received by them. You can shut the shutters against the light; you can close the vase against the stream. You cannot prevent its shining, you cannot prevent its flowing, but you can prevent yourself from receiving its loftiest and best blessings.

And another awful power that my sin has in reference to God's love is, that it can modify the form which God's love takes in its dealings with me. We may force Him to do 'His work,' 'His strange work,' as Isaiah calls it, and to punish when He would fain only succour and comfort and bless. Just as a fog in the sky does not touch the sun, but turns it to our eyes into a fiery ball, red and lurid, so the mist of my sin coming between me and God, may, to my apprehension and to my capacity of reception, solemnly make different that great love of His. But yet there is no difference in the fact of God's love to us.

III. Thirdly, there is no difference in the purpose and power of Christ's Cross for us all.

'He died for all.' The area over which the purpose and the power of Christ's death extend is precisely

conterminous with the area over which the power of
sin extends. It cannot be—blessed be God!—that the
raven Sin shall fly further than the dove with the
olive branch in its mouth. It cannot be that the
disease shall go wider than the cure. And so, dear
friends, I have to come to you now with this message.
No matter what a man is, how far he has gone, how
sinful he has been, how long he has stayed away from
the sweetness and grace of that great sacrifice on the
Cross, that death was for him. The power of Christ's
sacrifice makes possible the forgiveness of all the sins
of all the world, past, present, and to come. The worth
of that sacrifice, which was made by the willing surrender of the Incarnate Son of God to the death of the
Cross, is sufficient for the ransom price of all the sins
of all men.

Nor is it only the power of the Cross which is all
embracing, but its purpose also. In the very hour of
Christ's death, there stood, clear and distinct, before
His divine omniscience, each man, woman, and child
of the race. And for them all, grasping them all in the
tenderness of His sympathy and in the clearness of
His knowledge, in the design of His sufferings for them
all, He died, so that every human being may lay his
hand on the head of the sacrifice, and *know* 'his guilt
was there,' and may say, with as triumphant and
appropriating faith as Paul did, 'He loved *me*,' and in
that hour of agony and love 'gave Himself for *me*.'

To go back to a metaphor already employed, the
prisoners are gathered together in the prison, not that
they may be slain, but 'God hath included them all,'
shut them all up, 'that He might have mercy upon all.'
And so, as it was in the days of Christ's life upon earth,
so is it now, and so will it be for ever. All the crowd

may come to Him, and whosoever comes 'is made whole
of whatsoever disease he had.' There are no incurables
nor outcasts. 'There is no difference.'

IV. Lastly, there is no difference in the way which
we must take for salvation.

The only thing that unites men to Jesus Christ is
faith. You must trust Him, you must trust the power
of His sacrifice, you must trust the might of His living
love. You must trust Him with a trust which is self-
distrust. You must trust Him out and out. The people
with whom Paul is fighting, in this chapter, were quite
willing to admit that faith was the thing that made
Christians, but they wanted to tack on something besides. They wanted to tack on the rites of Judaism and
obedience to the moral law. And ever since men have
been going on in that erroneous rut. Sometimes it has
been that people have sought to add a little of their
own morality; sometimes to add ceremonies and sacra-
ments. Sometimes it has been one thing and sometimes it has been another; but there are not two ways
to the Cross of Christ, and to the salvation which He
gives.· There is only one road, and all sorts of men
have to come by it. You cannot lean half upon Christ
and half upon yourselves, like the timid cripple that is
not quite sure of the support of the friendly arm. You
cannot eke out the robe with which He will clothe you
with a little bit of stuff of your own weaving. It is an
insult to a host to offer to pay for entertainment.
The Gospel feast that Christ provides is not a social
meal to which every guest brings a dish. Our part is
simple reception, we have to bring empty hands if we
would receive the blessing.

We must put away superficial differences. The
Gospel is for the world, therefore the act by which we

receive it must be one which all men can perform, not one which only some can do. Not wisdom, nor righteousness, but faith joins us to Christ. And, therefore, people who fancy themselves wise or righteous are offended that 'special terms' are not made with them. They would prefer to have a private portion for them-selves. It grates against the pride of the aristocratic class, whether it be aristocratic by culture—and that is the most aristocratic of all—or by position, or anything else—it grates against their pride to be told: 'You have to go in by that same door that the beggar is going in at'; and 'there is no difference.' Therefore, the very width of the doorway, that is wide enough for all the world, gets to be thought narrowness, and becomes a hindrance to our entering. As Naaman's servant put a common-sense question to him, so may I to you. 'If the prophet had bid thee do some great thing, wouldest thou not have done it?' Ay! that you would! 'How much more when He says "Wash and be clean!"' There is only one way of getting dirt off, and that is by water. There is only one way of getting sin off, and that is by the blood of Jesus Christ. There is only one way of having that blood applied to your heart, and that is trusting Him. 'The common salvation' becomes ours when we exercise 'the common faith.' 'There is no difference' in our sins. Thank God! 'there is no difference' in the fact that He grasps us with His love. There is no difference in the fact that Jesus Christ has died for us all. Let there be no difference in our faith, or there will be a difference, deep as the difference between Heaven and Hell; the difference between them that believe and them that believe not, which will darken and widen into the difference between them that are saved and them that perish.

# 'LET US HAVE PEACE

'Let us have peace with God through our Lord Jesus Christ.'
ROMANS v. 1. (R.V.).

IN the rendering of the Revised Version, 'Let us have
peace with God through our Lord Jesus Christ,' the
alteration is very slight, being that of one letter in one
word, the substitution of a long 'o' for a short one.
The majority of manuscripts of authority read 'let us
have,' making the clause an exhortation and not a
statement. I suppose the reason why, in some inferior
MSS., the statement takes the place of the exhortation
is because it was felt to be somewhat of a difficulty to
understand the Apostle's course of thought. But I
shall hope to show you that the true understanding of
the context, as well as of the words I have taken
for my text, requires the exhortation and not the
affirmation.

One more remark of an introductory character: is it
not very beautiful to see how the Apostle here identifies himself, in all humility, with the Christians whom
he is addressing, and feels that he, Apostle as he is,
has the same need for the same counsel and stimulus
that the weakest of those to whom he is writing have?
It would have been so easy for him to isolate himself,
and say, 'Now you have peace with God; see that you
keep it.' But he puts himself into the same class as
those whom he is exhorting, and that is what all of
us have to do who would give advice that will be
worth anything or of any effect. He does not stand
upon a little molehill of superiority, and look down
upon the Roman Christians, and imply that they have

needs that he has not, but he exhorts himself too, saying, 'Let all of us who have obtained like precious faith, which is alike in an Apostle and in the humblest believer, have peace with God.'

Now a word, first, about the meaning of this somewhat singular exhortation.

There is a theory of man and his relation to God underlying it, which is very unfashionable at present, but which corresponds to the deepest things in human nature, and the deepest mysteries in human history, and that is, that something has come in to produce the totally unnatural and monstrous fact that between God and man there is not amity or harmony. Men, on their side, are alienated, because their wills are rebellious and their aims diverse from God's purpose concerning them. And—although it is an awful thing to have to say, and one from which the sentimentalism of much modern Christianity weakly recoils—on God's side, too, the relation has been disturbed, and 'we are by nature the children of wrath, even as others'; not of a wrath which is unloving, not of a wrath which is impetuous and passionate, not of a wrath which seeks the hurt of its objects, but of a wrath which is the necessary antagonism and recoil of pure love from such creatures as we have made ourselves to be. To speak as if the New Testament taught that 'reconciliation' was lop-sided—which would be a contradiction in terms, for reconciliation needs two to make it—to talk as if the New Testament taught that reconciliation was only man's putting away his false relation to God, is, as I humbly think, to be blind to its plainest teaching. So, there being this antagonism and separation between God and man, the Gospel comes to deal with it, and proclaims that Jesus Christ has abolished the enmity, and by His death on the Cross has become our peace; and that we, by faith in that Christ, and grasping in faith His death, pass from out of the condition of hostility into the condition of reconciliation.

With this by way of basis, let us come back to my text. It sounds strange; 'Therefore, being justified by faith, let us have peace.' 'Well,' you will say, 'but is not all that you have been saying just this, that to be justified by faith, to be declared righteous by reason of faith in Him who makes us righteous, is to have peace with God? Is not your exhortation an entirely superfluous one?' No doubt that is what the old scribe thought who originated the reading which has crept into our Authorised Version. The two things do seem to be entirely parallel. To be justified by faith is a certain process, to have peace with God is the inseparable and simultaneous result of that process itself. But that is going rather too fast. 'Being justified by faith let us have peace with God,' really is just this —see that you abide where you are; keep what you have. The exhortation is not to attain peace, but retain it. 'Hold fast that thou hast; let no man take thy crown.' 'Being justified by faith' cling to your treasure and let nothing rob you of it—'let us have peace with God.'

Now a word, in the next place, as to the necessity and importance of this exhortation.

There underlies it, this solemn thought, which Christian people, and especially some types of Christian doctrine, do need to have hammered into them over and over again, that we hold the blessed life itself, and all its blessings, only on condition of our own cooperation in keeping them; and that just as physical life dies, unless by reception of food we nourish and continue it, so a man that is in this condition of being justified by faith, and having peace with God, needs, in order to the permanence of that condition, to give his utmost effort and diligence. It will all go if he do not. All the old state will come back again if we are slothful and negligent. We cannot keep the treasure unless we guard it. And just because we have it, we need to put all our mind, the earnestness of our will, and the concentration of our efforts, into the specific work of retaining it.

For, consider how manifold and strong are the forces which are always working against our continual possession of this justification by faith, and consequent peace with God. There are all the ordinary cares and duties and avocations and fortunes of our daily life, which, indeed, may be so hallowed in their motives and in their activities, as that they may be turned into helps instead of hindrances, but which require a great deal of diligence and effort in order that they should not work like grains of dust that come between the parts of some nicely-fitting engine, and so cause friction and disaster. There are all the daily tasks that tempt us to forget the things that we only know by faith, and to be absorbed in the things that we can touch and taste and handle. If a man is upon an inclined plane, unless he is straining his muscles to go upwards, gravitation will make short work of him, and bring him down. And unless Christian men grip hard and continually that sense of having fellowship and peace with God, as sure as they are living they will lose the clearness of that consciousness, and the calm that comes from it. For we cannot go into the world and do the work that is laid upon us all without there being possible hostility to the Christian life in everything that we meet. Thank God there is possible help, too, and whether our daily calling is an enemy or a friend to our religion depends upon the earnestness and continuousness of our own efforts. But there is a worse force than these external distractions working to draw us away, one that we carry within, in our own vacillating wills and wayward hearts and treacherous affections and passions that usually lie dormant, but wake up sometimes at the most inopportune periods. Unless we keep a very tight hand upon ourselves, certainly these will rob us of this consciousness of being justified by faith which brings with it peace with God that passes understanding.

In the Isle of Wight massive cliffs rise hundreds of feet above the sea, and seem as if they were as solid as the framework of the earth itself. But they rest upon a sharply inclined plane of clay, and the moisture trickles through the rifts in the majestic cliffs above, and gets down to that slippery substance and makes it like the greased ways down which they launch a ship; and away goes the cliff one day, with its hundreds of feet of buttresses that have fronted the tempest for centuries, and it lies toppled in hideous ruin on the beach below. We have all a layer of 'blue slipper' in ourselves, and unless we take care that no storm-water finds its way down through the chinks in the rocks above they will slide into awful ruin. 'Being justified, let us have peace with God,' and remember that the exhortation is enforced not only by a consideration of the many strong forces which tend to deprive us of this peace, but also by a consideration of the hideous disaster that comes upon a man's whole

E

nature if he loses peace with God. For there is no
peace with ourselves, and there is no peace with man,
and there is no peace in face of the warfare of life
and the calamities that are certainly before us all,
unless, in the deepest sanctuary of our being, there is
the peace of God because in our consciences there is
peace with God. If I desire to be at rest—and there is
no blessedness but rest—if I desire to know the sovereign
joy of tranquillity, undisturbed by my own stormy
passions or by any human enmity, and to have even
the 'beasts of the field at peace with' me, and all things
my helpers and allies, there is but one way to realise
the desire, and that is the retention of peace with God
that comes with being justified by faith.

Lastly, a word or two as to the ways by which this
exhortation can be carried into effect.

· I have tried to explain how the peace of which my
text speaks comes originally through Christ's work
laid hold of by my faith, and now I would say only
three things.

Retain the peace by the exercise of that same faith
which at first brought it. Next, retain it by union
with that same Lord from whom you at first received
it. Very significantly, in the immediate context, we
have the Apostle drawing a broad distinction between
the benefits which we have received from Christ's
death, and those which we shall receive through His
life. And that is the best commentary on the words
of my text. 'If when we were enemies, we were
reconciled to God by the death of His Son, much more,
being reconciled, we shall be saved by His life.' So let
our faith grasp firmly the great twin facts of the
Christ who died that He might abolish the enmity, and
bring us peace; and of the Christ who lives in order that

He may pour into our hearts more and more of His own
life, and so make us more and more in His own image.
And the last word that I would say, in addition to
these two plain, practical precepts is, let your conduct
be such as will not disturb your peace with God.  For
if a man lets his own will rise up in rebellion against
God's, whether that divine will command duty or impose suffering, away goes all his peace.  There is no
possibility of the tranquil sense of union and communion with my Father in heaven lasting when I am
in rebellion against Him.  The smallest sin destroys,
for the time being, our sense of forgiveness and our
peace with God.  The blue surface of the lake, mirroring in its unmoved tranquillity the sky and the bright
sun, or the solemn stars, loses all that reflected heaven
in its heart when a cat's paw of wind ruffles its surface.
If we would keep our hearts as mirrors, in their peace,
of the peace in the heavens that shine down on them,
we must fence them from the winds of evil passions
and rebellious wills.  'Oh! that thou wouldest hearken
unto Me, then had thy peace been like a river.'

## ACCESS INTO GRACE

'By whom also we have access by faith into this grace wherein we stand.'
ROMANS v. 2.

I MAY be allowed to begin with a word or two of
explanation of the terms of this passage.  Note then,
especially, that *also* which sends us back to the previous
clause, and tells us that our text adds something to
what was spoken of there.  What was spoken of there?
'The peace of God' which comes to a man by Jesus

Christ through faith, the removal of enmity, and the declaration of righteousness. But that peace with God, which is the beginning of everything in the Christian view, is only the beginning, and there is much to follow. While, then, there is a progress clearly marked in the words of our text, and 'access into this grace wherein we stand' is something more than, and after, the 'peace with God,' mark next the similarity of the text and the preceding verse. The two great truths in the latter, Christ's mediation or intervention, and our faith as the condition by which we receive the blessings which are brought to us in and through Him, are both repeated, with no unmeaning tautology, but with profound significance in our text—' By whom also we have access'—as well as—'the peace of God'—'access *by faith* into this grace.' So then, for the initial blessing, and for all the subsequent blessings of the Christian life, the way is the same. The medium and channel is one, and the act by which we avail ourselves of the blessings coming through that one medium is the same. Now the language of my text, with its talking about access, faith, and grace, sounds to a great many of us, I am afraid, very hard and remote and technical. And there are not wanting people who tell us that all that terminology in the New Testament is like a dying brand in the fire, where the little kernel of glowing heat is getting covered thicker and thicker with grey ashes. Yes; but if you blow the ashes off, the fire is there all the same. Let us try if we can blow the ashes off.

This text seems to me in its archaic phraseology, only to need to be pondered in order to flash up into wonderful beauty. It carries in it a magnificent ideal of the Christian life, in three things: the Christian place,

'access into grace'; the Christian attitude, 'wherein
we stand'; and the Christian means of realising that
ideal, 'through Christ' and 'by faith.'  Now let us look
at these three points.

I. The Christian Place.

There is clearly a metaphor here, both in the word
'access' and in that other one 'stand.'  'The grace' is
supposed as some ample space into which a man is
led, and where he can continue, stand, and expatiate.
Or, we may say, it is regarded as a palace or treasure-
house into which we can enter.  Now, if we take that
great New Testament word 'grace,' and ponder its
meanings, we find that they run something in this
fashion.  The central thought, grand and marvellous,
which is enshrined in it, and which often is buried for
careless ears, is that of the active love of God poured
out upon inferiors who deserve something very different.  Then there follows a second meaning, which
covers a great part of the ground of the use of the
phrase in the New Testament, and that is the communication of that love to men, the specific and
individualised gifts which come out of that great
reservoir of patient, pardoning, condescending, and
bestowing love.  Then there may be taken into view a
meaning which is less prominent in Scripture but not
absent, namely, the resulting beauty of character.  A
gracious soul ought to be, and is, a graceful soul; a
supreme loveliness is imparted to human nature by
the communication to it of the gifts which are the
results of the undeserved, free, and infinite love of
God.

Now if we take all these three thoughts as blended
together in the grand metaphor of the Apostle, of the
ample space into which the Christian man passes, we

get such lessons as this. A Christian life may, and therefore should, be suffused with a continual consciousness of the love of God. That would change everything in it. Here is some great sweep of rolling country, perhaps a Highland moor : the little tarns on it are grey and cold, the vegetation is gloomy and dark, dreariness is over all the scene, because there is a great pall of cloud drawn beneath the blue. But the sun pierces with his lances through the grey, and crumples up the mists, and sends them flying beneath the horizon. Then what a change in the landscape! All the tarns that looked black and wicked are now infantile in their innocent blue and sunny gladness, and every dimple in the heights shows, and all the heather burns with the sunshine that falls upon it. So my lonely doleful life, if that light from God, the beam of His love, shines down upon it, rises into nobility, and flashes into beauty, and is calm and fair and great, as nothing else can make it. You may dwell in love by dwelling in God, and then your lives will be fair. You have access into the grace; see that you go there. They tell us that nightingales sing by the wayside by preference, and we may have in our lives, singing a quiet tune, the continual thought of the love of God, even whilst life's highway is dusty and rough, and our feet are often weary in treading it. A Christian life may be, and therefore should be, suffused with the sense of the abiding love of God.

Take the other meaning of the word, the secondary and derived meaning, the communication of that love to us, and that leads us to say that a Christian life may, and therefore should, be enriched with continual gifts from God's fullness. I said that the Apostle was using a metaphor here, regarding the grace as being an ample space into which a man was admitted, or we may say that he is thinking of it as a great treasure-house. We have the right of entrance there, where on every side, as it were, lie ingots of uncoined gold, and masses of treasure, and we may have just as much or as little as we choose. It is entirely in our own determination how much of the wealth of God we shall possess. We have access to the treasure-house; and this permit is put into our hands: 'Be it unto thee even as thou wilt.' The size of the sack that the man brings, in the old story, determined the amount of wealth that he carried away. Some of you bring very tiny baskets and expect little and desire little; you get no more than you desired and expected.

That wealth, the fullness of God, takes the shape of, as well as is determined in its measure by the magnitude of, the vessel into which it is put. It is multiform, and we get whatever we desire, and whatever either our characters or our circumstances require. The one gift assumes all forms, just as water poured into a vase takes the shape of the vase into which it is poured. The same gift unfolds itself in an infinite variety of manners, according to the needs of the man to whom it is given; just as the writer's pen, the carpenter's hammer, the farmer's ploughshare, are all made out of the same metal. So God's grace comes to you in a different shape from that in which it comes to me, according to our different callings and needs, as fixed by our circumstances, our duties, our sorrows, our temptations.

So, brethren, how shameful it is that, having the possibility of so much, we should have the actuality of so little. There is an old story about one of our generals in India long ago, who, when he came home, was accused of rapacity because he had brought away so much treasure from the Rajahs whom he had conquered, and his answer to the charge was, 'I was surprised at my own moderation.' Ah! there are a great many Christian people who ought to be ashamed of their moderation. They have gone into the treasure-house; stacks of jewels, jars of gold on all sides of them—and they have been content to come away with some one poor little coin, when they might have been 'rich beyond the dreams of avarice.' Brethren, you have 'access' to the fullness of God. Whose fault is it if you are empty?

Then, further, I said there was another meaning in these great words. The love which may suffuse our lives, the gifts, the consequence of that love, which may enrich our lives, should, and in the measure in which they are received will, adorn and make beautiful our lives. For 'grace' means loveliness as well as goodness, and the God who is the fountain of it all is the fountain of 'whatsoever things are fair,' as well as of whatsoever things are good. That suggests two considerations on which I have no time to dwell. One is that the highest beauty is goodness, and unless the art of a nation learns that, its art will become filthy and a minister of sin. They talk about 'Art for Art's sake.' Would that all these poets and painters who are trying to find beauty in corruption—and there is a phosphorescent glimmer in rotting wood, and a prismatic colouring on the scum of a stagnant pond—would that all those men who are seeking to find beauty apart from goodness, and so are turning a divine instinct into a servant of evil, would learn that the true gracefulness comes from the grace which is the fullness of God given unto men.

But there is another lesson, and that is that Christian people who say that they have their lives irradiated by the love of God, and who profess to be receiving gifts from His full hand, are bound to take care that their goodness is not 'harsh and crabbed,' as not only 'dull fools suppose' it to be, but as it sometimes is, but is musical and fair. You are bound to make your goodness attractive, and to show that the things that are 'of good report' are likewise the 'things that are lovely.'

II. And so, now, turn to the second point here, viz. the Christian attitude.

'The grace wherein ye *stand*'; that word is very emphatic here, and does not merely mean 'continue,' but it suggests what I have put into that phrase, the Christian attitude.

Two things are implied. One is that a life thus suffused by the love, and enriched by the gifts, and adorned by the loveliness that come from God, will be stable and steadfast. Resistance and stability are implied in the words. One very important item in determining a man's power of resistance, and of standing firm against whatever assaults may be hurled against him, is the sort of footing that he has. If you stand on slippery mud, or on the ice of a glacier, you will find it hard to stand firm; but if you plant your foot on the grace of God, then you will be able to 'withstand in the evil day, and having done all to stand.' And how does a man plant his foot on the grace of God? simply by trusting in God, and not in himself. So that the secret of all steadfastness of life, and of all successful resistance to the whirling onrush of temptations and of difficulties, is to set your foot upon that rock, and then your 'goings' will be established.

Jesus Christ brings to us, in the gift of life in Him, stability which will check the vacillations of our own hearts. We go up and down, we yield when pressure is brought to bear against us, we are carried off our feet often by the sudden swirl of the stream, and the fitful blast of the wind. But His grace comes in, and will make us able to stand against all assaults. . Our poor natures, necessarily changeable, and sinfully vacillating and weak, will be uniform, in the measure in which the grace of God comes into our hearts. Just as in these so-called petrifying wells, they take a bit of cloth, a bird's nest, a billet of wood, and plunge it into the water, and the mineral held in solution there infiltrates into the substance of the thing plunged in, and makes it firm and inflexible: so let us plunge our poor, changeful, vacillating resolutions, our wayward, wandering hearts, our passions, so easily excited by temptation, into that great fountain, and there will filter into our flexibility what will make it firm, and into our changefulness what will give in us some faint copy of the divine immutability, and we shall stand fast in the Lord and in the power of His might.

Further, in regard to this attitude, which is the result of the possession of grace, we may say that it indicates not only stability and steadfastness, but erectness, as in opposition to crouching or bowing. A man's independence is guaranteed by his dependence upon, and his possession of, that communicated grace of God. And so you have the fact that the phase of the Christian teaching which has laid most stress on the decrees and sovereign will of God, on divine grace in fact, and too little upon the human side—the phase which is roughly described as Calvinism—has underlain the liberties of Europe, and has stiffened men into the rejection of all

priestly and civic domination.  'Where the Spirit of
the Lord is, there is liberty,' and if a man has in his
heart the grace of God, then- he stands erect as a man.
'Ye are bought with a price; be ye not the servants of
men.'   The Christian democracy, the Christian rejection of all sacerdotal and other domination, flows from
the access of each individual Christian to the fountain
of all wisdom, the only source of law and command,
the inspirer of all strength, the giver of all grace.  By
faith ye stand.   'Stand fast therefore in the liberty
wherewith Christ has made you free.'

III. Lastly, and only a word; we have here the
Christian way of entrance into grace.

I have already remarked on the emphasis with
which, both in my text and in the preceding clause,
there are laid down the two conditions of possessing
this grace, or the peace which precedes it: 'By Christ
—through faith.'  Notice, too, that Jesus Christ gives
us 'access.'  Now that expression is but an imperfect
rendering of the original.   If it were not for its
trivial associations, one might read instead of 'access,'
introduction, 'by whom we have introduction into
this grace wherein we stand.'  The thought is that
Jesus Christ secures us entry into this ample space, this
treasure-house, as some court officer might take by the
the hand a poor rustic, standing on the threshold of the
palace, and lead him through all the glittering series
of unfamiliar splendour, and present him at last in the
central ring around the king.  The reality that underlies the metaphor is plain.  We sinners can never pass
into that central glory, nor ever possess those gifts of
grace, unless the barrier that stands between us and
God, between us and His highest gifts of love, is swept
away.

I recall an old legend where two knights are represented as seeking to enter a palace, where there is a mysterious fire burning in the middle of the portal. One of them tries to pass through, and recoils scorched; but when the other essays an entrance the fierce fire sinks, and the path is cleared. Jesus Christ has died, and I say it with all reverence, as His blood touches the fire it flickers down and the way is opened 'into the holiest of all, whither the Forerunner is for us entered.' He both brings the grace and makes it possible that we should go in where the grace is.

But Jesus Christ's work is nothing to you unless your personal faith comes in, and so that is pointed to in the second of the clauses here: ' *By faith* we have access.' That is no arbitrary appointment. It lies in the very nature of the gift and of the recipient. How can God give access into that grace to a man who shrinks from being near Him; who does not want 'access,' and who could not use the grace if he had it? How can God bestow inward and spiritual gifts upon any man who closes his heart against them, and will not have them? My faith is the condition; Christ is the Giver. If I ally myself to Him by my faith, He gives to me. If I do not, with all the will to do it, He cannot bestow His best gifts any more than a man who stretches out his hand to another sinking in the flood can lift him out, and set him on the safe shore, if the drowning man's hand is not stretched out to grasp the rescuer's outstretched hand.

Brethren, God is infinitely willing to give the choicest gifts of His love to us all, to gladden, to enrich, to adorn, to make stable and erect. But He cannot give them unless you will trust Him. 'It pleased the Father that in Him should all fullness dwell.'

That alabaster box is brought to earth. It was broken
on the Cross that 'the house' might be 'filled with the
odour of the ointment.' Our faith is the only condition;
it is only the condition, but it is the indispensable
condition, of our being anointed with that fragrant
anointing. He, and He only, can give us the fullness of
God.

## THE SOURCES OF HOPE

'We rejoice in hope of the glory of God. 3. And not only so, but we glory in
tribulations also: knowing that tribulation worketh patience; 4. And patience,
experience; and experience, hope.'—ROMANS v. 2-4.

WE have seen in a previous sermon that the Apostle in
the foregoing context is sketching a grand outline of
the ideal Christian life, as all rooted in 'being justified
by faith,' and flowering into 'peace with God,' 'access
into grace,' and a firm stand against all antagonists
and would-be masters. In our text he advances to
complete the outline by sketching the true Christian
attitude towards the future. I have ventured to take
so pregnant and large a text, because there is a very
striking and close connection throughout the verses,
which is lost unless we take them together. Note,
then, 'we rejoice in hope,' 'we glory in tribulation.'
Now, it is one word in the original which is diversely
rendered in these two clauses by 'rejoice' and 'glory.'
The latter is a better rendering than the former, because the original expression designates not only the
emotion of joy, but the expression of it, especially in
words. So it is frequently rendered in the New Testament by the word 'boast,' which, of course, has unpleasant associations, which scarcely fit it for use here.
So then you see Paul regards it as possible for, and

more than possibly characteristic of, a Christian, that
the very same emotion should be excited by that great
bright future hope, and by the blackness of present
sorrow.  That is strong meat; and so he goes on to
explain how he thinks it can and must be so, and points
out that trouble, through a series of results, arrives at
last at this, that if it is rightly borne, it flashes up
into greater brightness the hope which has grasped
the glory of God.  So then we have here, not only a
wonderful designation of the object around which
Christian hope twines its tendrils, but of the double
source from which that hope may come, and of the
one emotion with which Christian people should front
the darkness of the present and the brightness of the
future.  Ah! how different our lives would be if that
ideal of a steadfast hope and an untroubled joy were
realised by each of us.  It may be.  It should be.  So
I ask you to look at these three points which I have
suggested.

  .I. That wonderful designation of the one object of
Christian hope which should fill, with an uncoruscat-
ing and unflickering light, all that dark future.

  'We rejoice in hope of the glory of God.'  Now, I suppose I need not remind you that that phrase 'the glory
of God' is, in the Old Testament, used especially to mean
the light that dwelt between the cherubim above the
mercy-seat; the symbol of the divine perfections and
the token of the Divine Presence.  The reality of which
it was a symbol is the total splendour, so to speak, of
that divine nature, as it rays itself out into all the
universe.  And, says Paul, the true hope of the
Christian man is nothing less than that of that glory
he shall be, in some true sense, and in an eternally
growing degree, the real possessor.  It is a tremendous

claim, and one which leads us into deep places that I dare not venture into now, as to the resemblance between the human person and the Divine Person, notwithstanding all the differences which of course exist, and which only a presumptuous form of religion has ventured to treat as transitory or insignificant. Let me use a technical word, and say that it is no pantheistic absorption in an impersonal Light, no Nirvana of union with a vague whole, which the Apostle holds out here, but it is the closest possible union, personality being saved and individual consciousness being intensified. It is the clothing of humanity with so much of that glory as can be imparted to a finite creature. That means perfect knowledge, perfect purity, perfect love, and that means the dropping away of all weaknesses and the access of strange new powers, and that means the end of the schism between 'will' and 'ought,' and of the other schism between 'will' and 'can.' It means what this Apostle says: 'Whom He justified them He also glorified,' and what He says again, 'We all, beholding as in a glass'—or rather, perhaps, mirroring as a glass does—'the glory, are changed into the same image.'

The very heart of Christianity is that the Divine Light of which that Shekinah was but a poor and transitory symbol has 'tabernacled' amongst men in the Christ, and has from Him been communicated, and is being communicated in such measure as earthly limitations and conditions permit, and that these do point on assuredly to perfect impartation hereafter, when 'we shall be like Him, for we shall see Him as He is.' The Three could walk in the furnace of fire, because there was One with them, 'like unto the Son of God.' 'Who among us shall dwell with the everlasting fire,' the fire of that divine perfection? They who have had introduction by Christ into the grace, and who will be led by Him into the glory.

Now, brethren, it seems to me to be of great importance that this, the loftiest of conceptions of that future life, should be the main aspect under which we think of it. It is well to speak of rest from toil; it is well to speak of all the negations of present unfavourable, afflictive conditions which that future presents to us. And perhaps there is none of the aspects of it which appeals to deeper feelings in ourselves, than those which say 'there shall be no night there,' 'there shall be no tears there, neither sorrow nor sighing'; 'there shall be no toil there.' But we must rise above all that, for our heaven is to live in God, and to be possessors of His glory. Do not let us dwell upon the symbols instead of the realities. Do not let us dwell only on the oppositions and contradictions to earth. Let us rather rise high above symbols, high above negations, to the positive truth, and not contented with saying 'We shall be full of blessedness; we shall be full of purity; we shall be full of knowledge,' let us rather think of that which embraces them all—we shall be full of God.

So much, then, for the one object of Christian hope. We have here—

II. The double source of that hope.

Observe that the first clause of my text comes as the last term in a sequence. It began with 'being justified by faith.' The second round of the ladder was, 'we have peace with God.' The third, 'we have access into this grace.' The fourth, 'we stand,' and then comes, 'we rejoice in hope of the glory of God.' That is to say, to put it into general words, and, of course, presupposing the revelation in Jesus Christ as the basis of all, without which there is no assured hope of a future beyond the grave, then the facts of a Christian man's life are for him the best brighteners of the hope beyond. Of course, that is so. 'Justified by faith'—'peace with God'—'access into grace'; what, in the name of common-sense, can death do with these things? How can its blunted sword cut the bond that unites a soul that has had such experiences as these with the source of them all? Nothing can be more grotesque, nothing more incongruous, than to think that that subordinate and accidental fact, whose region is the physical, has anything whatever to do with this higher region of consciousness.

And, further than that, it is absolutely unthinkable to a man in the possession of these spiritual gifts, that they should ever come to a close; and the fact that in the precise degree in which we realise as our very own possession, here and now, these Christian emotions and blessings, we instinctively rise to the belief that they are 'not for an age, but for all time,' and not for all time, but for eternity, is itself, if not a proof, yet a very strong presumption, if you believe in God, that a man who thus 'feels he was not made to die' because he has grasped the Eternal, is right in so feeling. If, too, we look at the experiences themselves, they all have the stamp of incompleteness, and suggest completeness by their own incompleteness. The new moon with its ragged edge not more surely prophesies its completed silver round, than do the experiences of the Christian life here, in their greatness and in their smallness, declare that there come a time and an order of things in which what was thwarted tendency shall be accomplished result. The tender green spikelet, pushing up

F

through the brown clods, does not more surely prophesy the waving yellow ear, nor the broad highway on which a man comes in the wilderness more surely declare that there is a village at the end of it, than do the facts of the Christian life, here and now, attest the validity of the hope of the glory of God.

And so, brethren, if you wish to brighten that great light that fills the future, see to it that your present Christianity is fuller of 'peace with God,' 'access into grace,' and the firm, erect standing which flows from these. When the springs in the mountains dry up, the river in the valley shrinks; and when they are full, it glides along level with the top of its banks. So when our Christian life in the present is richest, our Christian hope of the future will be the brighter. Look into yourselves. Is there anything there that witnesses to that great future; anything there that is obviously incipient, and destined to greater power; anything there which is like a tropical plant up here in 45 degrees of north latitude, managing to grow, but with dwarfed leaves and scanty flowers and half shrivelled and sourish fruit, and that in the cold dreams of the warm native land? Reflecting telescopes show the stars in a mirror, and the observer looks down to see the heavens. Look into yourselves, and see whether, on the polished plate within, there are any images of the stars that move around the Throne of God.

But let us turn for a moment to the second source to which the Apostle traces the Christian hope here. I must not be tempted to more than just a word of explanation, but perhaps you will tolerate that. Paul says that trouble works patience, that is to say, not only passive endurance, but brave persistence in

a course, in spite of antagonisms. That is what
trouble does to a man when it is rightly borne. Of
course the Apostle is speaking here of its ideal operation, and not of the reality which alas! often is seen
when our tribulations lash us into impatience, or
paralyse our efforts. Tribulation worketh patience,
'and patience *experience.*' That is a difficult word to
put into English. There underlies it the frequent
thought which is familiar in Scripture, of trouble of all
kinds as testing a man, whether as the refiner's fire or
the winnower's fan. It tests a man, and if he bears the
trouble with patient persistence, then he has passed
the test and is approved. Patient perseverance thus
works approval, or proof of the man's Christianity,
and, still more, proof of the reality and power of the
Christ whom his Christianity grasps. And so from out
of that approval or proof which comes, through perseverance, from tribulation, there rises, of course, in
that heart that has been tested and has stood, a calm
hope that the future will be as the past, and that,
having fought through six troubles, by God's help the
seventh will be vanquished also, till at last troubles
will end, and heaven be won.

Brethren, there is the true point of view from which
to look, not only at tribulations, but at all the trials,
for they too bring trials, that lie in duty and in enjoyment, and in earthly things. They are meant to work
in us a conviction, by our experience of having been
able to meet them aright, of the reality of our grasp
of God, and of the reality and power of the God whom
we grasp. If we took that point of view in regard to
all the changes of this changeful life, we should not so
often be bewildered and upset by the darkest of our
sorrows. The shining lancets and cruel cutting instru-

ments that the surgeon lays out on his table before he begins the operation are very dreadful. But the way to think of them is that they are there in order to remove from a man what it does him harm to keep, and what, if it is not taken away, will kill him. So life, with its troubles, great and small, is all meant for this, to make us surer of, and bring us closer to, our God, and to brace and strengthen us in our own personal character. And if it does that, then blessed be everything that produces these results, and leads us thereby to glorying in the troubles by which shines out on us a brighter hope.

So there are the two sources, you see: the one is the blessedness of the Christian life, the other the sorrows of the outward life, and both may converge upon the brightening of our Christian hope. Our rainbow is the child of the marriage of the sun and the rain. The Christian hope comes from being 'justified by faith, having peace with God . . . and access into grace,' and it comes from tribulation, which 'worketh patience,' and patience which 'worketh approval.' The one spark is struck from the hard flint by the cold steel, and the other is kindled by the sun itself, but they are both fire.

And so, lastly, we have here—

III. The one emotion with which the Christian should front all the facts, inward and outward, of his earthly life.

'We glory in the hope,' 'we glory in tribulation.' I need not dwell upon the lesson which is taught us here by the fact that the Apostle puts as one in a series of Christian characteristics this of a steadfast and all-embracing joy. I do not believe that we Christian people half enough realise how imperative a Christian

duty, as well as how great a Christian privilege, it is to
be glad always.   You have no right to be anxious; you
are wrong to be hypochondriac and depressed, and
weary and melancholy.   True; there are a great many
occasions in our Christian life which minister sadness.
True; the Christian joy looks very gloomy to a worldly
eye.   But there are far more occasions which, if we were
right, would make joy instinctive, and which, whether
we are right or not, make it obligatory upon us.   I
need not speak of how, if that hope were brighter than
it commonly is with us, and if it were more constantly
present to our minds and hearts, we should sing
with gladness.   I need not dwell upon that great and
wonderful paradox by which the co-existence of sorrow
and of joy is possible.   The sorrows are on the surface; beneath there may be rest.   All the winds of
heaven may rave across the breast of ocean, and fret
it into clouds of spume against a storm-swept sky.   But
deep down there is stillness, and yet not stagnation,
because there is the great motion that brings life and
freshness; and so, though there will be wind-vexed
surfaces on our too-often agitated spirits, there ought
to be deeper than these the calm setting of the whole
ocean of our nature towards God Himself.   It is
possible, as this Apostle has it, to be 'sorrowful, yet
always rejoicing.'   It is possible, as his brother Apostle
has it, to 'rejoice greatly, though now for a season we
are in sorrow through manifold temptations.'   Look
back upon your lives from the point of view that your
tribulation is an instrument to produce hope, and you
will be able to thank God for all the way by which He
has led you.

Now, brethren, the plain lesson of all this is just that
we have here, in these texts, a linked chain, one end of

which is wrapped around our sinful hearts, and the
other is fastened to the Throne of God. You cannot
drop any of the links, and you must begin at the
beginning, if you are to be carried on to the end. If
we are to have a joy immovable, we must have a
'steadfast hope.' If we are to have a 'steadfast hope,'
we must have a present 'grace.' If we are to have a
present 'grace,' and 'access' to the fullness of God, we
must have 'peace with God.' If we are to have 'peace
with God,' we must have the condemnation and the
guilt taken away. If we are to have the condemnation
and the guilt taken away, Jesus Christ must take them.
If Jesus Christ is to take them away, we must have faith
in Him. Then you can work it backward, and begin at
your own end, and say, 'If I have faith in Jesus Christ,
then every link of the chain in due succession will pass
through my hand, and I shall have justifying, peace,
access, the grace, erectness, hope, and exultation, and
at last He will lead me by the hand into the glory for
which I dare to hope, the glory which the Father gave
to Him before the foundation of the world, and which
He will give to me when the world has passed away in
fervent heat.'

## A THREEFOLD CORD

' And hope maketh not ashamed; because the love of God is shed abroad in our
hearts by the Holy Ghost which is given unto us.'—ROMANS v. 5.

WE have seen in former sermons that, in the previous
context, the Apostle traces Christian hope to two
sources: one, the series of experiences which follow
'being justified by faith,' and the other, those which
follow on trouble rightly borne. Those two golden
chains together hold up the precious jewel of hope.

But a chain that is to bear a weight must have a staple, or it will fall to the ground. And so Paul here turns to yet another thought, and, going behind both our inward experiences and our outward discipline, falls back on that which precedes all. After all is said and done, the love of God, eternal, self-originated, the source of all Christian experiences because of the work of Christ which originates them all, is the root fact of the universe, and the guarantee that our highest anticipations and desires are not unsubstantial visions, but morning dreams, which are proverbially sure to be fulfilled. God is love; therefore the man who trusts Him shall not be put to shame.

But you will notice that here the Apostle not only adduces the love of God as the staple, so to speak, from which these golden chains hang, but that he traces the heart's being suffused with that love to its source, and as, of course, is always the case in the order of analysis, that which was last in time comes first in statement. We begin at the surface, and go down and down and down from effect to cause, and yet again to the cause of that cause which is itself effect. We strip off, as it were, layer after layer, until we get to the living centre—hope comes from the love, the love comes from the Spirit in the heart. And so to get at the order of time and of manifestation, we must reverse the order of analysis in my text, and begin where it ends. So we have here three things—the Spirit given, the love shed abroad by that Spirit, and the hope established by that love. Now just look at them for a moment.

I. The Spirit given.

Now, the first point to notice here is that the Revised Version presents the meaning of our text more accurately than the Authorised Version, because, instead of reading 'is given,' it correctly reads 'was given.' And any of you that can consult the original will see that the form of the language implies that the Apostle is thinking, not so much of a continuous bestowment, as of a definite moment when this great gift was bestowed upon the man to whom he is speaking.

So the first question is, when was that Spirit given to these Roman Christians? The Christian Church has been split in two by its answers to that question. One influential part, which has taken a new lease of life amongst us to-day, says 'in baptism,' and the other says 'at the moment of faith.' I am not going to be tempted into controversial paths now, for my purpose is a very different one, but I cannot help just a word about the former of these two answers. 'Given in baptism,' say our friends, and I venture to think that they thereby degrade Christianity into a system of magic, bringing together two entirely disparate things, an external physical act and a spiritual change. I do not say anything about the disastrous effects that have followed from such a conception of the medium by which this greatest of all Christian gifts is effected upon men. Since the Spirit who is given is life, the result of the gift of that Spirit is a new life, and we all know what disastrous and debasing consequences have followed from that dogma of regeneration by baptism. No doubt it is perfectly true that normally, in the early Church, the Divine Spirit was given at baptism; but for one thing, that general rule had exceptions, as in the case of Cornelius, and, for another thing, though it was given *at* baptism, it was not given *in* baptism, but it was given through faith, of which in those days baptism was the sequel and the sign.

But I pass altogether from this, and fall back on the great words which, to me at least, if there were no other, would determine the whole answer to this question as to when the Spirit was given: 'This spake He of the Holy Ghost, which they that *believe* on Him should receive'; and I would ask the modern upholders of the other theory the indignant question which the Apostle Paul fired off out of his heavy artillery at their ancient analogues, the circumcisers in the Galatian Church: 'This only would I know of you: Received ye the Holy Spirit by the works of the law, or by the hearing of faith?'

The answer which the evangelical Christian gives to this ancient question suggested by my text, 'When was that Divine Spirit bestowed?' is congruous with the spirituality of the Christian faith, and is eminently reasonable. For the condition required is the opening of the whole nature in willing welcome to the entrance of the Divine Spirit, and as surely as, wherever there is an indentation of the land, and a concavity of a receptive bay, the ocean will pour into it and fill it, so surely where a heart is open for God, God in His Divine Spirit will enter into that heart, and there will shed His blessed influences.

So, dear brethren, and this is the main point to which I wish to direct your attention, the Apostle here takes it for granted that all these Roman Christians knew in themselves the truth of what he was saying, and had an experience which confirmed his assertion that the Divine Spirit of God was given to them when they believed. Ah! I wonder if that is true about us professing Christians; if we are aware in any measure of a higher life than our own having been breathed into us; if we are aware in any measure of a Divine Spirit dwelling in our spirits, moulding, lifting, enlightening, guiding, constraining, and yet not coercing? We ought to be. 'Know ye not that the Spirit dwelleth in you, except ye be rejected?' Brethren, it seems to me to be of the very last importance, in this period of the Church's history, that the proportion between the Church's teaching as to the work of Christ on the Cross, and as to the consequent work of the Spirit of Christ in our hearts and spirits, should be changed. We must become more mystical if we are not to become less Christian. And the fact that so many of us seem to imagine that the whole Gospel lies in this, that 'He died for our sins according to the Scriptures, and have relegated the teaching that He, by His Spirit, lives in us, if we are His disciples, to a less prominent place, has done enormous harm, not only to the type of Christian life, but to the conception of what Christianity is, both amongst those who receive it, and amongst those who do not accept it, making it out to be nothing more than a means of escape from the consequences of our transgression, instead of recognising it for what it is, the impartation of a new life which will flower into all beauty, and bear fruit in all goodness.

There was a question put once to a group of disciples, in astonishment and incredulity, by this Apostle, when he said to the twelve disciples in Ephesus, 'Did you receive the Holy Ghost when you believed?' The question might well be put to a multitude of professing Christians amongst us, and I am afraid a great many of them, if they answered truly, would answer as those disciples did, 'We have not so much as heard whether there be any Holy Ghost.'

And now for the second point in my text—

II. The love which is shed abroad by that Spirit.

Now, I suppose I do not need to do more than point out that 'the love of God' here means His to us, and not ours to Him, and that the metaphor employed is but partially represented by that rendering 'shed abroad.' 'Poured out' would better convey Paul's image, which is that of a flood sent coursing through the heart, or, perhaps, rather lying there, as a calm deep lake on whose unruffled surface the heavens, with all their stars, are reflected. Of course, if God's love to us thus suffuses a heart, then there follows the consciousness of that love; though it is not the consciousness of the love that the Apostle is primarily speaking of, but that which lies behind it, the actual flowing into the human heart of that sweet and all-satisfying Love. This Divine Spirit that dwells in us, if we are trusting in Christ, will pour it in full streams into our else empty hearts. Surely there is nothing incongruous with the nature either of God or of man, in believing that thus a real communication is possible between them, and that by thoughts the occasions of which we cannot trace, by moments of elevation, by swift, piercing convictions, by sudden clear illuminations, God may speak, and will speak, in our waiting hearts.

> 'Such rebounds the inmost ear
> Catches often from afar.
> Listen, prize them, hold them dear;
> For of God, of God, they are.'

But we must not forget, too, that, according to the whole strain of New Testament thinking, the means by which that Divine Spirit does pour out the flashing flood of the love of God into a man's heart is, as Jesus Christ Himself has taught us, by taking the things of Christ and showing them to us.

Now, as I said about a former point of my sermon,

that the Apostle was taking for granted that this gift of the Spirit belonged to all Christian people: so here again he takes for granted that in every Christian heart there is, by a divine operation, the presence of the love, and of the consciousness of the love, of God. And, again, the question comes to some of us stunningly, to all of us warningly, Is that a transcript of our experience? It is the ideal of a Christian life; it is meant that it should be so, and should be so continuously. The stream that is poured out is intended to run summer and winter, not to be dried up in drought, nor made turbid and noisy in flood, but with equable flow throughout. I fear me that the experience of most good people is rather like one of those tropical wadies, or nullahs in Eastern lands, where there alternate times of spate and times of drought; and instead of a flashing stream, pouring life everywhere, and full to the top of its banks, there is for long periods a dismal stretch of white sun-baked stones, and a chaos of tumbled rocks with not a drop of water in the channel. The Spirit pours God's love into men's spirits, but there may be dams and barriers, so that no drop of the water comes into the empty heart.

Our Quaker friends have a great deal to say about 'waiting for the springing of the life within us.' Never mind about the phraseology: what is meant is profoundly true, that no Christian man will realise this blessing unless he knows how to sit still and meditate, and let the gracious influence soak into him. Thus being quiet, he may, he will, find rising in his heart the consciousness of the love of God. You will not, if you give only broken momentary sidelong glances; you will not, if you do not lie still. If you hold up a cup in a shaking hand beneath a fountain, and often

twitch it aside, you will get little water in it; and
unless we 'wait on the Lord,' we shall not 'renew our
strength.' You can build a dam as they do in Holland
that will keep out, not only the waters of a river, but
the waters of an ocean, and not a drop will come
through the dike. Brethren, we must keep ourselves
in the love of God.

Lastly, we have here—

III. The hope that is established by the love poured
out.

I need not dwell at any length upon this point,
because, to a large extent, it has been anticipated in
former sermons, but just a word or two may be permitted me. That love, you may be very sure, is not
going to lose its objects in the dust. The old Psalmist
who knew so much less than we do as to the love of
God, and knew nothing of the whispers of a Divine
Spirit within his heart charged with the message of
the love as it was manifested in Jesus Christ, had
risen to a height of confidence, the beauty of the
expression of which is often lost sight of, because we
insist upon dealing with it as merely being a Messianic
prophecy, which it is, but not merely: 'Thou wilt not
leave my soul in Sheol, neither wilt Thou suffer Thy
beloved' (for that is the real meaning of the word
translated 'thy Holy One')—'Thou wilt not suffer the
child of Thy love to see corruption.' Death's bony
fingers can untie all true lover's knots but one; and
they fumble at that one in vain. God will not lose His
child in the grave.

That love, we may be very sure, will not foster in us
hopes that are to be disappointed. Now, it is a fact
that the more a man feels that God loves him, the less
is it possible for him to believe that that love will ever

terminate, or that he shall 'all die.' In the lock of a
canal, as the water pours in, the vessel rises. In our
hearts, as the flood of the full love of God pours in, our
hopes are borne up and up, nearer and nearer to the
heavens. Since it is so, we must find in the fact that
the constant and necessary result of communion with
Him here on earth is a conviction of the immortality
of that communion, a very, very strong guarantee for
ourselves that the hope is not in vain. And if you say
that that is all merely subjective, yet I think that the
universality of the experience is a fact to be taken into
account even by those who doubt the reality of the
hope, and for ourselves, at all events, is a sufficient
ground on which to rest. We have the historical fact
of the Resurrection of Jesus Christ. We have the fact
that wherever there has been earthly experience of
true communion with God, there, and in the measure
in which it has been realised, the thermometer of our
hopes of immortality, so to speak, has risen. 'God is
love,' and God will not bring the man that trusts Him
to confusion.

And may we not venture to say that, contemplating
the analogous earthly love, we are permitted to believe
that that divine Lover of our souls desires to have His
beloved with Him, and desires that there be no separation between Him and them, either, if I might so say,
in place or in disposition? As certainly as husband and
wife, lover and friend, long to be together, and need it
for perfection and for rest, so surely will that divine
love not be satisfied until it has gathered all its children
to its breast and made them partakers of itself.

There are many, many hopes that put the men who
cherish them to shame, partly because they are never
fulfilled, partly because, though fulfilled, they are dis-

appointed, since the reality is so much less than the anticipation. Who does not know that the spray of blossom on the tree looks far more lovely hanging above our heads than when it is grasped by us? Who does not know that the fish struggling on the hook seems heavier than it turns out to be when lying on the bank? We go to the rainbow's end, and we find, not a pot of gold, but a huddle of cold, wet mist. There is one man that is entitled to say: 'To-morrow shall be as this day, and much more abundant.' Who is he? Only the man whose hope is in the Lord his God. If we open our hearts by faith, then these three lines of sequence of which we have been speaking will converge, and we shall have the hope that is the shining apex of 'being justified by faith,' and the hope that is the calm result of trouble and agitation, and the hope that, travelling further and higher than anything in our inward experience or our outward discipline, grasps the key-word of the universe, 'God is love,' and triumphantly makes sure that 'neither death nor life, nor angels, nor principalities, nor powers, nor things present, nor things to come, nor height, nor depth, nor any other creature, shall be able to separate us from the love of God which is in Christ Jesus our Lord.'

## WHAT PROVES GOD'S LOVE

'God commendeth His love toward us, in that, while we were yet sinners, Christ died for us.'—ROMANS v. 8.

WE have seen in previous sermons on the preceding context that the Apostle has been tracing various lines of sequence, all of which converge upon Christian hope. The last of these pointed to the fact that the

love of God, poured into a heart like oil into a lamp,
brightened that flame; and having thus mentioned the
great Christian revelation of God as love, Paul at
once passes to emphasise the historical fact on which
the conviction of that love rests, and goes on to say
that 'the love of God is shed abroad in our hearts by
the Holy Ghost which is given to us, *for* when we were
yet without strength, in due time Christ died for the
ungodly.'   Then there rises before him the thought
of how transcendent and unparalleled a love is that
which pours its whole preciousness on unworthy and
unresponsive hearts.  He thinks to himself—'We are
all ungodly; without strength—yet, He died for us.
Would any man do that?  No! for,' says he, 'it will be
a hard thing to find any one ready to die for a righteous
man—a man rigidly just and upright, and because
rigidly just, a trifle hard, and therefore not likely to
touch a heart to sacrifice; and even for a good man,
in whom austere righteousness has been softened and
made attractive, and become graciousness and beneficence, well! it is just within the limits of possibility
that somebody might be found even to die for a man
that had laid such a strong hand upon his affections.
But God commendeth His love in that while we were
yet sinners Christ died for us.'  Now, when Paul says
'commend,' he uses a very significant word which is
employed in two ways in the New Testament.  It
sometimes means to establish, or to prove, or to make
certain.  But 'prove' is a cold word, and the expression also means to recommend, to set forth in such a
way as to appeal to the heart, and God does both in
that great act.  He establishes the fact, and He, as it
were, sweeps it into a man's heart, on the bosom of
that full tide of self-sacrifice.

So there are two or three points that arise from these words, on which I desire to dwell now—to lay them upon our hearts, and not only upon our understandings. For it is a poor thing to prove the love of God, and we need that not only shall we be sure of it, but that we shall be softened by it. So now let me ask you to look with me, first, at this question—

I. What Paul thought Jesus Christ died for.

'Died *for* us.' Now that expression plainly implies two things: first, that Christ died of His own accord, and being impelled by a great motive, beneficence; and, second, that that voluntary death, somehow or other, is for our behoof and advantage. The word in the original, 'for,' does not define in what way that death ministers to our advantage, but it does assert that for those Roman Christians who had never seen Jesus Christ, and by consequence for you and me nineteen centuries off the Cross, there is benefit in the fact of that death. Now, suppose we quote an incident in the story of missionary martyrdom. There was a young lady, whom some of us knew and loved, in a Chinese mission station, who, with the rest of the missionary band, was flying. Her life was safe. She looked back, and saw a Chinese boy that her heart twined round, in danger. She returned to save him; they laid hold of her and flung her into the burning house, and her charred remains have never been found. That was a death for another, but 'Jesus died for us' in a deeper sense than that. Take another case. A man sets himself to some great cause, not his own, and he sees that in order to bless humanity, either by the proclamation of some truth, or by the origination of some great movement, or in some other way, if he is to carry out his purpose,

G

he must give his life. He does so, and dies a martyr. What he aimed at could only be done by the sacrifice of his life. The death was a means to his end, and he died for his fellows. That is not the depth of the sense in which Paul meant that Jesus Christ died for us. It was not that He was true to His message, and, like many another martyr, died. There is only one way, as it seems to me, in which any beneficial relation can be established between the Death of Christ and us, and it is that when He died He died for us, because 'He bare our sins in His own body on the tree.'

Dear brethren, I dare say some of you do not take that view, but I know not how justice can be done to the plain words of Scripture unless this is the point of view from which we look at the Cross of Calvary— that there the Lamb of Sacrifice was bearing, and bearing away, the sins of the whole world. I know that Christian men who unite in the belief that Christ's death was a sacrifice and an atonement diverge from one another in their interpretations of the way in which that came to be a fact, and I believe, for my part, that the divergent interpretations are like the divergent beams of light that fall upon men who stand round the same great luminary, and that all of them take their origin in, and are part of the manifestation of, the one transcendent fact, which passes all under- standing, and gathers into itself all the diverse con- ceptions of it which are formed by limited minds. He died for us because, in His death, our sins are taken away and we are restored to the divine favour.

I know that Jesus Christ is said to have made far less of that aspect of His work in the Gospels than His disciples have done in the Epistles, and that we are told that, if we go back to Jesus, we shall not find the

doctrine which for some of us is the first form in which
the Gospel finds its way into the hearts of men. I
admit that the fully-developed teaching followed the
fact, as was necessarily the case. I do not admit that
Jesus Christ 'spake nothing concerning Himself' as
the sacrifice for the world's sins. For I hear from
His lips—not to dwell upon other sayings which I could
quote—I hear from His lips, 'The Son of Man came not
to be ministered unto, but to minister'—that is only
half His purpose—'and to give His life a ransom
instead of the many.' You cannot strike the atoning
aspect of His death out of that expression by any fair
handling of the words.

And what does the Lord's Supper mean? Why did
Jesus Christ select that one point of His life as the
point to be remembered? Why did He institute the
double memorial, the body parted from the blood being
a sign of a violent death? I know of no explanation
that makes that Lord's Supper an intelligible rite
except the explanation which says that He came, to
live indeed, and in that life to be a sacrifice, but to
make the sacrifice complete by Himself bearing the
consequences of transgression, and making atonement
for the sins of the world.

Brethren, that is the only aspect of Christ's death
which makes it of any consequence to us. Strip it of
that, and what does it matter to me that He died, any
more than it matters to me that any philanthropist,
any great teacher, any hero or martyr or saint, should
have died? As it seems to me, nothing. Christ's
death is surrounded by tenderly pathetic and beautiful
accompaniments. As a story it moves the hearts of
men, and 'purges them, by pity and by terror.' But
the death of many a hero of tragedy does all that.

And if you want to have the Cross of Christ held
upright in its place as the Throne of Christ and the
attractive power for the whole world, you must not
tamper with that great truth, but say, 'He died for
our sins, according to the Scriptures.'

Now, there is a second question that I wish to ask,
and that is—

II. How does Christ's death 'commend' God's love?

That is a strange expression, if you will think about
it, that 'God commendeth His love towards us in that
Christ died.' If you take the interpretation of Christ's
death of which I have already been speaking, one
could have understood the Apostle if he had said,
'Christ commendeth His love towards us in that
Christ died.' But where is the force of the fact of a
man's death to prove God's love? Do you not see that
underlying that swift sentence of the Apostle there
is a presupposition, which he takes for granted? It
is so obvious that I do not need to dwell upon it to
vindicate his change of persons, viz. that 'God was in
Christ,' in such fashion as that whatsoever Christ did
was the revelation of God. You cannot suppose, at
least I cannot see how you can, that there is any
force of proof in the words of my text, unless you
come up to the full belief, 'God was in Christ reconciling the world to Himself.'

Suppose some great martyr who dies for his fellows.
Well, all honour to him, and the race will come to his
tomb for a while, and bring their wreaths and their
sorrow. But what bearing has his death upon our
knowledge of God's love towards us? None whatever,
or at most a very indirect and shadowy one. We
have to dig deeper down than that. 'God commends
His love . . . in that Christ died.' 'He that hath seen

Me hath seen the Father.' And we have the right and the obligation to argue back from all that is manifest in the tender Christ to the heart of God, and say, not only, ' God so loved the world that He' sent His Son, but to see that the love that was in Christ is the manifestation of the love of God Himself.

So there stands the Cross, the revelation to us, not only of a Brother's sacrifice, but of a Father's love; and that because Jesus Christ is the revelation of God as being the ' eradiation of His glory, and the express image of His person.' Friends! light does pour out from that Cross, whatever view men take of it. But the omnipotent beam, the all-illuminating radiance, the transforming light, the heat that melts, are all dependent on our looking at it—I do not only say, as Paul looked at it, nor do I even say as Christ looked at it, but as the deep necessities of humanity require that the world should look at it, as the altar whereon is laid the sacrifice for our sins, the very Son of God Himself. To me the great truths of the Incarnation and the Atonement of Jesus Christ are not points in a mere speculative theology; they are the pulsating vital centre of religion. And every man needs them in his own experience.

I was going to have said a word or two here—but it is not necessary—about the need that the love of God should be irrefragably established, by some plain and undeniable and conspicuous fact. I need not dwell upon the ambiguous oracles which—

> 'Nature, red in tooth and claw,
> With rapine'

gives forth, nor on how the facts of human life, our own sorrows, and the world's miseries, the tears that

swathe the earth, as it rolls on its orbit, like a misty
atmosphere, war against the creed that God is love.
I need not remind you, either, of how deep, in our own
hearts, when the conscience begins to speak its *not*
ambiguous oracles, there does rise the conviction that
there is much in us which it is impossible should be
the object of God's love.  Nor need I remind you how
all these difficulties in believing in a God who is love,
based on the contradictory aspects of nature, and the
mysteries of providence, and the whisperings of our
own consciousness, are proved to have been insuper-
able by the history of the world, where we find mytho-
logies and religions of all types and gods of every sort,
but nowhere in all the pantheon a God who is Love.

Only let me press upon you that that conviction of
the love of God, which is found now far beyond the
limits of Christian faith, and amongst many of us
who, in the name of that conviction itself, reject
Christianity, because of its sterner aspects, is historically the child of the evangelical doctrine of the
Incarnation and sacrifice of Jesus Christ.  And if it
still subsists, as I know it does, especially in this
generation, amongst many men who reject what seems
to me to be the very kernel of Christianity—subsists
like the stream cut off from its source, but still running, that only shows that men hold many convictions
the origin of which they do not know.  God is love.
You will not permanently sustain that belief against
the pressure of outward mysteries and inward sorrows,
unless you grasp the other conviction that Christ died
for our sins.  The two are inseparable.

And now lastly—

III. What kind of love does Christ's death declare
to us as existing in God?

A love that is turned away by no sin—that is the thing that strikes the Apostle here, as I have already pointed out. The utmost reach of human affection might be that a man would die for the good—he would scarcely die for the righteous. But God sends His Son, and comes Himself in His Son, and His Son died for the ungodly and the sinner. That death reveals a love which is its own origin and motive. We love because we discern, or fancy we do, something lovable in the object. God loves under the impulse, so to speak, of His own welling-up heart.

And yet it is a love which, though not turned away by any sin, is witnessed by that death to be rigidly righteous. It is no mere flaccid, flabby laxity of a loose-girt affection, no mere foolish indulgence like that whereby earthly parents spoil their children. God's love is not lazy good-nature, as a great many of us think it to be and so drag it in the mud, but it is rigidly righteous, and therefore Christ died. That Death witnesses that it is a love which shrinks from no sacrifices. This Isaac was not 'spared.' God gave up His Son. Love has its very speech in surrender, and God's love speaks as ours does. It is a love which, turned away by no sin, and yet rigidly righteous and shrinking from no sacrifices, embraces all ages and lands. 'God commendeth'—not 'commended.' The majestic present tense suggests that time and space are nothing to the swift and all-filling rays of that great Light. That love is 'towards us,' you and me and all our fellows. The Death is an historical fact, occurring in one short hour. The Cross is an eternal power, raying out light and love over all humanity and through all ages.

God lays siege to all hearts in that great sacrifice.

Do you believe that Jesus Christ died for *your* sins 'according to the Scriptures'? Do you see there the assurance of a love which will lift you up above all the cross-currents of earthly life, and the mysteries of providence, into the clear ether where the sunshine is unobscured? And above all, do you fling back the reverberating ray from the mirror of your own heart that directs again towards heaven the beam of love which heaven has shot down upon you? 'Herein is love, not that we loved God, but that He loved us, and gave His Son to be the propitiation for our sins.' Is it true of us that we love God because He first loved us?

## THE WARRING QUEENS

'As sin hath reigned unto death, even so might grace reign through righteousness unto eternal life by Jesus Christ our Lord.'—ROMANS v. 21.

I AM afraid this text will sound to some of you rather unpromising. It is full of well-worn terms, 'sin,' 'death,' 'grace,' 'righteousness,' 'eternal life,' which suggest dry theology, if they suggest anything. When they welled up from the Apostle's glowing heart they were like a fiery lava-stream. But the stream has cooled, and, to a good many of us, they seem as barren and sterile as the long ago cast out coils of lava on the sides of a quiescent volcano. They are so well-worn and familiar to our ears that they create but vague conceptions in our minds, and they seem to many of us to be far away from a bearing upon our daily lives. But you much mistake Paul if you take him to be a mere theological writer. He is an earnest evangelist, trying to draw men to love and trust in Jesus Christ. And his writings, however old-fashioned and doctrinally hard they may seem to you, are all

throbbing with life—instinct with truths that belong
to all ages and places, and which fit close to every one
of us.

I do not know if I can give any kind of freshness to
these words, but I wish to try. To begin with, I notice
the highly-imaginative and picturesque form into
which the Apostle casts his thoughts here. He, as it
were, draws back a curtain, and lets us see two royal
figures, which are eternally opposed and dividing the
dominion between them. Then he shows us the issues
to which these two rulers respectively conduct their
subjects; and the question that is trembling on his
lips is 'Under which of them do you stand?' Surely
that is not fossil theology, but truths that are of the
highest importance, and ought to be of the deepest
interest, to every one of us. They are to you the
former, whether they are the latter or not.

I. So, first, look at the two Queens who rule over
human life.

Sin and Grace are both personified; and they are
both conceived of as female figures, and both as exercising dominion. They stand face to face, and each recognises as her enemy the other. The one has established
her dominion: 'Sin *hath* reigned.' The other is fighting to establish hers: 'That Grace *might* reign.' And
the struggle is going on between them, not only on
the wide field of the world; but in the narrow lists of
the heart of each of us.

Sin reigns. The truths that underlie that solemn
picture are plain enough, however unwelcome they
may be to some of us, and however remote from the
construction of the universe which many of us are
disposed to take.

Now, let us understand our terms. Suppose a man

commits a theft. You may describe it from three
different points of view. He has thereby broken the
law of the land; and when we are thinking about
that we call it crime. He has also broken the law of
'morality,' as we call it; and when we are looking at
his deed from that point of view, we call it vice. Is
that all? He has broken something else. He has
broken the law of God; and when we look at it from
that point of view we call it sin. Now, there are a
great many things which are sins that are not crimes;
and, with due limitations, I might venture to say that
there are some things which are sins that are not
to be qualified as vices. Sin implies God. The Psalmist
was quite right when he said; 'Against Thee, Thee
only have I sinned'; although he was confessing a foul
injury he had done to Bathsheba, and a glaring crime
that he had committed against Uriah. It was as to
God, and in reference to Him only, that his crime and
his vice darkened and solidified into sin.

And what is it, in our actions or in ourselves considered in reference to God, that makes our actions
sins and ourselves sinners? Remember the prodigal
son. 'Father! Give me the portion of goods that
falleth to me.' There you have it all. He went away,
and 'wasted his substance in riotous living.' To claim
myself for my own; to act independently of, or
contrary to, the will of God; to try to shake myself
clear of Him; to have nothing to do with Him, even
though it be by mere forgetfulness and negligence,
and, in all my ways to comport myself as if I had no
relations of dependence on and submission to him
—that is sin. And there may be that oblivion or rebellion, not only in the gross vulgar acts which the law
calls crimes, or in those which conscience declares to be

vices, but also in many things which, looked at from a lower point of view, may be fair and pure and noble. If there is this assertion of self in them, or oblivion of God and His will in them, I know not how we are to escape the conclusion that even these fall under the class of sins. For there can be no act or thought, truly worthy of a man, situated and circumstanced as we are, which has not, for the very core and animating motive of it, a reference to God.

Now, when I come and say, as my Bible teaches me to say, that this is the deepest view of the state of humanity that sin reigns, I do not wish to fall into the exaggerations by which sometimes that statement has been darkened and discredited; but I do want to press upon you, dear brethren, this, as a matter of *personal* experience, that wherever there is a heart that loves, and leaves God out, and wherever there is a will that resolves, determines, impels to action, and does not bow itself before Him, and wherever there are hands that labour, or feet that run, at tasks and in paths self-chosen and unconsecrated by reference to our Father in heaven, no matter how great and beautiful subsidiary lustres may light up their deeds, the very heart of them all is transgression of the law of God. For this, and nothing else or less, is His law: 'Thou shalt love the Lord thy God with all thy heart, and with all thy soul, and with all thy strength, and with all thy mind.' I do not charge you with crimes. You know how far it would be right to charge you with vices. *I* do not charge you with anything; but I pray you to come with me and confess: 'We all have sinned, and come short of the glory of God.'

I suppose I need not dwell upon the difficulty of getting a lodgment for this conviction in men's hearts.

There is no sadder, and no more conclusive proof, of the tremendous power of sin over us, than that it has lulled us into unconsciousness, hard to be broken, of its own presence and existence. You remember the old stories—I suppose there is no truth in them, but they will do for an illustration—about some kind of a blood-sucking animal that perched upon a sleeping man, and with its leathern wings fanned him into deeper drowsiness whilst it drew from him his life-blood. That is what this hideous Queen does for men. She robes herself in a dark cloud, and sends out her behests from obscurity. And men fancy that they are free whilst all the while they are her servants. Oh, dear brethren! you may call this theology, but it is a simple statement of the facts of our condition. 'Sin hath reigned.'

And now turn to the other picture, 'Grace might reign.' Then there is an antagonistic power that rises up to confront the widespread dominion of this anarch of old. And this Queen comes with twenty thousand to war against her that has but ten thousand on her side.

Again I say, let us understand our terms. I suppose, there are few of the keywords of the New Testament which have lost more of their radiance, like quicksilver, by exposure in the air during the centuries than that great word Grace, which is always on the lips of this Apostle, and to him had music in its sound, and which to us is a piece of dead doctrine, associated with certain high Calvinistic theories which we enlightened people have long ago grown beyond, and got rid of. Perhaps Paul was more right than we when his heart leaped up within him at the very thought of all which he saw to lie palpitating and throbbing with eager desire to bless men, in that great word. What does he mean by it? Let me put it into the shortest possible terms. This antagonist Queen is nothing but the love of God raying. out for ever to us inferior creatures, who, by reason of our sinfulness, have deserved something widely different. Sin stands there, a hideous hag, though a queen; Grace stands here, 'in all her gestures dignity and love,' fair and self-communicative, though a sovereign. The love of God in exercise to sinful men: that is what the New Testament means by grace. And is it not a great thought?

Notice, for further elucidation of the Apostle's conception, how he sacrifices the verbal correctness of his antithesis in order to get to the real opposition. What is the opposite of Sin? Righteousness. Why does he not say, then, that 'as Sin hath reigned unto death, even so might Righteousness reign unto life'? Why? Because it is not man, or anything in man, that can be the true antagonist of, and victor over, the regnant Sin of humanity; but God Himself comes into the field, and only He is the foe that Sin dreads. That is to say, the only hope for a sin-tyrannised world is in the outthrob of the love of the great heart of God. For, notice the weapon with which He fights man's transgression, if I may vary the figure for a moment. It is only subordinately punishment, or law, or threatening, or the revelation of the wickedness of the transgression. All these have their places, but they are secondary places. The thing that will conquer a world's wickedness is nothing else but the manifested love of God. Only the patient shining down of the sun will ever melt the icebergs that float in all our hearts. And wonderful and blessed it is to think that, in whatsoever aspects man's sin may have been an interruption and a contradiction of the divine purpose, out of the evil has come a good; that the more obdurate and universal the rebellion, the more has it evoked a deeper and more wondrous tenderness. The blacker the thundercloud, the brighter glows the rainbow that is flung across it. So these two front each other, the one settled in her established throne—

'Fierce as ten furies, terrible as hell—'

the other coming on her adventurous errand to conquer the world to herself, and to banish the foul tyranny under which men groan. 'Sin hath reigned.' Grace is on her way to her dominion.

II. Notice the gifts of these two Queens to their subjects.

'Sin hath reigned in death' (as the accurate translation has it); 'Grace reigns unto eternal life.' The one has established her dominion, and its results are wrought out, her reign is, as it were, a reign in a cemetery; and her subjects are dead. If you want a modern instance to illustrate an ancient saw, think of Armenia. There is a reign whose gifts to its subjects are death. Sin reigns, says Paul, and for proof points to the fact that men die.

Now, I am not going to enter into the question here, and now, whether physical death passes over mankind because of the fact of transgression. I do not suppose that this is so. But I ask you to remember that when the Bible says that 'Death passed upon all men, for all have sinned,' it does not merely mean the physical fact of dissolution, but it means that fact along with the accompaniments of it, and the forerunners of it, in men's consciences. 'The sting of death is sin,' says Paul, in another place. By which he im-

plies, I presume, that, if it were not for the fact of
alienation from God and opposition to His holy will,
men might lie down and die as placidly as an animal
does, and might strip themselves for it 'as for a bed,
that longing they'd been sick for.' No doubt, there
was death in the world long before there were men in
it. No doubt, also, the complex whole phenomenon
gets its terror from the fact of men's sin.

But it is not so much that physical fact with its
accompaniments which Paul is thinking about when
he says that 'sin reigns in death,' as it is that solemn
truth which he is always reiterating, and which I pray
you, dear friends, to lay to heart, that, whatever
activity there may be in the life of a man who has rent
himself away from dependence upon God—however
vigorous his brain, however active his hand, however
full charged with other interests his life, in the very
depth of it it is a living death, and the right name for
it *is* death. So this is Sin's gift—that over our whole
nature there come mortality and decay, and that they
who live as her subjects are dead whilst they live.
Dear brethren, that may be figurative, but it seems to
me that it is absurd for you to turn away from such
thoughts, shrug your shoulders, and say, 'Old-fashioned
Calvinistic theology!' It is simply putting into a vivid
form the facts of your life and of your condition in
relation to God, if you are subjects of Sin.

Then, on the other hand, the other queenly figure
has her hands filled with one great gift which, like the
fatal bestowment which Sin gives to her subjects, has
two aspects, a present and a future one. Life, which
is given in our redemption from Death and Sin, and in
union with God; that is the present gift that the love
of God holds out to every one of us. That life, in its

very incompleteness here, carries in itself the prophecy
of its own completion hereafter, in a higher form and
world, just as truly as the bud is the prophet of the
flower and of the fruit; just as truly as a half-reared
building is the prophecy of its own completion when
the rooftree is put upon it. The men that here have,
as we all may have if we choose, the gift of life eternal
in the knowledge of God through Jesus Christ His
Son, must necessarily tend onwards and upwards to a
region where Death is beneath the horizon, and Life
flows and flushes the whole heaven. Brother! do you
put out your whole hand to take the poisoned gift
from the claw-like hand of that hideous Queen; or do
you turn and take the gift of life eternal from the
hands of the queenly Grace?

III. How this queenly Grace gives her gifts.

You observe that the Apostle, as is his wont—I was
going to say—gets himself entangled in a couple of
almost parenthetical or, at all events, subsidiary
sentences. I suppose when he began to write he
meant to say, simply, 'as Sin hath reigned unto death,
so Grace might reign unto life.' But notice that he
inserts two qualifications: 'through righteousness,'
'through Jesus Christ our Lord.' What does he mean
by these?

He means this, first, that even that great love of
God, coming throbbing straight from His heart, cannot
give eternal life as a mere matter of arbitrary will.
God can make His sun to shine and His rain to fall,
'on the unthankful and on the evil,' and if God could,
God would give eternal life to everybody, bad and good;
but He cannot. There must be righteousness if there
is to be life. Just as sin's fruit is death, the fruit of
righteousness is life.

: He means, in the next place, that whilst there is no life without righteousness, there is no righteousness without God's gift. You cannot break away from the dominion of Sin, and, as it were, establish yourselves in a little fortress of your own, repelling her assaults by any power of yours. Dear brethren, we cannot undo the past; we cannot strip off the poisoned garment that clings to our limbs; we can mend ourselves in many respects, but we cannot of our own volition and motion clothe ourselves with that righteousness of which the wearers shall be worthy to 'pass through the gate into the city.' There is no righteousness without God's gift.

And the other subsidiary clause completes the thought: 'through Christ.' In Him is all the grace, the manifest love, of God gathered together. It is not diffused as the nebulous light in some chaotic incipient system, but it is gathered into a sun that is set in the centre, in order that it may pour down warmth and life upon its circling planets. The grace of God is in Christ Jesus our Lord. In Him is life eternal; therefore, if we desire to possess it we must possess Him. In Him is righteousness; therefore, if we desire our own foulness to be changed into the holiness which shall see God, we must go to Jesus Christ. Grace reigns in life, but it is life through righteousness, which is through Jesus Christ our Lord.

So, then, brother, my message and my petition to each of you are—knit yourself to Him by faith in Him. Then He who is 'full of grace and truth' will come to you; and, coming, will bring in His hands righteousness and life eternal. If only we rest ourselves on Him, and keep ourselves close in touch with Him; then we shall be delivered from the tyranny of the

H

darkness, and translated into the Kingdom of the Son
of His love.

## 'THE FORM OF TEACHING'

'. . . Ye have obeyed from the heart that form of doctrine which was delivered
you.'—ROMANS vi. 17.

THERE is room for difference of opinion as to what
Paul precisely means by 'form' here. The word so
rendered appears in English as *type*, and has a similar
variety of meaning. It signifies originally a mark
made by pressure or impact; and then, by natural
transitions, a *mould*, or more generally a *pattern* or
*example*, and then the copy of such an example or
pattern, or the cast from such a mould. It has also
the other meaning which its English equivalent has
taken on very extensively of late years, such as, for
instance, you find in expressions like 'An English type
of face,' meaning thereby the general outline which
preserves the distinguishing characteristics of a thing.
Now we may choose between these two meanings in
our text. If the Apostle means type in the latter sense
of the word, then the rendering 'form' is adequate,
and he is thinking of the Christian teaching which
had been given to the Roman Christians as possessing
certain well-defined characteristics which distinguished
it from other kinds of teaching—such, for instance, as
Jewish or heathen.

But if we take the other meaning, then he is, in true
Pauline fashion, bringing in a vivid and picturesque
metaphor to enforce his thought, and is thinking of
the teaching which the Roman Christians had received
as being a kind of mould into which they were thrown,
a pattern to which they were to be conformed. And

that that is his meaning seems to me to be made a
little more probable by the fact that the last words of
my text would be more accurate if inverted, and
instead of reading, as the Authorised Version does,
'that form of doctrine which was delivered you,' we
were to read, as the Revised Version does, 'that form
whereunto ye were delivered.'

If this be the general meaning of the words before
us, there are three thoughts arising from them to
which I turn briefly.   First, Paul's Gospel was a
definite body of teaching; secondly, that teaching is
a mould for conduct and character; lastly, that teaching therefore demands obedience.   Take, then, these
three thoughts.

I. First, Paul's Gospel was a definite body of teaching.

Now the word 'doctrine,' which is employed in my
text, has, in the lapse of years since the Authorised
Version was made, narrowed its significance.   At the
date of our Authorised translation 'doctrine' was probably equivalent to 'teaching,' of whatever sort it
might be.   Since then it has become equivalent to a
statement of abstract principles, and that is not at all
what Paul means.   He does not mean to say that his
gospel was a form of doctrine in the sense of being a
theological system, but he means to say that it was a
body of teaching, the nature of the teaching not being
defined at all by the word.

Therefore we have to notice that the great, blessed
peculiarity of the Gospel is that it is a teaching, not of
abstract dry principles, but of concrete historical facts.
From these principles in plenty may be gathered, but
in its first form as it comes to men fresh from God it
is not a set of propositions, but a history of deeds that

were done upon earth. And, therefore, is it fitted to be the food of every soul and the mould of every character.

Jesus Christ did not come and talk to men about God, and say to them what His Apostles afterwards said, 'God is love,' but He lived and died, and that mainly was His teaching about God. He did not come to men and lay down a theory of atonement or a doctrine of propitiation, or theology about sin and its relations to God, but He went to the Cross and gave Himself for us, and that was His teaching about sacrifice. He did not say to men 'There is a future life, and it is of such and such a sort,' but He came out of the grave and He said 'Touch Me, and handle Me. A spirit hath not flesh and bones,' and *therefore* He brought life and immortality to light, by no empty words but by the solid realities of facts. He did not lecture upon ethics, but He lived a perfect human life out of which all moral principles that will guide human conduct may be gathered. And so, instead of presenting us with a *hortus siccus*, with a botanic collection of scientifically arranged and dead propositions, He led us into the meadow where the flowers grow, living and fair. His life and death, with all that they imply, are the teaching.

Let us not forget, on the other hand, that the history of a fact is not the mere statement of the outward thing that has happened. Suppose four people, for instance, standing at the foot of Christ's Cross; four other 'evangelists' than the four that we know. There is a Roman soldier; there is a Pharisee; there is one of the weeping crowd of poor women, not disciples; and there is a disciple. The first man tells the fact as he saw it: 'A Jewish rebel was crucified this morning.'

The second man tells the fact: 'A blaspheming apostate suffered what he deserved to-day.' The woman tells the fact: 'A poor, gentle, fair soul was martyred to-day.' And the fourth one tells the fact: 'Jesus Christ, the Son of God, died for our sins.' The three tell the same fact; the fourth preaches the Gospel— that is to say, Christian teaching is the facts plus their explanation; and it is that which differentiates it from the mere record which is of no avail to anybody. So Paul himself in one of his other letters puts it. This is his gospel: Jesus of Nazareth ' died for *our* sins according to the Scriptures, and He was buried, and rose again the third day, according to the Scriptures.' That is what turns the bald story of the facts into teaching, which is the mould for life.

So on the one hand, dear brethren, do not let us fall into the superficial error of fancying that our religion is a religion of emotion and morality only. It is a religion with a basis of divine truth, which, being struck away, all the rest goes. There is a revolt against dogma to-day, a revolt which in large measure is justified as an essential of progress, and in large measure as an instance of progress; but human nature is ever prone to extremes, and in the revolt from man's dogma there is danger of casting away God's truth. Christianity is not preserved when we hold by the bare facts of the outward history, unless we take with these facts the interpretation of them, which declares the divinity and the sacrifice of the Son of God.

And on the other hand, let us keep very clear in our minds the broad and impassable gulf of separation between the Christian teaching as embodied in the Scripture and the systems which Christianity has evolved therefrom. Men's intellects must work upon the pabulum that is provided for them, and a theology in a systematised form is a necessity for the intellectual and reasonable life of the Christian Church. But there is all the difference between man's inferences from and systematising of the Christian truth and the truth that lies here. The one is the golden roof that is cast over us; the other is too often but the spiders' webs that are spun across and darken its splendour. It is a sign of a wholesome change in the whole sentiment and attitude of the modern Christian mind that the word 'doctrine,' which has come to mean men's inferences from God's truth, should have been substituted as it has been in our Revised Version of my text, by the wholesome Christian word 'teaching.' The teaching is the facts with the inspired commentary on them.

II. Secondly, notice that this teaching is in Paul's judgment a mould or pattern according to which men's lives are to be conformed.

There can be no question but that, in that teaching as set forth in Scripture, there does lie the mightiest formative power for shaping our lives, and emancipating us from our evil.

Christ is *the* type, the mould into which men are to be cast. The Gospel, as presented in Scripture, gives us three things. It gives us the perfect mould; it gives us the perfect motive; it gives us the perfect power. And in all three things appears its distinctive glory, apart from and above all other systems that have ever tried to affect the conduct or to mould the character of man.

In Jesus Christ we have in due combination, in perfect proportion, all the possible excellences of humanity. As in other cases of perfect symmetry, the

very precision of the balanced proportions detracts
from the apparent magnitude of the statue or of the
fair building, so to a superficial eye there is but little
beauty there that we should desire Him, but as we
learn to know Him, and live nearer to Him, and get
more familiar with all His sweetness, and with all His
power, He towers before us in ever greater and yet
never repellent or exaggerated magnitude, and never
loses the reality of His brotherhood in the completeness of His perfection. We have in the Christ the one
type, the one mould and pattern for all striving, the
'glass of form,' the perfect Man.

And that likeness is not reproduced in us by pressure
or by a blow, but by the slow and blessed process of
gazing until we become like, beholding the glory until
we are changed into the glory.

It is no use having a mould and metal unless you
have a fire. It is no use having a perfect Pattern
unless you have a motive to copy it. Men do not go to
the devil for want of examples; and morality is not at
a low ebb by reason of ignorance of what the true type
of life is. But nowhere but in the full-orbed teaching
of the New Testament will you find a motive strong
enough to melt down all the obstinate hardness of the
'northern iron' of the human will, and to make it
plastic to His hand. If we can say, 'He loved me and
gave Himself for me,' then the sum of all morality, the
old commandment that 'ye love one another,' receives
a new stringency, and a fresh motive as well as a
deepened interpretation, when His love is our pattern.
The one thing that will make men willing to be like
Christ is their faith that Christ is their Sacrifice and
their Saviour. And sure I am of this, that no form of
mutilated Christianity, which leaves out or falteringly

proclaims the truth that Christ died on the Cross for the sins of the world, will ever generate heat enough to mould men's wills, or kindle motives powerful enough to lead to a life of growing imitation of and resemblance to Him. The dial may be all right, the hours most accurately marked in their proper places, every minute registered on the circle, the hands may be all right, delicately fashioned, truly poised, but if there is no main-spring inside, dial and hands are of little use, and a Christianity which says, 'Christ is the Teacher; do you obey Him?' is as impotent as the dial face with the broken main-spring. What we need, and what, thank God, in 'the teaching' we have, is the pattern brought near to us, and the motive for imitating the pattern, set in motion by the great thought, 'He loved me and gave Himself for me.'

Still further, the teaching is a power to fashion life, inasmuch as it brings with it a gift which secures the transformation of the believer into the likeness of his Lord. Part of 'the teaching' is the fact of Pentecost; part of the teaching is the fact of the Ascension; and the consequence of the Ascension and the sure promise of the Pentecost is that all who love Him, and wait upon Him, shall receive into their hearts the 'Spirit of life in Christ Jesus' which shall make them free from the law of sin and death.

So, dear friends, on the one hand, let us remember that our religion is meant to work, that we have nothing in our creed that should not be in our character, that all our *credenda* are to be our *agenda*; everything *believed* to be something *done*; and that if we content ourselves with the simple acceptance of the teaching, and make no effort to translate that teaching into life, we are hypocrites or self-deceivers.

And, on the other hand, do not let us forget that religion is the soul of which morality is the body, and that it is impossible in the nature of things that you shall ever get a true, lofty, moral life which is not based upon religion. I do not say that men cannot be sure of the outlines of their duty without Christianity, though I am free to confess that I think it is a very maimed and shabby version of human duty, which is supplied, minus the special revelation of that duty which Christianity makes; but my point is, that the knowledge will not work without the Gospel.

The Christian type of character is a distinct and manifestly separate thing from the pagan heroism or from the virtues and the righteousnesses of other systems. Just as the musician's ear can tell, by half a dozen bars, whether that strain was Beethoven's, or Handel's, or Mendelssohn's, just as the trained eye can see Raffaelle's magic in every touch of his pencil, so Christ, the Teacher, has a style; and all the scholars of His school carry with them a certain mark which tells where they got their education and who is their Master, if they are scholars indeed. And that leads me to the last word.

III. This mould demands obedience.

By the very necessity of things it is so. If the 'teaching' was but a teaching of abstract truths it would be enough to assent to them. I believe that the three angles of a triangle are equal to two right angles, and I have done my duty by that proposition when I have said 'Yes! it is so.' But the 'teaching' which Jesus Christ gives and is, needs a good deal more than that. By the very nature of the teaching, assent drags after it submission. You can please yourself whether you let Jesus Christ into your minds or not, but if you do let Him in, He will be Master. There is no such thing as taking Him in and not obeying.

, And so the requirement of the Gospel which we call faith has in it quite as much of the element of obedience as of the element of trust. And the presence of that element is just what makes the difference between a sham and a real faith. 'Faith which has not works is dead, being alone.' A faith which is all trust and no obedience is neither trust nor obedience.

And that is why so many of us do not care to yield ourselves to the faith that is in Jesus Christ. If it simply came to us and said, 'If you will trust Me you will get pardon,' I fancy there would be a good many more of us honest Christians than are so. But Christ comes and says, 'Trust Me, follow Me, and take Me for your Master; and be like Me,' and one's will kicks, and one's passions recoil, and a thousand of the devil's servants within us prick their ears up and stiffen their backs in remonstrance and opposition. 'Submit' is Christ's first word; submit by faith, submit in love.

That heart obedience, which is the requirement of Christianity, means freedom. The Apostle draws a wonderful contrast in the context between the slavery to lust and sin, and the freedom which comes from obedience to God and to righteousness. Obey the Truth, and the Truth, in your obeying, shall make you free, for freedom is the willing submission to the limitations which are best. 'I will walk at liberty for I keep Thy precepts.' Take Christ for your Master, and, being His servants, you are your own masters, and the world's to boot. For 'all things are yours if ye are Christ's.' Refuse to bow your necks to that yoke which is easy, and to take upon your shoulders that burden which is light, and you do not buy liberty, though you

buy licentiousness, for you become the slaves and
downtrodden vassals of the world and the flesh and
the devil, and while you promise yourselves liberty,
you become the bondsmen of corruption. Oh! then,
let us obey from the heart that mould of teaching to
which we are delivered, and so obeying, we shall be
free indeed.


### 'THY FREE SPIRIT'

'The law of the Spirit of life in Christ Jesus hath made me free from the law of
sin and death.'—ROMANS viii. 2.

WE have to distinguish two meanings of law. In the
stricter sense, it signifies the authoritative expressions of the will of a ruler proposed for the obedience
of man; in the wider, almost figurative sense, it means
nothing more than the generalised expression of constant similar facts. For instance, objects attract one
another in certain circumstances with a force which
in the same circumstances is always the same. When
that fact is stated generally, we get the law of gravitation. Thus the word comes to mean little more than
a regular process. In our text the word is used in a
sense much nearer the latter than the former of these
two. 'The law of sin and of death' cannot mean a
series of commandments; it certainly does not mean
the Mosaic law. It must either be entirely figurative,
taking sin and death as two great tyrants who
domineer over men; or it must mean the continuous
action of these powers, the process by which they
work. These two come substantially to the same
idea. The law of sin and of death describes a certain
constancy of operation, uniform and fixed, under the

dominion of which men are struggling. But there is
another constancy of operation, uniform and fixed
too, a mighty antagonistic power, which frees from the
dominion of the former: it is 'the law of the Spirit
of life in Christ Jesus.'

I. The bondage.

The Apostle is speaking about himself as he was, and
we have our own consciousness to verify his transcript
of his own personal experience. Paul had found that,
by an inexorable iron sequence, sin worked in himself
the true death of the soul, in separation from God, in
the extinction of good and noble capacities, in the
atrophying of all that was best in himself, in the death
of joy and peace. And this iron sequence he, with an
eloquent paradox, calls a 'law,' though its very
characteristic is that it is lawless transgression of the
true law of humanity. He so describes it, partly,
because he would place emphasis on its dominion over
us. Sin rules with iron sway; men madly obey it, and
even when they think themselves free, are under a
bitter tyranny. Further, he desires to emphasise the
fact that sin and death are parts of one process which
operates constantly and uniformly. This dark anarchy
and wild chaos of disobedience and transgression has
its laws. All happens there according to rule. Rigid
and inevitable as the courses of the stars, or the fall
of the leaf from the tree, is sin hurrying on to its
natural goal in death. In this fatal dance, sin leads in
death; the one fair spoken and full of dazzling
promises, the other in the end throws off the mask,
and slays. It is true of all who listen to the tempting
voice, and the deluded victim 'knows not that the
dead are there, and that her guests are in the depth
of hell.'

II. The method of deliverance.

The previous chapter sounded the depths of human impotence, and showed the tragic impossibility of human efforts to strip off the poisoned garment. Here the Apostle tells the wonderful story of how he himself was delivered, in the full rejoicing confidence that what availed for his emancipation would equally avail for every captived soul. Because he himself has experienced a divine power which breaks the dreadful sequence of sin and of death, he knows that every soul may share in the experience. No mere outward means will be sufficient to emancipate a spirit; no merely intellectual methods will avail to set free the passions and desires which have been captured by sin. It is vain to seek deliverance from a perverted will by any republication, however emphatic, of a law of duty. Nothing can touch the necessities of the case but a gift of power which becomes an abiding influence in us, and develops a mightier energy to overcome the evil tendencies of a sinful soul.

That communicated power must impart life. Nothing short of a Spirit of life, quick and powerful, with an immortal and intense energy, will avail to meet the need. Such a Spirit must give the life which it possesses, must quicken and bring into action dormant powers in the spirit that it would free. It must implant new energies and directions, new motives, desires, tastes, and tendencies. It must bring into play mightier attractions to neutralise and deaden existing ones; as when to some chemical compound a substance is added which has a stronger affinity for one of the elements, a new thing is made.

Paul's experience, which he had a right to cast into general terms and potentially to extend to all mankind,

had taught him· that such a new life for such a spirit
had come to him by union with Jesus Christ. Such a
union, deep and mystical as it is, is, thank God, an experience universal in all true Christians, and constitutes the very heart of the Gospel which Paul rejoiced
to believe was entrusted to his hands for the world. His
great message of 'Christ in us' has been wofully cur-
tailed and mangled when his other message of 'Christ
for us' has been taken, as it too often has been, to be
the whole of his Gospel. They who take either of
these inseparable elements to be the whole, rend into
two imperfect halves the perfect oneness of the Gospel
of Christ.

We are often told that Paul was the true author
of Christian doctrine, and are bidden to go back from
him to Jesus. If we do so, we hear His grave sweet
voice uttering in the upper-room the deep words, 'I
am the Vine, ye are the branches'; and, surely, Paul
is but repeating, without metaphor, what Christ, once
for all, set forth in that lovely emblem, when he says
that 'the law of the Spirit of life in Christ Jesus made
me free from the law of sin and of death.' The
branches in their multitude make the Vine in its unity,
and the sap which rises from the deep root through
the brown stem, passes to every tremulous leaf, and
brings bloom and savour into every cluster. Jesus
drew His emblem from the noblest form of vegetative
life; Paul, in other places, draws his from the highest
form of bodily life, when he points to the many members in one body, and the Head which governs all, and
says, 'So also is Christ.' In another place he points to
the noblest form of earthly love and unity. The
blessed fellowship and sacred oneness of husband and
wife are an emblem sweet, though inadequate, of the

fellowship in love and unity of spirit between Christ
and His Church.

And all this mysterious oneness of life has an intensely practical side.  In Jesus, and by union with
Him, we receive a power that delivers from sin and
arrests the stealthy progress of sin's follower, death.
Love to Him, the result of fellowship with Him, and
the consequence of life received from Him, becomes
the motive which makes the redeemed heart delight to
do His will, and takes all the power out of every
temptation.  We are in Him, and He in us, on condition, and by means, of our humble faith; and because
my faith thus knits me to Him it is 'the victory that
overcomes the world,' and breaks the chains of many
sins.  So this communion with Jesus Christ is the way
by which we shall increase that triumphant spiritual
life, which is the only victorious antagonist of the
else inevitable consequence which declares that the
'soul that sinneth it shall die,' and die even in sinning.

III. The process of the deliverance.

Following the R.V. we read ' made me free,' not ' hath
made me.'  The reference is obviously, as the Greek
more clearly shows, to a single historical event, which
some would take to be the Apostle's baptism, but
which is more properly supposed to be his conversion.
His strong bold language here does not mean that he
claims to be sinless.  The emancipation is effected,
although it is but begun.  He holds that at that
moment when Jesus appeared to him on the road to
Damascus, and he yielded to Him as Lord, his deliverance was real, though not complete.  He was conscious
of a real change of position in reference to that law of
sin and of death.  Paul distinguishes between the true
self and the accumulation of selfish and sensual habits

which make up so much of ourselves. The deeper and purer self may be vitalised in will and heart, and set free even while the emancipation is not worked out in the life. The parable of the leaven applies in the individual renewal; and there is no fanaticism, and no harm, in Paul's point of view, if only it be remembered that sins by which passion and externals overbear my better self are mine in responsibility and in consequences. Thus guarded, we may be wholly right in thinking of all the evils which still cleave to the renewed Christian soul as not being part of it, but destined to drop away.

And this bold declaration is to be vindicated as a prophetic confidence in the supremacy and ultimate dominion of the new power which works even through much antagonism in an imperfect Christian. Paul, too, calls 'things that are not as though they were.' If my spirit of life is the 'Spirit of life in Christ,' it will go on to perfection. It is Spirit, therefore it is informing and conquering the material; it is a divine Spirit, therefore it is omnipotent; it is the Spirit of life, leading in and imparting life like itself, which is kindred with it and is its source; it is the Spirit of life in Christ, therefore leading to life like His, bringing us to conformity with Him because the same causes produce the same effects; it is a life in Christ having a law and regular orderly course of development. So, just as if we have the germ we may hope for fruit, and can see the infantile oak in the tightly-shut acorn, or in the egg the creature which shall afterwards grow there, we have in this gift of the Spirit, the victory. If we have the cause, we have the effects implicitly folded in it; and we have but to wait further development.

The Christian life is to be one long effort, partial, and gradual, to unfold the freedom possessed. Paul knew full well that his emancipation was not perfect. It was, probably, after this triumphant expression of confidence that he wrote, 'Not as though I had already attained, either were already perfect.' The first stage is the gift of power, the appropriation and development of that power is the work of a life; and it ought to pass through a well-marked series and cycle of growing changes. The way to develop it is by constant application to the source of all freedom, the life-giving Spirit, and by constant effort to conquer sins and temptations. There is no such thing in the Christian conflict as a painless development. We must mortify the deeds of the body if we are to live in the Spirit. The Christian progress has in it the nature of a crucifixion. It is to be effort, steadily directed for the sake of Christ, and in the joy of His Spirit, to destroy sin, and to win practical holiness. Homely moralities are the outcome and the test of all pretensions to spiritual communion.

We are, further, to perfect holiness in the fear of the Lord, by 'waiting for the Redemption,' which is not merely passive waiting, but active expectation, as of one who stretches out a welcoming hand to an approaching friend. Nor must we forget that this accomplished deliverance is but partial whilst upon earth. 'The body is dead because of sin, but the spirit is life because of righteousness.' But there may be indefinite approximation to complete deliverance. The metaphors in Scripture under which Christian progress is described, whether drawn from a conflict or a race, or from a building, or from the growth of a tree, all suggest the idea of constant advance against hindrances, which yet, constant though it is, does not reach the goal here. And this is our noblest earthly condition—not to be pure, but to be tending towards it and conscious of impurity. Hence our tempers should be those of humility, strenuous effort, firm hope. We are as slaves who have escaped, but are still in the wilderness, with the enemies' dogs baying at our feet; but we shall come to the land of freedom, on whose sacred soil sin and death can never tread.


## CHRIST CONDEMNING SIN

'For what the law could not do, in that it was weak through the flesh, God sending His own Son in the likeness of sinful flesh, and for sin, condemned sin in the flesh.'—ROMANS viii. 3.

IN the first verse of this chapter we read that 'There is no condemnation to them that are in Christ Jesus.' The reason of that is, that they are set free from the terrible sequence of cause and effect which constitutes 'the law of sin and death'; and the reason why they are freed from that awful sequence by the power of Christ is, because He has 'condemned sin in the flesh.' The occurrence of the two words 'condemnation' (ver. 1) and 'condemned' (ver. 3) should be noted. Sin is personified as dwelling in the flesh, which expression here means, not merely the body, but unregenerate human nature. He has made his fortress there, and rules over it all. The strong man keeps his house and his goods are in peace. He laughs to scorn the attempts of laws and moralities of all sorts to cast him out. His dominion is death to the human nature over which he tyrannises. Condemnation is inevitable to the men over whom he rules. They or he must

perish. If he escape they die. If he could be slain
they might live. Christ comes, condemns the tyrant,
and casts him out. So, he being condemned, we are
acquitted; and he being slain there is no death for
us. Let us try to elucidate a little further this great
metaphor by just pondering the two points prominent
in it—Sin tyrannising over human nature and resisting all attempts to overcome it, and Christ's condemnation and casting out of the tyrant.

I. Sin tyrannising over human nature, and resisting
all attempts to overcome it.

Paul is generalising his own experience when he
speaks of the condemnation of an intrusive alien
force that holds unregenerate human nature in
bondage. He is writing a page of his own auto-
biography, and he is sure that all the rest of us have
like pages in ours. Heart answereth unto heart as in
a mirror. If each man is a unity, the poison must
run through all his veins and affect his whole nature.
Will, understanding, heart, must all be affected and
each in its own way by the intruder; and if men
are a collective whole, each man's experience is
repeated in his brother's.

The Apostle is equally transcribing his own experience when in the text he sadly admits the futility
of all efforts to shake the dominion of sin. He has
found in his own case that even the loftiest revelation in the Mosaic law utterly fails in the attempt
to condemn sin. This is true not only in regard
to the Mosaic law but in regard to the law of
conscience, and to moral teachings of any kind.
It is obvious that all such laws do condemn sin in the
sense that they solemnly declare God's judgment about
it, and His sentence on it; but in the sense of real

condemnation, or casting out, and depriving sin of its
power, they all are impotent.  The law may deter
from overt acts or lead to isolated acts of obedience;
it may stir up antagonism to sin's tyranny, but after
that it has no more that it can do.  It cannot give
the purity which it proclaims to be necessary, nor
create the obedience which it enjoins.  Its thunders
roll terrors, and no fruitful rain follows them to soften
the barren soil.  There always remains an unbridged
gulf between the man and the law.

And this is what Paul points to in saying that it
'was weak through the flesh.'  It is good in itself, but
it has to work through the sinful nature.  The only
powers to which it can appeal are those which are
already in rebellion.  A discrowned king whose only
forces to conquer his rebellious subjects are the rebels
themselves, is not likely to regain his crown.  Because
law brings no new element into our humanity, its
appeal to our humanity has little more effect than
that of the wind whistling through an archway.  It
appeals to conscience and reason by a plain declaration
of what is right; to will and understanding by an
exhibition of authority; to fears and prudence by
plainly setting forth consequences.  But what is to
be done with men who know what is right but have no
wish to do it, who believe that they ought but will
not, who know the consequences but 'choose rather
the pleasures of sin for a season,' and shuffle the
future out of their minds altogether?  This is the
essential weakness of all law.  The tyrant is not
afraid so long as there is no one threatening his reign,
but the unarmed herald of a discrowned king.  His
citadel will not surrender to the blast of the trumpet
blown from Sinai.

II. Christ's condemnation and casting out of the tyrant.

The Apostle points to a triple condemnation.

'In the likeness of sinful flesh,' Jesus condemns sin by His own perfect life. That phrase, 'the likeness of the flesh of sin,' implies the real humanity of Jesus, and His perfect sinlessness; and suggests the first way in which He condemns sin in the flesh. In His life He repeats the law in a higher fashion. What the one spoke in words the other realised in 'loveliness of perfect deeds'; and all men own that example is the mightiest preacher of righteousness, and that active goodness draws to itself reverence and sways men to imitate. But that life lived in human nature gives a new hope of the possibilities of that nature even in us. The dream of perfect beauty 'in the flesh' has been realised. What the Man Christ Jesus was, He was that we may become. In the very flesh in which the tyrant rules, Jesus shows the possibility and the loveliness of a holy life.

But this, much as it is, is not all. There is another way in which Christ condemns sin in the flesh, and that is by His perfect sacrifice. To this also Paul points in the phrase, 'the flesh of sin.' The example of which we have been speaking is much, but it is weak for the very same reason for which law is weak—that it operates only through our nature as it is; and that is not enough. Sin's hold on man is twofold—one that it has perverted his relation to God, and another that it has corrupted his nature. Hence there is in him a sense of separation from God and a sense of guilt. Both of these not only lead to misery, but positively tend to strengthen the dominion of sin. The leader of the mutineers keeps them true to him by remind-

ing them that the mutiny laws decree death without
mercy. Guilt felt may drive to desperation and hopeless continuance in wrong. The cry, 'I am so bad that
it is useless to try to be better,' is often heard. Guilt
stifled leads to hardening of heart, and sometimes to
desire and riot. Guilt slurred over by some easy
process of absolution may lead to further sin. Similarly
separation from God is the root of all evil, and thoughts
of Him as hard and an enemy, always lead to sin.
So if the power of sin in the past must be cancelled,
the sense of guilt must be removed, and the wall of
partition between man and God thrown down. What
can law answer to such a demand? It is silent; it
can only say, 'What is written is written.' It has no
word to speak that promises 'the blotting out of the
handwriting that is against us'; and through its
silence one can hear the mocking laugh of the tyrant
that keeps his castle.

But Christ has come 'for sin'; that is to say His
Incarnation and Death had relation to, and had it
for their object to remove, human sin. He comes to
blot out the evil, to bring God's pardon. The recognition of His sacrifice supplies the adequate motive to
copy His example, and they who see in His death
God's sacrifice for man's sin, cannot but yield themselves to Him, and find in obedience a delight. Love
kindled at His love makes likeness and transmutes
the outward law into an inward 'spirit of life in Christ
Jesus.'

Still another way by which God 'condemns sin in
the flesh' is pointed to by the remaining phrase of
our text, 'sending His own Son.' In the beginning
of this epistle Jesus is spoken of as 'being declared
to be the Son of God with power according to the

Spirit of holiness'; and we must connect that saying with our text, and so think of Christ's bestowal
of His perfect gift to humanity of the Spirit which
sanctifies as being part of His condemnation of
sin in the flesh.  Into the very region where the
tyrant rules, the Son of God communicates a new
nature which constitutes a real new power.  The
Spirit operates on all our faculties, and redeems them
from the bondage of corruption.  All - the springs
in the land are poisoned; but a new one, limpid and
pure, is opened.  By the entrance of the Spirit of
holiness into a human spirit, the usurper is driven from
the central fortress: and though he may linger in
the outworks and keep up a guerilla warfare, that is
all that he can do.  We never truly apprehend Christ's
gift to man until we recognise that He not merely
'died for our sins,' but lives to impart the principle
of holiness in the gift of His Spirit.  The dominion of
that imparted Spirit is gradual and progressive.  The
Canaanite may still be in the land, but a growing
power, working in and through us, is warring against
all in us that still owns allegiance to that alien power,
and there can be no end to the victorious struggle
until the whole body, soul, and spirit, be wholly under
the influence of the Spirit that dwelleth in us, and
nothing shall hurt or destroy in what shall then be all
God's holy mountain.

Such is, in the most general terms, the statement of
what Christ does 'for us'; and the question comes to
be the all-important one for each, Do I let Him do
it for me?  Remember the alternative.  There must
either be condemnation for us, or for the sin that
dwelleth in us.  There is no condemnation for them
who are in Christ Jesus, because there is condemna-

tion for the sin that dwells in them.  It must be slain,
or it will slay us.  It must be cast out, or it will cast
us out from God.  It must be separated from us, or
it will separate us from Him.  We need not be condemned, but if it be not condemned, then we shall be.

## THE WITNESS OF THE SPIRIT

'The Spirit itself beareth witness with our spirit, that we are the children of
God.'—ROMANS viii. 16.

THE sin of the world is a false confidence, a careless,
complacent taking for granted that a man is a Christian when he is not.  The fault, and sorrow, and weakness of the Church is a false diffidence, an anxious fear
whether a man be a Christian when he is.  There are
none so far away from false confidence as those who
tremble lest they be cherishing it.  There are none so
inextricably caught in its toils as those who are all
unconscious of *its* existence and of *their* danger.  The
two things, the false confidence and the false diffidence,
are perhaps more akin to one another than they look
at first sight.  Their opposites, at all events—the true
confidence, which is faith in Christ; and the true diffidence, which is utter distrust of myself—are identical.
But there may sometimes be, and there often is, the
combination of a real confidence and a false diffidence,
the presence of faith, and the doubt whether it be
present.  Many Christians go through life with this as
the prevailing temper of their minds—a doubt sometimes arising almost to agony, and sometimes dying
down into passive patient acceptance of the condition
as inevitable—a doubt whether, after all, they be not,
as they say, 'deceiving themselves'; and in the per-
verse ingenuity with which that state of mind is con-

stantly marked, they manage to distil for themselves a
bitter vinegar of self-accusation out of grand words in
the Bible, that were meant to afford them but the wine
of gladness and of consolation.

Now this great text which I have ventured to take—
not with the idea that I can exalt it or say anything
worthy of it, but simply in the hope of clearing away
some misapprehensions—is one that has often and
often tortured the mind of Christians. They say of
themselves, 'I know nothing of any such evidence: I
am not conscious of any Spirit bearing witness with
my spirit.' Instead of looking to other sources to
answer the question whether they are Christians or
not—and then, having answered it, thinking thus, 'That
text asserts that *all* Christians have this witness,
therefore certainly I have it in some shape or other,'
they say to themselves, 'I do not feel anything that
corresponds with my idea of what such a grand, supernatural voice as the witness of God's Spirit in my
spirit must needs be; and therefore I doubt whether I
am a Christian at all.' I should be thankful if the
attempt I make now to set before you what seems to
me to be the true teaching of the passage, should be,
with God's help, the means of lifting some little part of
the burden from some hearts that are right, and that
only long to know that they are, in order to be at
rest.

'The Spirit itself beareth witness with our spirit, that
we are the children of God.' The general course of
thought which I wish to leave with you may be summed
up thus: Our cry 'Father' is the witness that we are
sons. That cry is not simply ours, but it is the voice of
God's Spirit. The divine Witness in our spirits is subject to the ordinary influences which affect our spirits.

Let us take these three thoughts, and dwell on them for a little while.

I. Our cry 'Father' is the witness that we are sons.

Mark the terms of the passage: 'The Spirit itself beareth witness *with* our spirit—.' It is not so much a revelation made to my spirit, considered as the recipient of the testimony, as a revelation made in or with my spirit considered as co-operating in the testimony. It is not that my spirit says one thing, bears witness that I am a child of God; and that the Spirit of God comes in by a distinguishable process, with a separate evidence, to say Amen to my persuasion; but it is that there is one testimony which has a conjoint origin—the origin from the Spirit of God as true source, and the origin from my own soul as recipient and co-operant in that testimony. From the teaching of this passage, or from any of the language which Scripture uses with regard to the inner witness, it is not to be inferred that there will rise up in a Christian's heart, from some origin consciously beyond the sphere of his own nature, a voice with which he has nothing to do; which at once, by its own character, by something peculiar and distinguishable about it, by something strange in its nature, or out of the ordinary course of human thinking, shall certify itself to be not *his* voice at all, but *God's* voice. That is not the direction in which you are to look for the witness of God's Spirit. It is evidence borne, indeed, by the Spirit of God; but it is evidence borne not only to our spirit, but through it, with it. The testimony is one, the testimony of a man's own emotion, and own conviction, and own desire, the cry, Abba, Father! So far, then, as the form of the evidence goes, you are not to look for it in anything ecstatic, arbitrary, parted off from your own experience by a broad line of demarcation; but you are to look into the experience which at first sight you would claim most exclusively for your own, and to try and find out whether *there* there be not working with your soul, working through it, working beneath it, distinct from it but not distinguishable from it by anything but its consequences and its fruitfulness—a deeper voice than yours—a 'still small voice,' —no whirlwind, nor fire, nor earthquake—but the voice of God speaking in secret, taking the voice and tones of your own heart and your own consciousness, and saying to you, 'Thou art my child, inasmuch as, operated by My grace, and Mine inspiration alone, there rises, tremblingly but truly, in thine own soul the cry, Abba, Father.'

So much, then, for the form of this evidence—my own conviction. Then with regard to the substance of it: conviction of what? The text itself does not tell us what is the evidence which the Spirit bears, and by reason of which we have a right to conclude that we are the children of God. The previous verse tells us. I have partially anticipated what I have to say on that point, but it will bear a little further expansion. 'Ye have not received the spirit of bondage again to fear; but ye have received the Spirit of adoption, whereby we cry Abba, Father.' 'The Spirit itself,' by this means of our cry, Abba, Father, 'beareth witness with our spirit, that we are the children of God.' The substance, then, of the conviction which is lodged in the human spirit by the testimony of the Spirit of God is not primarily directed to our relation or feelings to God, but to a far grander thing than that—to God's feelings and relation to us. Now I want you to think for one moment, before I pass on, how entirely different the

whole aspect of this witness of the Spirit of which
Christian men speak so much, and sometimes with so
little understanding, becomes according as you regard
it mistakenly as being the direct testimony to you that
you are a child of God, or rightly as being the direct
testimony to you that God is your Father. The two
things seem to be the same, but they are not. In the
one case, the false case, the mistaken interpretation,
we are left to this, that a man has no deeper certainty
of his condition, no better foundation for his hope,
than what is to be drawn from the presence or absence
of certain emotions within his own heart. In the other
case, we are admitted into this 'wide place,' that all
which is our own is second and not first, and that the
true basis of all our confidence lies not in the thought
of what we are and feel to God, but in the thought of
what God is and feels to us. And instead, therefore, of
being left to labour for ourselves, painfully to search
amongst the dust and rubbish of our own hearts, we
are taught to sweep away all that crumbled, rotten
surface, and to go down to the living rock that lies
beneath it; we are taught to say, in the words of the
book of Isaiah, 'Doubtless Thou art our Father—we
are all an unclean thing; our iniquities, like the wind,
have carried us away'; there is nothing stable in us;
our own resolutions, they are swept away like the
chaff of the summer threshing-floor, by the first gust
of temptation; but what of that?—'in those is continuance, and we shall be saved!' Ah, brethren! expand
this thought of the conviction that God is my Father,
as being the basis of all my confidence that I am His
child, into its widest and grandest form, and it leads
us up to the blessed old conviction, I am nothing, my
holiness is nothing, my resolutions are nothing, my

faith is nothing, my energies are nothing; I stand
stripped, and barren, and naked of everything, and I
fling myself out of myself into the merciful arms of my
Father in heaven! There is all the difference in the
world between searching for evidence of my sonship,
and seeking to get the conviction of God's Fatherhood.
The one is an endless, profitless, self-tormenting task;
the other is the light and liberty, the glorious liberty,
of the children of God.

And so the *substance* of the Spirit's evidence is the
direct conviction based on the revelation of God's infinite love and fatherhood in Christ the Son, that God
is my Father; from which direct conviction I come to
the conclusion, the inference, the second thought, Then
I may trust that I am His son. But why? Because of
anything in me? No: because of Him. The very
emblem of fatherhood and sonship might teach us that
*that* depends upon the Father's will and the Father's
heart. The Spirit's testimony has for form my own
conviction: and for substance my humble cry, 'Oh Thou,
my Father in heaven!' Brethren, is not that a far
truer and nobler kind of thing to preach than saying,
Look into your own heart for strange, extraordinary,
distinguishable signs which shall mark you out as
God's child—and which are proved to be His Spirit's,
because they are separated from the ordinary human
consciousness? Is it not far more blessed for us, and
more honouring to Him who works the sign, when we
say, that it is to be found in no out-of-rule, miraculous
evidence, but in the natural (which is in reality supernatural) working of His Spirit in the heart which is
its recipient, breeding there the conviction that God is
my Father? And oh, if I am speaking to any to whom
that text, with all its light and glory, has seemed to

lift them up into an atmosphere too rare and a height
too lofty for their heavy wings and unused feet, if I am
speaking to any Christian man to whom this word has
been like the cherubim and flaming sword, bright and
beautiful, but threatening and repellent when it speaks
of a Spirit that bears witness with our spirit—I ask
you simply to take the passage for yourself, and carefully and patiently to examine it, and see if it be not
true what I have been saying, that your trembling conviction—sister and akin as it is to your deepest distrust and sharpest sense of sin and unworthiness—
that your trembling conviction of a love mightier than
your own, everlasting and all-faithful, is indeed the
selectest sign that God can give you that you *are* His
child.   Oh, brethren and sisters! be confident; for it
is not false confidence: be confident if up from the
depths of that dark well of your own sinful heart
there rises sometimes, through all the bitter waters,
unpolluted and separate, a sweet conviction, forcing
itself upward, that God hath love in His heart, and
that God is *my* Father.   Be confident; 'the Spirit itself
beareth witness with your spirit.'

II. And now, secondly, That cry is not simply ours,
but it is the voice of God's Spirit.

Our own convictions are ours because they are
God's.   Our own souls possess these emotions of
love and tender desire going out to God—our own
spirits possess them; but our own spirits did not
originate them.   They are ours by property; they
are His by source.   The spirit of a Christian man
has no good thought in it, no true thought, no perception of the grace of God's Gospel, no holy desire,
no pure resolution, which is not stamped with the sign
of a higher origin, and is not the witness of God's

Spirit in his spirit. The passage before us tells us that the sense of Fatherhood which is in the Christian's heart, and becomes his cry, comes from God's Spirit. This passage, and that in the Epistle to the Galatians which is almost parallel, put this truth very forcibly, when taken in connection. 'Ye have received,' says the text before us, 'the Spirit of adoption, whereby *we* cry, Abba, Father.' The variation in the Epistle to the Galatians is this: 'Because ye are sons, God hath sent forth the Spirit of His Son into your hearts, *crying* (the Spirit crying), Abba, Father.' So in the one text, the cry is regarded as the voice of the believing heart; and in the other the same cry is regarded as the voice of God's Spirit. And these two things are both true; the one would want its foundation if it were not for the other; the cry of the Spirit is nothing for me unless it be appropriated by me. I do not need to plunge here into metaphysical speculation of any sort, but simply to dwell upon the plain practical teaching of the Bible—a teaching verified, I believe, by every Christian's experience, if he will search into it—that everything in him which makes the Christian life, is not his, but is God's by origin, and his only by gift and inspiration. And the whole doctrine of my text is built on this one thought—without the Spirit of God in your heart, you never can recognise God as your Father. That in us which runs, with love, and childlike faith, and reverence, to the place 'where His honour dwelleth,' that in us which says 'Father,' is kindred with God, and is not the simple, unhelped, unsanctified human nature. There is no ascent of human desires above their source. And wherever in a heart there springs up heavenward a thought, a wish, a prayer, a trembling confidence, it is because that came down first from heaven, and rises to seek its level again. All that is divine in man comes from God. All that tends towards God in man is God's voice in the human heart; and were it not for the possession and operation, the sanctifying and quickening, of a living divine Spirit granted to us, our souls would for ever cleave to the dust and dwell upon earth, nor ever rise to God and live in the light of His presence. Every Christian, then, may be sure of this, that howsoever feeble may be the thought and conviction in his heart of God's Fatherhood, *he* did not work it, he received it only, cherished it, thought of it, watched over it, was careful not to quench it; but in origin it was God's, and it is now and ever the voice of the Divine Spirit in the child's heart.

But, my friends, if this principle be true, it does not apply only to this one single attitude of the believing soul when it cries, Abba, Father; it must be widened out to comprehend the whole of a Christian's life, outward and inward, which is not sinful and darkened with actual transgression. To all the rest of his being, to everything in heart and life which is right and pure, the same truth applies. 'The Spirit itself beareth witness with our spirit' in every perception of God's word which is granted, in every revelation of His counsel which dawns upon our darkness, in every aspiration after Him which lifts us above the smoke and dust of this dim spot, in every holy resolution, in every thrill and throb of love and desire. Each of these is mine—inasmuch as in my heart it is experienced and transacted; it is mine, inasmuch as I am not a mere dead piece of matter, the passive recipient of a magical and supernatural grace; but it is God's; and therefore, and therefore only, has it come to be mine!

And if it be objected, that this opens a wide door to all manner of delusion, and that there is no more dangerous thing than for a man to confound his own thoughts with the operations of God's Spirit, let me just give you (following the context before us) the one guarantee and test which the Apostle lays down. He says, 'There is a witness from God in your spirits.' You may say, That witness, if it come in the form of these convictions in my own heart, I may mistake and falsely read. Well, then, here is an outward guarantee. 'As many as are led by the Spirit of God, they are the sons of God'; and so, on the regions both of heart and of life the consecrating thought,—God's work, and God's Spirit's work—is stamped. The heart with its love, the head with its understanding, the conscience with its quick response to the law of duty, the will with its resolutions,—these are all, as sanctified by Him, the witness of His Spirit; and the life with its strenuous obedience, with its struggles against sin and temptation, with its patient persistence in the quiet path of ordinary duty, as well as with the times when it rises into heroic stature of resignation or allegiance, the martyrdom of death and the martyrdom of life, this too is all (in so far as it is pure and right) the work of that same Spirit. The test of the inward conviction is the outward life; and they that have the witness of the Spirit within them have the light of their life lit by the Spirit of God, whereby they may read the handwriting on the heart, and be sure that it is God's and not their own.

III. And now, lastly, this divine Witness in our spirits is subject to the ordinary influences which affect our spirits.

The notion often prevails that if there be in the

K

heart this divine witness of God's Spirit, it must needs be perfect, clearly indicating its origin by an exemption from all that besets ordinary human feelings, that it must be a strong, uniform, never flickering, never darkening, and perpetual light, a kind of vestal fire burning always on the altar of the heart! The passage before us, and all others that speak about the matter, give us the directly opposite notion. The Divine Spirit, when it enters into the narrow room of the human spirit, condescends to submit itself, not wholly, but to such an extent as practically for our present purpose *is* wholly to submit itself to the ordinary laws and conditions and contingencies which befall and regulate our own human nature. Christ came into the world divine: He was 'found in fashion as a man,' in form a servant; the humanity that He wore limited (if you like), regulated, modified, the manifestation of the divinity that dwelt in it. And not otherwise is the operation of God's Holy Spirit when it comes to dwell in a human heart. There too, working through man, *it* 'is found in fashion as a man'; and though the origin of the conviction be of God, and though the voice in my heart be not only my voice, but God's voice there, it will obey those same laws which make human thoughts and emotions vary, and fluctuate, flicker and flame up again, burn bright and burn low, according to a thousand circumstances. The witness of the Spirit, if it were yonder in heaven, would shine like a perpetual star; the witness of the Spirit, here in the heart on earth, burns like a flickering flame, never to be extinguished, but still not always bright, wanting to be trimmed, and needing to be guarded from rude blasts. Else, brother, what does an Apostle mean when he says to you and me, 'Quench

not the Spirit'? what does he mean when he says to
us, 'Grieve not the Spirit'? What does the whole
teaching which enjoins on us, 'Let your loins be girded
about, and your lights burning,' and 'What I say to
you, I say to all, Watch!' mean, unless it means this,
that God-given as (God be thanked!) that conviction of
Fatherhood is, it is not given in such a way as that,
irrespective of our carefulness, irrespective of our
watching, it shall burn on—the same and unchange-
able? The Spirit's witness comes from God, therefore
it is veracious, divine, omnipotent; but the Spirit's
witness from God is in man, therefore it may be
wrongly read, it may be checked, it may for a time be
kept down, and prevented from showing itself to be
what it is.

And the practical conclusion that comes from all
this, is just the simple advice to you all: Do not wonder,
in the first place, if that evidence of which we speak,
vary and change in its clearness and force in your own
hearts. 'The flesh lusteth against the spirit, and the
spirit against the flesh.' Do not think that it cannot be
genuine, because it is changeful. There is a sun in the
heavens, but there are heavenly lights too that wax
and wane; they *are* lights, they *are* in the heavens
though they change. You have no reason, Christian
man, to be discouraged, cast down, still less despon-
dent, because you find that the witness of the Spirit
changes and varies in your heart. Do not despond
because it does; watch it, and guard it, lest it do;
live in the contemplation of the Person and the fact
that calls it forth, that it may not. You will never
'brighten your evidences' by polishing at them. To
polish the mirror ever so assiduously does not secure
the image of the sun on its surface. The only way to

do that is to carry the poor bit of glass out into the
sunshine. It will shine then, never fear. It is weary
work to labour at self-improvement with the hope of
drawing from our own characters evidences that we
are the sons of God. To have the heart filled with the
light of Christ's love to us is the only way to have the
whole being full of light. If you would have clear and
irrefragable, for a perpetual joy, a glory and a defence,
the unwavering confidence, 'I am Thy child,' go to
God's throne, and lie down at the foot of it, and let the
first thought be, 'My Father in heaven,' and *that* will
brighten, that will stablish, that will make omnipotent
in your life the witness of the Spirit that you are the
child of God.

## SONS AND HEIRS

'If children, then heirs; heirs of God, and joint-heirs with Christ.'
ROMANS viii. 17.

GOD Himself is His greatest gift. The loftiest blessing
which we can receive is that we should be heirs,
possessors of God. There is a sublime and wonderful
mutual possession of which Scripture speaks much
wherein the Lord is the inheritance of Israel, and Israel
is the inheritance of the Lord. 'The Lord hath taken
you to be to Him a people of inheritance,' says Moses;
'Ye are a people for a possession,' says Peter. And,
on the other hand, 'The Lord is the portion of my
inheritance,' says David; 'Ye are heirs of God,' echoes
Paul. On earth and in heaven the heritage of the
children of the Lord is God Himself, inasmuch as He
is with them for their delight, in them to make them
'partakers of the divine nature,' and for them in all His
attributes and actions.

This being clearly understood at the outset, we shall
be prepared to follow the Apostle's course of thought
while he points out the conditions upon which the .
possession of that inheritance depends. It is children
of God who are heirs of God. It is by union with
Christ Jesus, the Son, to whom the inheritance belongs,
that they who believe on His name receive power to
become the sons of God, and with that power the
possession of the inheritance. Thus, then, in this
condensed utterance of the text there appear a series
of thoughts which may perhaps be more fully unfolded
in some such manner as the following, that there is no
inheritance without sonship, that there is no sonship
without a spiritual birth, that there is no spiritual birth
without Christ, and that there is no Christ for us
without faith.

I. First, then, the text tells us, no inheritance without
sonship.

In general terms, spiritual blessings can only be
given to those who are in a certain spiritual condition. Always and necessarily the capacity or organ of
reception precedes and determines the bestowment of
blessings. The light falls everywhere, but only the eye
drinks it in. The lower orders of creatures are shut
out from all participation in the gifts which belong to
the higher forms of life, simply because they are so
made and organised as that these cannot find entrance
into their nature. They are, as it were, walled up all
round; and the only door they have to communicate
with the outer world is the door of sense. Man has
higher gifts simply because he has higher capacities.
All creatures are plunged in the same boundless ocean
of divine beneficence and bestowment, and into each
there flows just that, and no more, which each, by

the make and constitution that God has given it, is
capable of receiving. In the man there are more
windows and doors opened out than in the animal.
He is capable of receiving intellectual impulses, spiritual emotions; he can think, and feel, and desire, and
will, and resolve: and so he stands on a higher level
than the beast below him.

Not otherwise is it in regard to God's kingdom, 'which
is righteousness, and peace, and joy in the Holy Ghost.'
The gift and blessing of salvation is primarily a spiritual
gift, and only involves outward consequences second-
arily and subordinately. It mainly consists in the
heart being at peace with God, in the whole soul being
filled with divine affections, in the weight and bondage
of transgression being taken away, and substituted by
the impulse and the life of the new love. Therefore,
neither God can give, nor man can receive, that gift
upon any other terms, than just this, that the heart
and nature be fitted and adapted for it. Spiritual
blessings require a spiritual capacity for the reception
of them; or, as my text says, you cannot have the
inheritance unless you are sons. If salvation consisted
simply in a change of place; if it were merely that by
some expedient or arrangement, an outward penalty,
which was to fall or not to fall at the will of an
arbitrary judge, were prevented from coming down,
why then, it would be open to Him who held the power
of letting the sword fall, to decide on what terms He
might choose to suspend its infliction. But inasmuch
as God's deliverance is not a deliverance from a mere
arbitrary and outward punishment: inasmuch as God's
salvation, though it be deliverance from the penalty as
well as from the guilt of sin, is by no means chiefly a
deliverance from outward consequences, but mainly a

removal of the nature and disposition that makes these outward consequences certain,—therefore a man cannot be saved, God's love cannot save him, God's justice will not save him, God's power stands back from saving him, upon any other condition than this, that his soul shall be adapted and prepared for the reception and enjoyment of the blessing of a spiritual salvation.

But the inheritance which my text speaks about is also that which a Christian hopes to receive and enter upon in heaven. The same principle precisely applies there. There is no inheritance of heaven without sonship; because all the blessings of that future life are of a spiritual character. The joy and the rapture and the glory of that higher and better life have, of course, connected with them certain changes of bodily form, certain changes of local dwelling, certain changes which could perhaps be granted equally to a man, of whatever sort he was. But, friends, it is not the golden harps, not the pavement of 'glass mingled with fire,' not the cessation from work, not the still composure, and changeless indwelling, not the society even, that makes the heaven of heaven. All these are but the embodiments and rendering visible of the inward facts, a soul at peace with God in the depths of its being, an eye which gazes upon the Father, and a heart which wraps itself in His arms. Heaven is no heaven except in so far as it is the possession of God. That saying of the Psalmist is not an exaggeration, nor even a forgetting of the other elements of future blessedness, but it is a simple statement of the literal fact of the case, 'I have none in heaven but Thee!' God is the heritage of His people. To dwell in His love, and to be filled with His light, and to walk for ever in the glory of His

sunlit face, to do His will, and to bear His character
stamped upon our foreheads—*that* is the glory and the
perfectness to which we are aspiring.   Do not then
rest in the symbols that show us, darkly and far off,
what that future glory is.   Do not forget that the
picture is a shadow.   Get beneath all these figurative
expressions, and feel that whilst it may be true that
for us in our present earthly state, there can be no
higher, no purer, no more spiritual nor any truer
representations of the blessedness which is to come,
than those which couch it in the forms of earthly
experience, and appeal to sense as the minister of
delight—yet that all these things are *representations*,
and not adequate presentations.   The inheritance of
the servants of the Lord is the Lord Himself, and they
dwell in Him, and *there* is their joy.

Well then, if that be even partially true—admitting
all that you may say about circumstances which go to
make some portion of the blessedness of that future
life—if it be true that God is the true blessing given by
His Gospel upon earth, that He Himself is the greatest
gift that can be bestowed, and that He is the true
Heaven of heaven—what a flood of light does it cast
upon that statement of my text, 'If children, then
heirs'; no inheritance without sonship!   For who can
possess God but they who love Him? who can love,
but they who know His love? who can have Him
working in their hearts a blessed and sanctifying
change, except the souls that lie thankfully quiet
beneath the forming touch of His invisible hand, and
like flowers drink in the light of His face in their still
joy?   How can God dwell in any heart except a heart
which has in it a love of purity?   Where can He make
His temple except in the 'upright heart and pure'?   How

can there be fellowship betwixt Him and any one
except the man who is a son because he hath received
of the divine nature, and in whom that divine nature
is growing up into a divine likeness? 'What fellowship hath Christ with Belial?' is not only applicable as
a guide for our practical life, but points to the principle
on which God's inheritance belongs to God's sons alone.
'Blessed are the pure in heart, for they shall see God';
and those only who love, and are children, to them
alone does the Father come and does the Father belong.

So much, then, for the first principle: No inheritance
without sonship.

II. Secondly, the text leads us to the principle that
there is no sonship without a spiritual birth.

The Apostle John in that most wonderful preface to
his Gospel, where all deepest truths concerning the
Eternal Being in itself and in the solemn march of His
progressive revelations to the world are set forth in
language simple like the words of a child and inexhaustible like the voice of a god, draws a broad distinction
between the relation to the manifestations of God
which every human soul by virtue of his humanity
sustains, and that into which some, by virtue of their
faith, enter. Every man is lighted by the true light
because he is a man. They who believe in His name
receive from Him the prerogative to become the sons
of God. Whatever else may be taught in John's words,
surely they do teach us this, that the sonship of which
he speaks does not belong to man as man, is not a
relation into which we are born by natural birth, that
we *become* sons after we *are* men, that those who
become sons do not include all those who are lighted
by the Light, but consist of so many of that greater
number as receive Him, and that such become sons

by a divine act, the communication of a spiritual life, whereby they are born of God.

The same Apostle, in his Epistles, where the widest love is conjoined with the most firmly drawn lines of moral demarcation between the great opposites—life, light, love—death, darkness, hate—contrasts in the most unmistakable antithesis the sons of God who are known for such because they do righteousness, and the world which knew not Christ, nor knows those who, dimly beholding, partially resemble Him. Nay, he goes further, and says in strange contradiction to the popular estimate of his character, but in true imitation of that Incarnate love which hated iniquity, 'In this the children of God are manifested and the children of the devil'—echoing thus the words of Him whose pitying tenderness had sometimes to clothe itself in sharpest words, even as His hand of powerful love had once to grasp the scourge of small cords. 'If God were your Father, ye would love Me: ye are of your father, the devil.'

These are but specimens of a whole cycle of Scripture statements which in every form of necessary implication, and of direct statement, set forth the principle that he who is born again of the Spirit, and he only, is a son of God.

Nothing in all this contradicts the belief that all men are the children of God, inasmuch as they are shaped by His divine hand and He has breathed into their nostrils the breath of life. They who hold that sonship is obtained on the condition which these passages seem to assert, do also rejoice to believe and to preach that the Father's love broods over every human heart as the dovelike Spirit over the primeval chaos. They rejoice to proclaim that Christ has come that all, that each, may receive the adoption of sons. They do not feel that their message to, nor their hope for, the world is less blessed, less wide, because while they call on all to come and take the things that are freely given to them of God, they believe that those only who do come and take possess the blessing. Every man may become a son and heir of God by faith in Jesus Christ.

But notwithstanding all the mercies that belong to us all, notwithstanding the divine beneficence, which, like the air and the light, pervades all nature, and underlies all our lives, notwithstanding the universal adaptation and intention of Christ's work, notwithstanding the wooing of His tender voice and the unceasing beckoning of His love, it still remains true that there are men in the world, created by God, loved and cared for by Him, for whom Christ died, who might be, but are not, sons of God.

Fatherhood! what does that word itself teach us? It speaks of the communication of a life, and the reciprocity of love. It rests upon a divine act, and it involves a human emotion. It involves that the father and the child shall have kindred life—the father bestowing and the child possessing a life which is derived; and because derived, kindred; and because kindred, unfolding itself in likeness to the father that gave it. And it requires that between the father's heart and the child's heart there shall pass, in blessed interchange and quick correspondence, answering love, flashing backwards and forwards, like the lightning that touches the earth and rises from it again. A simple appeal to your own consciousness will decide if that be the condition of all men. Are you, my brother, conscious of anything within you higher than the common life that belongs to you because you are an

immortal soul?  Can you say, 'From God's hand I have
received the granting and implantation of a new and
better life?'. Is your claim verified by this, that you
are kindred with God in holy affections, in like purposes, loving what He loves, hating what He hates,
doing what He wills, accepting what He sends, longing
for Himself, and blessed in His presence?  Is your
sonship proved by the depth and sincerity, the simplicity and power, of your throbbing heart of love to
your Father in heaven?   Or are all these emotions
empty words to you, things that are spoken in pulpits,
but to which you have nothing in your life corresponding?  Oh then, my friend, what am I to say to you?
What but this?  no sonship except by that spiritual
birth; and if not such sonship, then the spirit of
bondage.  If not such sonship, why then, by all the
tendencies of your nature, and by all the affinities of
your moral being, if you are not holding of heaven,
you are holding of hell; if you are not drawing your
life, your character, your emotions, your affections,
from the sacred well that lies up yonder, you are
drawing them from the black one that lies down there.
There are heaven, hell, and the earth that lies between,
ever influenced either from above or from below.  You
are sons because born again, or slaves and ' enemies by
wicked works.'  It is a grim alternative, but it is a fact.

III. Thirdly, no spiritual birth without Christ.

We have seen that the sonship which gives power of
possessing the inheritance and which comes by spiritual
birth, rests upon the giving of life, spiritual life, from
God; and unfolds itself in certain holy characters, and
affections, and desires, the throbbing of the whole soul
in full accord and harmony with the divine character
and will.  Well then, it looks very clear that a man

cannot make that new life for himself, cannot do it because of the habit of sin, and cannot do it because of the guilt and punishment of sin. If for sonship there must be a birth again, why, surely, the very symbol might convince you that such a process does not lie within our own power. There must come down a divine leaven into the mass of human nature, before this new being can be evolved in any one. There must be a gift of God. A divine energy must be the source and fountain of all holy and of all Godlike life. Christ comes, comes to make you and me live again as we never lived before; live possessors of God's love; live tenanted and ruled by a divine Spirit; live with affections in our hearts which *we* never could kindle there; live with purposes in our souls which *we* never could put there.

And I want to urge this thought, that the centre point of the Gospel is this regeneration; because if we understand, as we are too much disposed to do, that the Gospel simply comes to make men live better, to work out a moral reformation,—why, there is no need for a Gospel at all. If the change were a simple change of habit and action on the part of men, we could do without a Christ. If the change simply involved a bracing ourselves up to behave better for the future, we could manage somehow or other about as well as or better than we have managed in the past. But if redemption be the giving of life from God; and if redemption be the change of position in reference to God's love and God's law as well, neither of these two changes can a man effect for himself. You cannot gather up the spilt water; you cannot any more gather up and re-issue the past life. The sin remains, the guilt remains. The inevitable law of God will go

on its crashing way in spite of all penitence, in spite of
all reformation, in spite of all desires after newness of
life.  There is but one Being who can make a change
in our position in regard to God, and there is but one
Being who can make the change by which man shall
become a 'new creature.'  The Creative Spirit that
shaped the earth must shape its new being in my soul;
and the Father against whose law I have offended,
whose love I have slighted, from whom I have turned
away, must effect the alteration that I can never
effect—the alteration in my position to His judgments
and justice, and to the whole sweep of His government.   No new birth without Christ; no escape
from the old standing-place, of being 'enemies to God
by, wicked works,' by anything that we can do:
no hope of the inheritance unless the Lord and the
Man, the 'second Adam from heaven,' have come!
He *has* come, and He has 'dwelt with us,' and He
has worn this life of ours, and He has walked in the
·midst of this world, and He knows all about our
human condition, and He has effected an actual change
in the possible aspect of the divine justice and government to us; and He has carried in the golden urn of
His humanity a new spirit and a new life which He
has set down in the midst of the race; and the urn was
broken on the cross of Calvary, and the water flowed
out, and whithersoever that water comes there is life,
and whithersoever it comes not there is death!

 IV. Last of all, no Christ without faith.

It is not enough, brethren, that we should go through
all these previous steps, if we then go utterly astray at
the end, by forgetting that there is only one way by
which we become partakers of any of the benefits and
blessings that Christ has wrought out.  It is much to say

that for inheritance there must be sonship. It is much to
say that for sonship there must be a divine regeneration. It is much to say that the power of this regeneration is all gathered together in Christ Jesus. But there
are plenty of people that would agree to all that, who
go off at that point, and content themselves with *this*
kind of thinking—that in some vague mysterious way,
they know not how, in a sort of half-magical manner,
the benefit of Christ's death and work comes to all in
Christian lands, whether there be an act of faith or
not! Now I am not going to talk theology at present,
at this stage of my sermon; but what I want to leave
upon all your hearts is this profound conviction,—Unless
we are wedded to Jesus Christ by the simple act of
trust in His mercy and His power, Christ is nothing to
us. Do not let us, my friends, blink that deciding test
of the whole matter. We may talk about Christ for
ever; we may set forth aspects of His work, great and
glorious. He may be to us much that is very precious;
but the one question, the question of questions, on
which everything else depends, is, Am I trusting to
Him as my divine Redeemer? am I resting in Him as
the Son of God? Some of us here now have a sort
of nominal connection with Christ, who have a kind
of imaginative connection with Him; traditional,
ceremonial, by habit of thought, by attendance on
public worship, and by I know not what other
means. Ceremonies are nothing, notions are nothing, beliefs are nothing, formal participation in
worship is nothing. Christ is everything to him
that trusts Him. Christ is nothing but a judge and a
condemnation to him who trusts Him not. And here
is the turning-point, Am I resting upon that Lord for
my salvation? If so, you can begin upon that step,

the low one on which you can put your foot, the
humble act of faith, and with the foot there, can climb
up. If faith, then new birth; if new birth, then
sonship; if sonship, then 'an heir of God, and a joint-
heir with Christ.' But if you have not got your foot
upon the lowest round of the ladder, you will never
come within sight of the blessed face of·Him who
stands at the top of it, and who looks down to you at
this moment, saying to you, 'My child, *wilt* thou not
cry unto Me " Abba, Father?"'

## SUFFERING WITH CHRIST, A CONDITION OF 'GLORY WITH CHRIST

'. . . Joint heirs with Christ: if so be that we suffer with Him, that we may
be also glorified together.'—ROMANS viii. 17.

IN the former part of this verse the Apostle tells us
that in order to be heirs of God, we must become sons
through and joint-heirs with Christ. He seems at first
sight to add in these words of our text another condition to those already specified, namely, that of
suffering with Christ.

Now, of course, whatever may be the operation of
suffering in fitting for the possession of the Christian inheritance, either here or in another world, the sonship
and the sorrows do not stand on the same level in regard
to that possession. The one is the indispensable condition of all; the other is but the means for the operation
of the condition. The one—being sons, 'joint-heirs with
Christ,'—is the root of the whole matter; the other—
the 'suffering with Him,'—is but the various process by
which from the root there come 'the blade, and the
ear, and the full corn in the ear.' Given the sonship
—if it is to be worked out into power and beauty,

there must be suffering with Christ. But unless there be sonship, there is no possibility of inheriting God; discipline and suffering will be of no use at all.

The chief lesson which I wish to gather from this text now is that all God's sons must suffer with Christ; and in addition to this principle, we may complete our considerations by adding briefly, that the inheritance must be won by suffering, and that if we suffer with Him, we certainly shall receive the inheritance.

I. First, then, sonship with Christ necessarily involves suffering with Him.

I think that we entirely misapprehend the force of this passage before us, if we suppose it to refer principally or merely to the outward calamities, what you call trials and afflictions, which befall people, and see in it only the teaching, that the sorrows of daily life may have in them a sign of our being children of God, and some power to prepare us for the glory that is to come. There is a great deal more in the thought than that, brethren. This is not merely a text for people who are in affliction, but for all of us. It does not merely contain a law for a certain part of life, but it contains a law for the whole of life. It is not merely a promise that in all our afflictions Christ will be afflicted, but it is a solemn injunction that we seek to know 'the fellowship of His sufferings, and be made conformable to the likeness of His death,' if we expect to be 'found in the likeness of His Resurrection,' and to have any share in the community of His glory. In other words, the foundation of it is not that Christ shares in our sufferings; but that we, as Christians, in a deep and real sense do necessarily share and participate in Christ's. We 'suffer with Him'; *not* He suffers with us.

L

Now, do not let us misunderstand each other, or the Apostle's teaching.   Do not suppose that I am forgetting, or wishing you to account as of small importance, the awful sense in which Christ's suffering stands as a thing by itself and unapproachable, a solitary pillar rising up, above the waste of time, to which all men everywhere are to turn with the one thought, 'I can do nothing like that; I need to do nothing like it; it has been done once, and once for all; and what I have to do is, simply to lie down before Him, and let the power and the blessings of that death and those sufferings flow into my heart.' The Divine Redeemer makes eternal redemption.   The sufferings of Christ—the sufferings of His life, and the sufferings of His death—both because of the nature which bore them, and of the aspect which they wore in regard to us, are in their source, in their intensity, in their character, and consequences, unapproachable, incapable of repetition, and needing no repetition whilst the world shall stand.   But then, do not let us forget that the very books and writers in the New Testament that preach most broadly Christ's sole, all-sufficient, eternal redemption for the world by His sufferings and death, turn round and say to us too, '"Be planted together in the likeness of His death": you are "crucified to the world" by the Cross of Christ; you are to "fill up that which is behind of the sufferings of Christ."'   He Himself speaks of our drinking of the cup that He drank of, and being baptized with the baptism that He was baptized with, if we desire to sit yonder on His throne, and share with Him in His glory.

Now what do the Apostles, and what does Christ Himself, in that passage that I have quoted, mean, by such solemn words as these? Some people shrink from them, and say that it is trenching upon the central doctrine of the Gospel, when we speak about drinking of the cup which Christ drank of. They ask, Can it be? Yes, it can be, if you will think thus:—If a Christian has the Spirit and life of Christ in him, his career will be moulded, imperfectly but really, by the same Spirit that dwelt in his Lord; and similar causes will produce corresponding effects. The life of Christ which— divine, pure, incapable of copy and repetition—in one aspect has ended for ever for men, remains to be lived, in another view of it, by every Christian, who in like manner has to fight with the world; who in like manner has to resist temptation; who in like manner has to stand, by God's help, pure and sinless, in so far as the new nature of him is concerned, in the midst of a world that is full of evil. For were the sufferings of the Lord only the sufferings that were wrought upon Calvary? Were the sufferings of the Lord only the sufferings which came from the 'contradiction of sinners against Himself'? Were the sufferings of the Lord only the sufferings which were connected with His bodily afflictions and pain, precious and priceless as they were, and operative causes of our redemption as they were? Oh no. Conceive of that perfect, sinless, really human life, in the midst of a system of things that is all full of corruption and of sin; coming ever and anon against misery, and wrong-doing, and rebellion; and ask yourselves whether part of His sufferings did not spring from the contact of the sinless Son of man with a sinful world, and the apparently vain attempt to influence and leaven that sinful world with care for itself and love for the Father. If there had been nothing more

than that, yet Christ's sufferings as the Son of God
in the midst of sinful men would have been deep and
real. 'O faithless generation, how long shall I be
with you? how long shall I suffer you?' was wrung
from Him by the painful sense of want of sympathy
between His aims and theirs. 'Oh that I had wings
like a dove, for then I would fly away and be at rest,'
must often be the language of those who are like Him
in spirit, and in consequent sufferings.

And then again, another branch of the 'sufferings
of Christ' is to be found in that deep and mysterious
fact on which I durst not venture to speak beyond
what the actual words of Scripture put into my lips—
the fact that Christ wrought out His perfect obedience
as a man, through temptation and by suffering. There
was no sin *within* Him, no tendency to sin, no yielding
to the evil that assailed. 'The Prince of this world
cometh, and hath nothing in Me.' But yet, when that
dark Power stood by His side, and said, 'If thou be
the Son of God, cast Thyself down,' it was a real
temptation and not a sham one. There was no wish to
do it, no faltering for a moment, no hesitation. There
was no rising up in that calm will of even a moment's
impulse to do the thing that was presented;—but yet
it was presented, and, when Christ triumphed, and the
tempter departed for a season, there had been a
temptation and there had been a conflict. And though
obedience be a joy, and the doing of His Father's
will was His delight, as it must needs be in pure and
in purified hearts; yet obedience which is sustained in
the face of temptation, and which never fails, though
its path lead to bodily pains and the 'contradiction
of sinners,' may well be called suffering. We cannot
speak of our Lord's obedience as the surrender of His

own will to the Father's, with the implication that these two wills ever did or could move except in harmony. There was no place in Christ's obedience for that casting out of sinful self which makes our submission a surrender joined with suffering, but He knew temptation. Flesh, and sense, and the world, and the prince of this world, presented it to Him; and therefore His obedience too was suffering, even though to do the will of His Father was His meat and His drink, His sustenance and His refreshment.

But then, let me remind you still further, that not only does the life of Christ, as sinless in the midst of sinful men, and the life of Christ, as sinless whilst yet there was temptation presented to it—assume the aspect of being a life of suffering, and become, in that respect, the model for us; but that also the Death of Christ, besides its aspect as an atonement and sacrifice for sin, the power by which transgression is put away and God's love flows out upon our souls, has another power given to it in the teaching of the New Testament. The Death of Christ is a type of the Christian's life, which is to be one long, protracted, and daily dying to sin, to self, to the world. The crucifixion of the old manhood is to be the life's work of every Christian, through the power of faith in that Cross by which 'the world is crucified unto Me, and I unto the world.' That thought comes over and over again in all forms of earnest presentation in the Apostle's teaching. Do not slur it over as if it were a mere fanciful metaphor. It carries in its type a most solemn reality. The truth is, that, if a Christian, you have a double life. There is Christ, with His power, with His Spirit, giving you a nature which is pure and sinless, incapable of transgression, like His own. The new man, that which is born of God, sinneth not, cannot sin. But side by side with it, working through it, working in it, leavening it, indistinguishable from it to your consciousness, by anything but this that the one works righteousness and the other works transgression, there is the 'old man,' 'the flesh,' 'the old Adam,' your own godless, independent, selfish, proud being. And the one is to slay the other! Ah, let me tell you, these words—crucifying, casting out the old man, plucking out the right eye, maiming self of the right hand, mortifying the deeds of the body—they are something very much deeper and more awful than poetical symbols and metaphors. They teach us this, that there is no growth without sore sorrow. Conflict, not progress, is the word that defines man's path from darkness into light. No holiness is won by any other means than this, that wickedness should be slain day by day, and hour by hour. In long lingering agony often, with the blood of the heart pouring out at every quivering vein, you are to cut right through the life and being of that sinful self; to do what the Word does, pierce to the dividing asunder of the thoughts and intents of the heart, and get rid by crucifying and slaying—a long process, a painful process—of your own sinful self. And not until you can stand up and say, 'I live, yet not I, but Christ liveth in me,' have you accomplished that to which you are consecrated and vowed by your sonship—'being conformed unto the likeness of His death,' and 'knowing the fellowship of His sufferings.'

It is this process, the inward strife and conflict in getting rid of evil, which the Apostle designates here with the name of 'suffering with Christ, that we may be also glorified together.' On this high level, and not upon the lower one of the consideration that Christ will help us to bear outward infirmities and afflictions, do we find the true meaning of all that Scripture teaching which says indeed, 'Yes, our sufferings are *His*'; but lays the foundation of it in this, 'His sufferings are *ours*.' It begins by telling us that Christ has done a work and borne a sorrow that no second can ever do. Then it tells us that Christ's life of obedience—which, because it *was* a life of obedience, was a life of suffering, and brought Him into a condition of hostility to the men around Him—is to be repeated in us. It sets before us the Cross of Calvary, and the sorrows and pains that were felt there;—and it says to us, Christian men and women, if you want the power for holy living, have fellowship in that atoning death; and if you want the pattern of holy living, look at that Cross and feel, 'I am crucified to the world by it; and the life that I live in the flesh I live by the faith of the Son of God.'

Such considerations as these, however, do not necessarily exclude the other one (which we may just mention and dwell on for a moment), namely, that where there is this spiritual participation in the sufferings of Christ, and where His death is reproduced and perpetuated, as it were, in our daily mortifying ourselves in the present evil world—there Christ is with us in our afflictions. God forbid that I should try to strike away any word of consolation that has come, as these words of my text have come, to so many sorrowing hearts in all generations, like music in the night and like cold waters to a thirsty soul. We need not hold that there is no reference here to that comforting thought, 'In all our affliction He is afflicted.' Brethren, you and I have, each of us—one in one way,

and one in another, all in some way, all in the right
way, none in too severe a way, none in too slight a
way—to tread the path of sorrow; and is it not a
blessed thing, as we go along through that dark valley
of the shadow of death down into which the sunniest
paths go sometimes, to come, amidst the twilight and
the gathering clouds, upon tokens that Jesus has been
on the road before us? They tell us that in some
trackless lands, when one friend passes through the
pathless forests, he breaks a twig ever and anon as he
goes, that those who come after may see the traces of
his having been there, and may know that they are
not out of the road. Oh, when we are journeying
through the murky night, and the dark woods of
affliction and sorrow, it is something to find here and
there a spray broken, or a leafy stem bent down with
the tread of His foot and the brush of His hand as He
passed, and to remember that the path He trod He
has hallowed, and thus to find lingering fragrances
and hidden strengths in the remembrance of Him as
'in all points tempted like as we are,' bearing grief *for*
us, bearing grief *with* us, bearing grief *like* us.

Oh, do not, do not, my brethren, keep these sacred
thoughts of Christ's companionship in sorrow, for the
larger trials of life. If the mote in the eye be large
enough to annoy you, it is large enough to bring out
His sympathy; and if the grief be too small for Him
to compassionate and share, it is too small for you to
be troubled by it. If you are ashamed to apply that
divine thought, 'Christ bears this grief with me,' to
those petty molehills that you sometimes magnify into
mountains, think to yourselves that then it is a shame
for you to be stumbling over them. But on the other
hand, never fear to be irreverent or too familiar in

the thought that Christ is willing to bear, and help you to bear, the pettiest, the minutest, and most insignificant of the daily annoyances that may come to ruffle you. Whether it be a poison from one serpent sting, or whether it be poison from a million of buzzing tiny mosquitoes, if there be a smart, go to Him, and He will help you to endure it. He will do more, He will bear it with you, for if so be that we suffer with Him, He suffers with us, and our oneness with Christ brings about a community of possessions whereby it becomes true of each trusting soul in its relations to Him, that 'all mine (joys and sorrows alike) are thine, and all thine are mine.'

II. There remain some other considerations which may be briefly stated, in order to complete the lessons of this text. In the second place, this community of suffering is a necessary preparation for the community of glory.

I name this principally for the sake of putting in a caution. The Apostle does not mean to tell us, of course, that if there were such a case as that of a man becoming a son of God, and having no occasion or opportunity afterwards, by brevity of life or other causes, for passing through the discipline of sorrow, his inheritance would be forfeited. We must always take such passages as this—which seem to make the discipline of the world an essential part of the preparing of us for glory—in conjunction with the other undeniable truth which completes them, that when a man has the love of God in his heart, however feebly, however newly, there and then he is fit for the inheritance. I think that Christian people make vast mistakes sometimes in talking about 'being made meet for the inheritance of the saints in light,' about being 'ripe for glory,' and the like. One thing at any rate is very certain, it is not the discipline that fits. That which fits goes before the discipline, and the discipline only develops the fitness. 'God hath made us meet for the inheritance of the saints in light,' says the Apostle. That is a past act. The preparedness for heaven comes at the moment—if it be a momentary act—when a man turns to Christ. You may take the lowest and most abandoned form of human character, and in one moment (it is possible, and it is often the case) the entrance into that soul of the feeble germ of that new affection shall at once change the whole moral habitude of that man. Though it be true, then, that heaven is only open to those who are capable—by holy aspirations and divine desires—of entering into it, it is equally true that such aspirations and desires may be the work of an instant, and may be superinduced in a moment in a heart the most debased and the most degraded. 'This day shalt thou be with Me in Paradise,'—*fit* for the inheritance!

And, therefore, let us not misunderstand such words as this text, and fancy that the necessary discipline, which we have to go through before we are ready for heaven, is necessary in anything like the same sense in which it is necessary that a man should have faith in Christ in order to be saved. The one may be dispensed with, the other cannot. A Christian at any period of his Christian experience, if it please God to take him, is fit for the kingdom. The life *is* life, whether it be the budding beauty and feebleness of childhood, or the strength of manhood, or the maturity and calm peace of old age. But 'add to your faith,' that 'an entrance may be ministered unto you

*abundantly.*' Remember that though the root of the
matter, the seed of the kingdom, may be in you; and
that though, therefore, you have a right to feel that,
at any period of your Christian experience, if it please
God to take you out of this world, you are fit for
heaven—yet in His mercy He is leaving you here,
training you, disciplining you, cleansing you, making
you to be polished shafts in His quiver; and that all
the glowing furnaces of fiery trial and all the cold
waters of affliction are but the preparation through
which the rough iron is to be passed before it becomes tempered steel, a shaft in the Master's hand.

And so learn to look upon all trial as being at once
the seal of your sonship, and the means by which
God puts it within your power to win a higher place,
a loftier throne, a nobler crown, a closer fellowship
with Him 'who hath suffered, being tempted,' and who
will receive into His own blessedness and rest them
that are tempted. 'The child, though he be an heir,
differeth nothing from a servant, though he be lord
of all; but is under tutors and governors.' God puts
us in the school of sorrow under that stern tutor and
governor here, and gives us the opportunity of 'suffering with Christ,' that by the daily crucifixion of our
old nature, by the lessons and blessings of outward
calamities and change, there may grow up in us a still
nobler and purer, and perfecter divine life; and that
we may so be made capable—more capable, and capable of more—of that inheritance for which the only
necessary thing is the death of Christ, and the only
fitness is faith in His name.

III. Finally, that inheritance is the necessary result
of the suffering that has gone before.

The suffering results from our union with Christ.

That union must needs culminate in glory.  It is not only because the joy hereafter seems required in order to vindicate God's love to His children, who here reap sorrow from their sonship, that the discipline of life cannot but end in blessedness.  That ground of mere compensation is a low one on which to rest the certainty of future bliss.  But the inheritance is sure to all who here suffer with Christ, because the one cause—union with the Lord—produces both the present result of fellowship in His sorrows, and the future result of joy in His joy, of possession of His possessions.  The inheritance is sure because Christ possesses it now.  The inheritance is sure because earth's sorrows not merely require to be repaid by its peace, but because they have an evident design to fit us for it, and it would be destructive to all faith in God's wisdom, and God's knowledge of His own purposes, not to believe that what He has wrought us for will be given to us.  Trials have no meaning, unless they are means to an end.  The end is the inheritance, and sorrows here, as well as the Spirit's work here, are the earnest of the inheritance.  Measure the greatness of the glory by what has preceded it.  God takes all these years of life, and all the sore trials and afflictions that belong inevitably to an earthly career, and works them in, into the blessedness that *shall* come.  If a fair measure of the greatness of any result of productive power be the length of time that was taken for getting it ready, we can dimly conceive what that joy must be for which seventy years of strife and pain and sorrow are but a momentary preparation; and what must be the weight of that glory which is the counterpoise and consequence to the afflictions of this lower world.  The further the pendulum swings on the one side, the further it goes up on the other. The deeper God plunges the comet into the darkness out yonder, the closer does it come to the sun at its nearest distance, and the longer does it stand basking and glowing in the full blaze of the glory from the central orb. So in *our* revolution, the measure of the distance from the farthest point of our darkest earthly sorrow, *to* the throne, may help us to the measure of the closeness of the bright, perfect, perpetual glory above, when we are *on* the throne : for if so be that we are sons, we *must* suffer with Him ; if so be that we suffer, we *must* be glorified together !

## THE REVELATION OF SONS

'For the earnest expectation of the creature waiteth for the manifestation of the sons of God.'—ROMANS viii. 19.

THE Apostle has been describing believers as 'sons' and 'heirs.' He drops from these transcendent heights to contrast their present apparent condition with their true character and their future glory. The sad realities of suffering darken his lofty hopes, even although these sad realities are to his faith tokens of joint-heirship with Jesus, and pledges that if our inheritance is here manifested by suffering with him, that very fact is a prophecy of common glory hereafter. He describes that future as the revealing of a glory, to which the sufferings of this present time are not worthy to be compared; and then, in our text he varies the application of that thought of revealing and thinks of the subjects of it as being the 'sons of God.' They will be revealed when the glory which they have as joint-heirs with Christ is revealed in them. They walk, as it were, compassed with mist and cloud, but the splendour which will fall on them will scatter the envious darkness, and 'when Christ who is our life shall appear, then shall His co-heirs also appear with Him in glory.'

We may consider—

I. The present veil over the sons of God.

There is always a difference between appearance and reality, between the ideal and its embodiments. For all men it is true that the full expression of oneself is impossible. Each man's deeds fall short of disclosing the essential self in the man. Every will is hampered by the fleshly screen of the body. 'I would that my tongue could utter the thoughts that arise in me,' is the yearning of every heart that is deeply moved. Contending principles successively sway every personality and thwart each other's expression. For these, and many other reasons, the sum-total of every life is but a shrouded representation of the man who lives it; and we, all of us, after all efforts at self-revelation, remain mysteries to our fellows and to ourselves. All this is eminently true of the sons of God. They have a life-germ hidden in their souls, which in its very nature is destined to fill and expand their whole being, and to permeate with its triumphant energy every corner of their nature. But it is weak and often overborne by its opposite. The seed sown is to grow in spite of bad weather and a poor soil and many weeds, and though it is destined to overcome all these, it may to-day only be able to show on the surface a little patch of pale and struggling growth. When we think of the cost at which the life of Christ was imparted to men, and of the divine source from which it comes, and of the sedulous and protracted discipline

through which it is being trained, we cannot but
conclude that nothing short of its universal dominion
over all the faculties of its imperfect possessors can be
the goal of its working.  Hercules in his cradle is still
Hercules, and strangles snakes.  Frost and sun may
struggle in midwinter, and the cold may seem to
predominate, but the sun is steadily enlarging its
course in the sky, and increasing the fervour of its
beams, and midsummer day is as sure to dawn as the
shortest day was.

The sons of God, even more truly than other men,
have contending principles fighting within them.  It
was the same Apostle who with oaths denied that he
'knew the man,' and in a passion of clinging love and
penitence fell at His feet; but for the mere onlooker it
would be hard to say which was the true man and
which would conquer.  The sons of God, like other
men, have to express themselves in words which are
never closely enough fitted to their thoughts and
feelings.  David's penitence has to be contented with
groans which are not deep enough; and John's calm
raptures on his Saviour's breast can only be spoken by
shut eyes and silence.  The sons of God never fully
correspond to their character, but always fall somewhat beneath their desire, and must always be somewhat less than their intention.  The artist never wholly
embodies his conception.  It is only God who 'rests
from His works,' because the works fully embody
His creative design and fully receive the benediction
of His own satisfaction with them.

From all such thoughts there arises a piece of plain
practical wisdom, which warns Christian men not
to despond or despair if they do not find themselves
living up to their ideal.  The sons of God are 'veiled'

because the world's estimate of them is untrue. The old commonplace that the world knows nothing of its greatest men is verified in the opinions which it holds about the sons of God. It is not for their Christianity that they get any of the world's honours and encomiums, if such fall to their share. They are *unknown* and yet *well*-known. They live for the most part veiled in obscurity. 'The light shineth in darkness, and the darkness comprehendeth it not.' They are God's hidden ones. If they are wise, they will look for no recognition nor eulogy from the world, and will be content to live, as unknown by the princes of this world as was the Lord of glory, whom they slew because their dim eyes could not see the flashing of the glory 'through the veil, that is to say, His flesh.' But no consciousness of imperfection in our revelation of an indwelling Christ must ever be allowed to diminish our efforts to live out the life that is in us, and to shine as lights in the world; nor must the consciousness that we walk as 'veiled,' lead us to add to the thick folds the criminal one of voluntary silence and cowardly hiding in dumb hearts the secret of our lives.

II. The unveiling of the sons of God.

That unveiling is in the text represented as coming along with the glory which shall be revealed to us-ward, and as being contemporaneous with the deliver-ance of the creation itself from the bondage of corrup-tion, and its passing into the liberty of the glory of the children of God. It coincides with the vanishing of the pain in which the whole creation now groans and travails, and with the adoption—that is, the redemption of our body. Then hope will be seen and will pass into still fruition. All this points to the time when

Jesus Christ is revealed, and His servants are revealed with Him in glory. That revelation brings with it of necessity the manifestation of the sons of God for what they are—the making visible in the life of what God sees them to be.

That revelation of the sons of God is the result of the entire dominion and transforming supremacy of the Spirit of God in them. In the whole sweep of their consciousness there will in that day be nothing done from other motives; there will be no sidelights flashing in and disturbing the perfect illumination from the candle of the Lord set on high in their being; there will be no contradictions in the life. It will be one and simple, and therefore perfectly intelligible. Such is the destined issue of the most imperfect Christian life. The Christian man who has in his experience to-day the faintest and most interrupted operation of the spirit of life in Christ Jesus has therein a pledge of immortality, because nothing short of an endless life of progressive and growing purity will be adequate to receive and exemplify the power which can never terminate until it is made like Him and perfectly seeing Him as He is.

But that unveiling further guarantees the possession of fully adequate means of expression. The limitations and imperfections of our present bodily life will all drop away in putting on 'the body of glory' which shall be ours. The new tongue will perfectly utter the new knowledge and rapture of the new life; new hands will perfectly realise our ideals; and on every forehead will be stamped Christ's new name.

That unveiling will be further realised by a divine act indicating the characters of the sons of God by their position. Earth's judgments will be reversed by that divine voice, and the great promise, which through weary ages has shone as a far-off star,—'I will set him on high because he hath known my name'—will then be known for the sun near at hand. Many names loudly blown through the world's trumpet will fall silent then. Many stars will be quenched, but 'they that be wise shall shine as the brightness of the firmament.'

That revelation will be more surprising to no one than to those who are its subjects, when they see themselves mirrored in that glass, and so unlike what they are here. Their first impulse will be to wonder at the form they see, and to ask, almost with incredulity, 'Lord, is it I?' Nor will the wonder be less when they recognise many whom they knew not. The surprises when the family of God is gathered together at last will be great. The Israel of Captivity lifts up her wondering eyes as she sees the multitudes flocking to her side as the doves to their windows, and, half-ashamed of her own narrow vision, exclaims, 'I was left alone; these, where had they been?' Let us rejoice that in the day when the sons of God are revealed, many hidden ones from many dark corners will sit at the Father's table. That revelation will be made to the whole universe; we know not how, but we know that it shall be; and, as the text tells us, that revelation of the sons of God is the hope for which 'the earnest expectation of the creature waits' through the weary ages.

# THE REDEMPTION OF THE BODY

'The adoption, to wit, the redemption of our body.'—ROMANS viii. 23.

IN a previous verse Paul has said that all true
Christians have received 'the Spirit of adoption.'
They become sons of God through Christ the Son.
They receive a new spiritual and divine life from God
through Christ, and that life is like its source. In so
far as that new life vitalises and dominates their
nature, believers have received 'the Spirit of adoption,'
and by it they cry 'Abba, Father.' But the body still
remains a source of weakness, the seat of sin. It is
sluggish and inapt for high purposes; it still remains
subject to 'the law of sin and death'; and so is not
like the Father who breathed into it the breath of life.
It remains in bondage, and has not yet received the
adoption. This text, in harmony with the Apostle's
whole teaching, looks forward to a change in the body
and in its relations to the renewed spirit, as the crown
and climax of the work of redemption, and declares
that till that change is effected, the condition of
Christian men is imperfect, and is a waiting, and often
a groaning.

In dealing with some of the thoughts that arise
from this text, we note—

I. That a future bodily life is needed in order to give
definiteness and solidity to the conception of immortality.

Before the Gospel came men's belief in a future life
was vague and powerless, mainly because it had no
Gospel of the Resurrection, and so nothing tangible to
lay hold on. The Gospel has made the belief in a
future state infinitely easier and more powerful,

179

mainly because of the emphasis with which it has
proclaimed an actual resurrection and a future bodily
life. Its great proof of immortality is drawn, not
merely from ethical considerations of the manifest
futility of earthly life which has no sequel beyond
the grave, nor from the intuitions and longings of
men's souls, but from the historical fact of the
Resurrection of Jesus Christ, and of His Ascension in
bodily form into heaven. It proclaims these two facts
as parts of His experience, and asserts that when He
rose from the dead and ascended up on high, He did so
as 'the first-born among many brethren,' their forerunner and their pattern. It is this which gives the
Gospel its power, and thus transforms a vague and
shadowy conception of immortality into a solid faith,
for which we have already an historical guarantee.
Stupendous mysteries still veil the nature of the resurrection process, though these are exaggerated into
inconceivabilities by false notions of what constitutes
personal identity; but if the choice lies between accepting the Christian doctrine of a resurrection and the
conception of a finite spirit disembodied and yet active,
there can be no doubt as to which of these two is the
more reasonable and thinkable. Body, soul, and spirit
make the complete triune man.

The thought of the future life as a bodily life satisfies
the longings of the heart. Much natural shrinking
from death comes from unwillingness to part company
with an old companion and friend. As Paul puts it in
2nd Corinthians, 'Not for that we would be unclothed,
but clothed upon.' All thoughts of the future which do
not give prominence to the idea of a bodily life open
up but a ghastly and uninviting mode of existence,
which cannot but repel those who are accustomed to

the fellowship of their bodies, and they feel that they cannot think of themselves as deprived of that which was their servant and instrument, through all the years of their earthly consciousness.

II. 'The body that shall be' is an emancipated body.

The varied gifts of the Spirit bestowed upon the Christian Church served to quicken the hope of the yet greater gifts of that indwelling Spirit which were yet to come. Chief amongst these our text considers the transformation of the earthly into a spiritual body. This transformation our text regards as being the participation by the body in the redemption by which Christ has bought us with the great price of His blood. We have to interpret the language here in the light of the further teaching of Paul in the great Resurrection chapter of 1st Corinthians, which distinctly lays stress, not on the identity of the corporeal frame which is laid in the grave with 'the body of glory,' but upon the entire contrast between the 'natural body,' which is fit organ for the lower nature, and is informed by it, and the 'spiritual body,' which is fit organ for the spirit. We have to interpret 'the resurrection of the body' by the definite apostolic declaration, 'Thou sowest not that body that shall be . . . but God giveth it a body as it hath pleased Him'; and we have to give full weight to the contrasts which the Apostle draws between the characteristics of that which is 'sown' and of that which is 'raised.' The one is 'sown in corruption and raised in incorruption.' Natural decay is contrasted with immortal youth. The one is 'sown in dishonour,' the other is 'raised in glory.' That contrast is ethical, and refers either to the subordinate position of the body here in relation to the spirit, or to the natural sense of shame, or to the ideas of degradation

which are attached to the indulgence of the appetites.
The one is 'sown in weakness,' the other is 'raised in
power'; the one is 'sown a natural body,' the other is
'raised a spiritual body.' Is not Paul in this whole
series of contrasts thinking primarily of the vision
which he saw on the road to Damascus when the risen
Christ appeared before him? And had not the years
which had passed since then taught him to see in the
ascended Christ the prophecy and the pattern of what
His servants should become? We have further to
keep in view Paul's other representation in 2nd Corinthians v., where he strongly puts the contrast between
the corporeal environment of earth and 'the body of
glory,' which belongs to the future life, in his two
images: 'the earthly house of this tabernacle,'—a clay
hut which lasts but for a time,—and 'the building of
God, the house not made with hands and eternal.' The
body is an occasion of separation from the Lord.

These considerations may well lead us to, at least,
general outlines on which a confident and peaceful
hope may fix. For example, they lead us to the thought
that that redeemed body is no more subject to decay
and death, is no more weighed upon by weakness and
weariness, has no work beyond its strength, needs
no sustenance by food, and no refreshment of sleep.
'The Lamb which is in the midst of the throne shall
feed them,' suggests strength constantly communicated
by a direct divine gift. And from all these negative
characteristics there follows that there will be in that
future bodily life no epochs of age marked by bodily
changes. The two young men who were seen sitting
in the sepulchre of Jesus had lived before Adam, and
would seem as young if we saw them to-day.

Similarly the redeemed body will be a more perfect

instrument for communication with the external universe. We know that the present body conditions our
knowledge, and that our senses do not take cognisance
of all the qualities of material things. Microscopes
and telescopes have enlarged our field of vision, and
have brought the infinitely small and the infinitely
distant within our range. Our ear hears vibrations
at a certain rate per second, and no doubt if it were
more delicately organised we could hear sounds where
now is silence. Sometimes the creatures whom we
call 'inferior' seem to have senses that apprehend much
of which we are not aware. Balaam's ass saw the
obstructing angel before Balaam did. Nor is there any
reason to suppose that all the powers of the mind find
tools to work with in the body. It is possible that that
body which is the fit instrument of the spirit may
become its means of knowing more deeply, thinking
more wisely, understanding more swiftly, comprehend-
ing more widely, remembering more firmly and judging
more soundly. It is possible that the contrast between
then and now may be like the contrast between telegraph and slow messenger in regard to the rapidity,
between photograph and poor daub in regard to the
truthfulness, between a full-orbed circle and a frag-
mentary arc in regard to the completeness of the
messages which the body brings to the indwelling self.

But, once more, the body unredeemed has appetites
and desires which may lead to their own satisfaction,
which do lead to sordid cares and weary toil. 'The
flesh lusts against the spirit and the spirit against the
flesh.' The redeemed body will have in it nothing to
tempt and nothing to clog, but will be a helper to the
spirit and a source of strength. Glorious work of God
as the body is, it has its weaknesses, its limitations,

and its tendencies to evil. We must not be tempted into brooding over unanswered questions as to 'How do the dead rise, and with what body do they come?' But we can lift our eyes to the mountain-top where Jesus went up to pray. 'And as He prayed the fashion of His countenance was altered, and His raiment became white and dazzling'; and He was capable of entering into the Shekinah cloud and holding fellowship therein with the Father, who attested His Sonship and bade us listen to His voice. And we can look to Olivet and follow the ascending Jesus as He lets His benediction drop on the upturned faces of His friends, until He again passes into the Shekinah cloud, and leaving the world, goes to the Father. And from both His momentary transfiguration and His permanent Ascension we can draw the certain assurance that 'He shall fashion anew the body of our humiliation, that it may be conformed to the body of His glory, according to the working whereby He is able even to subdue all things unto Himself.'

III. The redeemed body is a consequence of Christ's indwelling Spirit.

It is no natural result of death or resurrection, but is the outcome of the process begun on earth, by which, 'through faith and the righteousness of faith,' the spirit is life. The context distinctly enforces this view by its double use of 'adoption,' which in one aspect has already been received, and is manifested by the fact that 'now are we the sons of God,' and in another aspect is still 'waited' for. The Christian man in his regenerated spirit has been born again; the Christian man still waits for the completion of that sonship in a time when the regenerated spirit will no longer dwell in the clay cottage of 'this tabernacle,' but will inhabit a congruous dwelling in 'the building of God not made with hands, eternal in the heavens.'

Scripture is too healthy and comprehensive to be contented with a merely spiritual regeneration, and is withal too spiritual to be satisfied with a merely material heaven. It gives full place to both elements, and yet decisively puts all belonging to the latter second. It lays down the laws that for a complete humanity there must be body as well as spirit; that there must be a correspondence between the two, and as is the spirit so must the body be, and further, that the process must begin at the centre and work outwards, so that the spirit must first be transformed, and then the body must be participant of the transformation.

All that Scripture says about 'rising in glory' is said about believers. It is represented as a spiritual process. They who have the Spirit of God in their spirits because they have it receive the glorified body which is like their Saviour's. It is not enough to die in order to 'rise glorious.' 'If the Spirit of Him that raised up Jesus from the dead dwell in you, He that raised up Christ from the dead shall also quicken your mortal bodies by His Spirit that dwelleth in you.' The resurrection is promised for all mankind, but it may be a resurrection in which there shall be endless living and no glory, nor any beauty and no blessedness. But the body may be 'sown in weakness,' and in weakness raised; it may be 'sown in dishonour' and in dishonour raised; it may be sown dead, and raised a living death. 'Many of them that sleep in the dust of the earth shall awake, some to everlasting life, and some to shame and everlasting contempt.' Does that mean nothing? 'They that have done evil to the resurrection of condemnation.' Does that mean nothing?

.There are dark mysteries in these and similar words of Scripture which should make us all pause and solemnly reflect. The sole way which leads to the resurrection of glory is the way of faith in Jesus Christ. If we yield ourselves to Him, He will plant His Spirit in our spirits, will guide and growingly sanctify us through life, will deliver us by the indwelling of the Spirit of life in Him from the law of sin and death. Nor will His transforming power cease till it has pervaded our whole being with its fiery energy, and we stand at the last men like Christ, redeemed in body, soul, and spirit, 'according to the mighty working whereby He is able to subdue all things unto Himself.'

## THE INTERCEDING SPIRIT

'The Spirit itself maketh intercession for us with groanings which cannot be uttered.'—ROMANS viii. 26.

PENTECOST was a transitory sign of a perpetual gift. The tongues of fire and the rushing mighty wind, which were at first the most conspicuous results of the gifts of the Spirit, tongues, and prophecies, and gifts of healing, which were to the early Church itself and to onlookers palpable demonstrations of an indwelling power, were little more lasting than the fire and the wind. Does anything remain? This whole great chapter is Paul's triumphant answer to such a question. The Spirit of God dwells in every believer as the source of his true life, is for him 'the Spirit of adoption,' and witnesses with his spirit that he is a child of God, and a joint-heir with Christ. Not only does that Spirit co-operate with the human spirit in this witness-bearing, but the verse, of which our text is a part, points to another form of co-operation: for the word rendered in the earlier part of the verse 'helpeth' in the original suggests more distinctly that the Spirit of God in His intercession for us works in association with us.

First, then—

I. The Spirit's intercession is not carried on apart from us.

Much modern hymnology goes wrong in this point, that it represents the Spirit's intercession as presented in heaven rather than as taking place within the personal being of the believer. There is a broad distinction carefully observed throughout Scripture between the representations of the work of Christ and that of the Spirit of Christ. The former in its character and revelation and attainment was wrought upon earth, and in its character of intercession and bestowment of blessings is discharged at the right hand of God in heaven; the whole of the Spirit's work, on the other hand, is wrought in human spirits here. The context speaks of intercession expressed in 'groanings which cannot be uttered,' and which, unexpressed though they are, are fully understood 'by Him who searches the heart.' Plainly, therefore, these groanings come from human hearts, and as plainly are the Divine Spirit's voicing them.

II. The Spirit's intercession in our spirits consists in our own divinely-inspired longings.

The Apostle has just been speaking of another groaning within ourselves, which is the expression of 'the earnest expectation' of 'the adoption, to wit, the redemption of our body'; and he says that that longing will be the more patient the more it is full of hope. This, then, is Paul's conception of the normal attitude of a Christian soul; but that attitude is hard to keep up in one's own strength, because of the distractions of time and sense which are ever tending to disturb the continuity and fixity of that onward look, and to lead us rather to be satisfied with the gross, dull present. That redemption of the body, with all which it implies and includes, ought to be the supreme object to which each Christian heart should ever be turning, and Christian prayers should be directed. But our own daily experience makes us only too sure that such elevation above, and remoteness from earthly thoughts, with all their pettinesses and limitations, is impossible for us in our own strength. As Paul puts it here, 'We know not what to pray for'; nor can we fix and focus our desires, nor present them 'as we ought.' It is to this weakness and incompleteness of our desires and prayers that the help of the Spirit is directed. He strengthens our longings by His own direct operation. The more vivid our anticipations and the more steadfast our hopes, and the more our spirits reach out to that future redemption, the more are we bound to discern something more than human imaginings in them, and to be sure that such visions are too good not to be true, too solid to be only the play of our own fancy. The more we are conscious of these experiences as our own, the more certain we shall be that in them it is not we that speak, but 'the Spirit of the Father that speaketh in us.'

III. These divinely-inspired longings are incapable of full expression.

They are shallow feelings that can be spoken. Language breaks down in the attempt to express our deepest emotions and our truest love. For all the deepest things in man, inarticulate utterance is the most self-revealing.  Grief can say more in a sob and a tear than in many weak words; love finds its tongue in the light of an eye and the clasp of a hand.  The groanings which rise from the depths of the Christian soul cannot be forced into the narrow frame-work of human language; and just because they are unutterable are to be recognised as the voice of the Holy Spirit.

But where amidst the Christian experience of to-day shall we find anything in the least like these unutterable longings after the redemption of the body which Paul here takes it for granted are the experience of all Christians?  There is no more startling condemnation of the average Christianity of our times than the calm certainty with which through all this epistle the Apostle takes it for granted that the experience of the Roman Christians will universally endorse his statements.  Look for a moment at what these statements are.  Listen to the briefest summary of them : 'We cry, Abba, Father'; 'We are children of God'; 'We suffer with Him that we may be glorified with Him'; 'Glory shall be revealed to usward'; 'We have the first-fruits of the Spirit'; 'We ourselves groan within ourselves'; 'By hope were we saved'; 'We hope for that which we see not'; 'Then do we with patience wait for it'; 'We know that to them that love God all things work together for good'; 'In all these things we are more than conquerors'; 'Neither death nor life . . . nor any other creature shall be able to separate us from the love of God.'  He believed that in these rapturous and triumphant words he was gathering together the experience of every Roman Christian, and would evoke from their lips a confident 'Amen.'  Where are the communities to-day

in whose hearing these words could be reiterated with
the like assurance? How few among us there are
who know anything of these 'groanings which cannot
be uttered!' How few among us there are whose
spirits are stretching out eager desires towards the
land of perpetual summer, like migratory birds in
northern latitudes when the autumn days are shorten-
ing and the temperature is falling!

But, however we must feel that our poor experience
falls far short of the ideal in our text, an ideal which
was to some extent realised in the early Christian
Church, we must beware of taking the imperfections of
our experience as any evidence of the unreality of our
Christianity. They are a proof that we have limited
and impeded the operation of the Spirit within us.
They teach us that He will not intercede 'with groanings which cannot be uttered,' unless we let Him speak
through our voices. Therefore, if we find that in our
own consciousness there is little to correspond to those
unuttered groanings, we should take the warning:
'Quench not the Spirit.' 'Grieve not the Holy Spirit
of God in whom ye were sealed unto the day of
redemption.'

IV. The unuttered longings are sure to be answered.

He that searcheth the heart knows the meaning
of the Spirit's unspoken prayers; and looking into
the depths of the human spirit interprets its longings,
discriminating between the mere human and partial
expression and the divinely-inspired desire which may
be unexpressed. If our prayers are weak, they are
answered in the measure in which they embody in
them, though perhaps mistaken by us, a divine longing.
Apparent disappointment of our petitions may be
real answers to our real prayer. It was because Jesus

loved Mary and Martha and Lazarus that He abode
still in the same place where He was, to let Lazarus
die that He might be raised again. That was the true
answer to the sisters' hope of His immediate coming.
God's way of giving to us is to breathe within us a
desire, and then to answer the desire inbreathed. So,
longing is the prophecy of fulfilment when it is
longing according to the will of God. They who
'hunger and thirst after righteousness' may ever be
sure that their bread shall be given them, and their
water will be made sure. The true object of our
desires is often not clear to us, and so we err in trans-
lating it into words. Let us be thankful that we pray
to a God who can discern the prayer within the prayer,
and often gives the substance of our petitions in the
very act of refusing their form.

## THE GIFT THAT BRINGS ALL GIFTS

'He that spared not His own Son, but delivered Him up for us all, how shall He
not with Him also freely give us all things?'—ROMANS viii. 32.

WE have here an allusion to, if not a distinct quotation from, the narrative in Genesis, of Abraham's
offering up of Isaac. The same word which is employed in the Septuagint version of the Old Testament,
to translate the Hebrew word rendered in our Bible as
'withheld,' is employed here by the Apostle. And
there is evidently floating before his mind the thought
that, in some profound and real sense, there is an
analogy between that wondrous and faithful act of
giving up and the transcendent and stupendous gift to
the world, from God, of His Son.

If we take that point of view, the language of my

text rises into singular force, and suggests many very
deep thoughts, about which, perhaps, silence is best.
But led by that analogy, let us deal with these words.

I. Consider this mysterious act of divine surrender.

The analogy seems to suggest to us, strange as it may
be, and remote from the cold and abstract ideas of the
divine nature which it is thought to be philosophical
to cherish, that something corresponding to the pain
and loss that shadowed the patriarch's heart flitted
across the divine mind when the Father sent the Son
to be the Saviour of the world. Not merely to give,
but to give up, is the highest crown and glory of love,
as we know it. And who shall venture to say that we
so fully apprehend the divine nature as to be warranted in declaring that some analogy to that is
impossible for Him? Our language is, 'I will not
offer unto God that which doth cost me nothing.' Let
us bow in silence before the dim intimation that seems
to flicker out of the words of my text, that so He says
to us, 'I will not offer unto you that which doth cost
Me nothing.' 'He *spared* not His own Son'; withheld
Him not from us.

But passing from that which, I dare say, many of you
may suppose to be fanciful and unwarranted, let us
come upon the surer ground of the other words of my
text. And notice how the reality of the surrender is
emphasised by the closeness of the bond which, in the
mysterious eternity, knits together the Father and the
Son. As with Abraham, so in this lofty example, of
which Abraham and Isaac were but as dim, wavering
reflections in water, the Son is His own Son. It seems
to me impossible, upon any fair interpretation of the
words before us, to refrain from giving to that epithet
here its very highest and most mysterious sense. It

cannot be any mere equivalent for Messiah, it cannot merely mean a man who was like God in purity of nature and in closeness of communion. For the force of the analogy and the emphasis of that word which is even more emphatic in the Greek than in the English 'His *own* Son,' point to a community of nature, to a uniqueness and singleness of relation, to a closeness of intimacy, to which no other is a parallel. And so we have to estimate the measure of the surrender by the tenderness and awfulness of the bond. 'Having one Son, His well-beloved, He sent Him.'

Notice, again, how the greatness of the surrender is made more emphatic by the contemplation of it in its double negative and positive aspect, in the two successive clauses. 'He spared not His Son, but delivered Him up,' an absolute, positive giving of Him over to the humiliation of the life and to the mystery of the death.

And notice how the tenderness and the beneficence that were the sole motive of the surrender are lifted into light in the last words, 'for us all.' The single, sole reason that bowed, if I may so say, the divine purpose, and determined the mysterious act, was a pure desire for our blessing. No definition is given as to the manner in which that surrender wrought for our good. The Apostle does not need to dwell upon that. His purpose is to emphasise the entire unselfishness, the utter simplicity of the motive which moved the divine will. One great throb of love to the whole of humanity led to that transcendent surrender, before which we can only bow and say, 'Thanks be unto God for His unspeakable gift.'

And now, notice how this mysterious act is grasped by the Apostle here as what I may call the illuminat-

N

ing fact as to the whole divine nature. From it, and
from it alone, there falls a blaze of light on the deepest
things in God. We are accustomed to speak of Christ's
perfect life of unselfishness, and His death of pure
beneficence, as being the great manifestation to us all
that in His heart there is an infinite fountain of love to
us. We are, further, accustomed to speak of Christ's
mission and death as being the revelation to us of the
love of God as well as of the Man Christ Jesus, because
we believe that 'God was in Christ reconciling the
world,' and that He has so manifested and revealed the
very nature of divinity to us, in His life and in His
person, that, as He Himself says, 'He that hath seen
Me hath seen the Father.' And every conclusion that
we draw as to the love of Christ is, *ipso facto*, a conclusion as to the love of God. But my text looks at
the matter from rather a different point of view, and
bids us see, in Christ's mission and sacrifice, the
great demonstration of the love of God, not only
because 'God was in Christ,' but because the Father's
will, conceived of as distinct from, and yet harmonious
with, the will of the Son, gives Him up for us. And
we have to say, not only that we see the love of God
*in* the love of Christ, but 'God so loved the world that
He sent His only begotten Son' that we might have
life through Him.

These various phases of the love of Christ as
manifesting the divine love, may not be capable of
perfect harmonising in our thoughts, but they do
blend into one, and by reason of them all, 'God commendeth His love toward us in that while we were yet
sinners, Christ died for us.' We have to think not only
of Abraham who gave up, but of the unresisting,
innocent Isaac, bearing on his shoulders the wood for

the burnt offering, as the Christ bore the Cross on His, and suffering himself to be bound upon the pile, not only by the cords that tied his limbs, but by the cords of obedience and submission, and in both we have to bow before the Apocalypse of divine love.

II. So, secondly, look at the power of this divine surrender to bring with it all other gifts.

'How shall He not with Him also freely give us all things?' The Apostle's triumphant question requires for its affirmative answer only the belief in the unchangeableness of the Divine heart, and the uniformity of the Divine purpose. And if these be recognised, their conclusion inevitably follows. 'With Him He will freely give us all things.'

It is so, because the greater gift implies the less. We do not expect that a man who hands over a million of pounds to another, to help him, will stick at a farthing afterwards. If you give a diamond you may well give a box to keep it in. In God's gift the lesser will follow the lead of the greater; and whatsoever a man can want, it is a smaller thing for Him to bestow, than was the gift of His Son.

There is a beautiful contrast between the manners of giving the two sets of gifts implied in words of the original, perhaps scarcely capable of being reproduced in any translation. The expression that is rendered 'freely give,' implies that there is a grace and a pleasantness in the act of bestowal. God gave in Christ, what we may reverently say it was something like pain to give. Will He not give the lesser, whatever they may be, which it is the joy of His heart to communicate? The greater implies the less.

Farther, this one great gift draws all other gifts after it, because the purpose of the greater gift cannot be

attained without the bestowment of the lesser. He
does not begin to build being unable to finish; He does
not miscalculate His resources, nor stultify Himself by
commencing upon a large scale, and having to stop
short before the purpose with which He began is
accomplished. Men build great palaces, and are bank-
rupt before the roof is, put on. God lays His plans
with the knowledge of His powers, and having first of
all bestowed this large gift, is not going to have it
bestowed in vain for want of some smaller ones to
follow it up. Christ puts the same argument to us,
beginning only at the other end of the process. Paul
says, 'God has laid the foundation in Christ.' Do you
think He will stop before the headstone is put on?
Christ said, 'It is your Father's good pleasure to give
you the Kingdom.' Do you think He will not give you
bread and water on the road to it? Will He send
out His soldiers half-equipped; will it be found when
they are on their march that they have been started
with a defective commissariat, and with insufficient
trenching tools? Shall the children of the King, on
the road to their thrones, be left to scramble along
anyhow, in want of what they need to get there?
That is not God's way of doing. He that hath begun
a good work will also perfect the same, and when He .
gave to you and me His Son, He bound Himself to give
us every subsidiary and secondary blessing which was
needed to make that Son's work complete in each
of us.

Again, this great blessing draws after it, by necessary consequence, all other lesser and secondary gifts,
inasmuch as, in every real sense, everything is included and possessed in the Christ when we receive
Him. 'With Him,' says Paul, as if that gift once laid

in a man's heart actually enclosed within it, and had
for its indispensable accompaniment the possession of
every smaller thing that a man can need, Jesus Christ
is, as it were, a great Cornucopia, a horn of abundance,
out of which will pour, with magic affluence, all
manner of supplies according as we require. This
fountain flows with milk, wine, and water, as men
need. Everything is given us when Christ is given to
us, because Christ is the Heir of all things, and we
possess all things in Him; as some poor village maiden
married to a prince in disguise, who, on the morrow of
her wedding finds that she is lady of broad lands, and
mistress of a kingdom. 'He that spared not His own
Son,' not only 'with Him will give,' but in Him has
'given us all things.'

And so, brethren, just as that great gift is the
illuminating fact in reference to the divine heart, so is
it the interpreting fact in reference to the divine dealings. Only when we keep firm hold of Christ as the
gift of God, and the Explainer of all that God does,
can we face the darkness, the perplexities, the torturing questions that from the beginning have harassed
men's minds as they looked upon the mysteries of
human misery. If we recognise that God has given us
His Son, then all things become, if not plain, at least
lighted with some gleam from that great gift; and we
feel that the surrender of Christ is the constraining
fact which shapes after its own likeness, and for its
own purpose, all the rest of God's dealings with men.
That gift makes anything believable, reasonable,
possible, rather than that He should spare not His
own Son, and then should counterwork His own act by
sending the world anything but good.

III. And now, lastly, take one or two practical issues

from these thoughts, in reference to our own belief and conduct.

First, I would say, Let us correct our estimates of the relative importance of the two sets of gifts. On the one side stands the solitary Christ; on the other side are massed all delights of sense, all blessings of time, all the things that the vulgar estimation of men unanimously recognises to be good. These are only make-weights. They are all lumped together into an 'also.' They are but the golden dust that may be filed off from the great ingot and solid block. They are but the outward tokens of His far deeper and true preciousness. They are secondary; He is the primary. What an inversion of our notions of good! Do *you* degrade all the world's wealth, pleasantness, ease, prosperity, into an 'also?' Are you content to put it in the secondary place, as a result, if it please Him, of Christ? Do you live as if you did? Which do you hunger for most? Which do you labour for hardest? 'Seek ye first the Kingdom' and the King, and all 'these things shall be added unto you.'

Let these thoughts teach us that sorrow too is one of the gifts of the Christ. The words of my text, at first sight, might seem to be simply a promise of abundant earthly good. But look what lies close beside them, and is even part of the same triumphant burst. 'Shall tribulation, or distress, or persecution, or famine, or nakedness, or peril, or sword?' These are some of the 'all things' which Paul expected that God would give him and his brethren. And looking upon all, he says, 'They all work together for good'; and in them all we may be more than conquerors. It would be a poor, shabby issue of such a great gift as that of which we have been speaking, if it were only to be followed by the sweetnesses and prosperity and wealth of this world. But here is the point that we have to keep hold of—inasmuch as He gives us all things, let us take all the things that come to us as being as distinctly the gifts of His love, as is the gift of Christ Himself. A wise physician, to an ignorant onlooker, might seem to be acting in contradictory fashions when in the one moment he slashes into a limb, with a sharp, gleaming knife, and in the next sedulously binds the wounds, and closes the arteries, but the purpose of both acts is one.

The diurnal revolution of the earth brings the joyful sunrise and the pathetic sunset. The same annual revolution whirls us through the balmy summer days and the biting winter ones. God's purpose is one. His methods vary. The road goes straight to its goal; but it sometimes runs in tunnels dank and dark and stifling, and sometimes by sunny glades and through green pastures. God's purpose is always love, brother. His withdrawals are gifts, and sorrow is not the least of the benefits which come to us through the Man of Sorrows.

So again, let these thoughts teach us to live by a very quiet and peaceful faith. We find it a great deal easier to trust God for Heaven than for earth—for the distant blessings than for the near ones. Many a man will venture his soul into God's hands, who would hesitate to venture to-morrow's food there. Why? Is it not because we do not really trust Him for the greater that we find it so hard to trust Him for the less? Is it not because we want the less more really than we want the greater, that we can put ourselves off with faith for the one, and want something more solid to grasp for the other? Live in the calm con-

fidence that God gives all things; and gives us for
to-morrow as for eternity; for earth as for heaven.

And, last of all, make you quite sure that you have
taken *the* great gift of God. He gives it to all the
world, but they only have it who accept it by faith.
Have you, my brother? I look out upon the lives of the
mass of professing Christians; and this question weighs
on my heart, judging by conduct—have they really got
Christ for their own? 'Wherefore do ye spend your
money for that which is not bread, and your labour
for that which satisfieth not?' Look how you are all
fighting and scrambling, and sweating and fretting, to
get hold of the goods of this present life, and here is a
gift gleaming before you all the while that you will
not condescend to take. Like a man standing in a
market-place offering sovereigns for nothing, which
nobody accepts because they think the offer is too
good to be true, so God complains and wails: I have
stretched out My hands all the day, laden with gifts,
and no man regarded.

> 'It is only heaven may be had for the asking;
>     It is only God that is given away.'

He gives His Son. Take Him by humble faith in
His sacrifice and Spirit; take Him, and with Him He
freely gives you all things.


## MORE THAN CONQUERORS

'Nay, in all these things we are more than conquerors through Him that loved
us.'—ROMANS viii. 37.

IN order to understand and feel the full force of this
triumphant saying of the Apostle, we must observe that
it is a negative answer to the preceding questions,

'Who shall separate us from the love of Christ? Shall tribulation, or distress, or persecution, or famine, or nakedness, or peril, or sword?' A heterogeneous mass the Apostle here brigades together as an antagonistic army. They are alike in nothing except that they are all evils. There is no attempt at an exhaustive enumeration, or at classification. He clashes down, as it were, a miscellaneous mass of evil things, and then triumphs over them, and all the genus to which they belong, as being utterly impotent to drag men away from Jesus Christ. To ask the question is to answer it, but the form of the answer is worth notice. Instead of directly replying, 'No! no such powerless things as these can separate us from the love of Christ,' he says, 'No! In all these things, whilst weltering amongst them, whilst ringed round about by them, as by encircling enemies, "we are more. than conquerors."' Thereby, he suggests that there is something needing to be done by us, in order that the foes may not exercise their natural effect. And so, taking the words of my text in connection with that to which they are an answer, we have three things—the impotent enemies of love; the abundant victory of love; 'We are more than conquerors'; and the love that makes us victorious. Let us look then at these three things briefly.

I. First of all, the impotent enemies of love.

There is contempt in the careless massing together of the foes which the Apostle enumerates. He begins with the widest word that covers everything—'affliction.' Then he specifies various forms of it—'distress,' *straitening*, as the word might be rendered, then he comes to evils inflicted for Christ's sake by hostile men—'persecution,' then he names purely physical

evils, 'hunger' and 'nakedness,' then he harks back
again to man's antagonism, 'peril,' and 'sword.' And
thus carelessly, and without an effort at logical order,
he throws together, as specimens of their class, these
salient points, as it were, and crests of the great sea,
whose billows threaten to roll over us; and he laughs
at them all, as impotent and nought, when compared
with the love of Christ, which shields us from them all.

Now it must be noticed that here, in his triumphant
question, the Apostle means not our love to Christ but
His to us; and not even our sense of that love, but the
fact itself. And his question is just this:—Is there
any evil in the world that can make Christ stop loving
a man that cleaves to Him? And, as I said, to ask the
question is to answer it. The two things belong to
two different regions. They have nothing in common.
The one moves amongst the low levels of earth; the
other dwells up amidst the abysses of eternity, and to
suppose that anything that assails and afflicts us here
has any effect in making that great heart cease to love
us is to fancy that the mists can quench the sunlight,
is to suppose that that which lies down low in the
earth can rise to poison and to darken the heavens.

There is no need, in order to rise to the full height of
the Christian contempt for calamity, to deny any of its
terrible power. These things can separate us from
much. They can separate us from joy, from hope,
from almost all that makes life desirable. They can
strip us to the very quick, but the quick they cannot
touch. The frost comes and kills the flowers, browns
the leaves, cuts off the stems, binds the sweet music of
the flowing rivers in silent chains, casts mists and
darkness over the face of the solitary grey world, but
it does not touch the life that is in the root.

And so all these outward sorrows that have power
over the whole of the outward life, and can slay joy
and all but stifle hope, and can ban men into irrevoc-
able darkness and unalleviated solitude, they do not
touch in the smallest degree the secret bond that binds
the heart to Jesus, nor in any measure affect the flow
of His love to us.  Therefore we may front them and
smile at them and say:

> 'Do as thou wilt, devouring time,
> With this wide world, and all its fading sweets';

'my flesh and my heart faileth, but God is the strength
of my heart, and my portion for ever.'

You need not be very much afraid of anything being
taken from you as long as Christ is left you.  You
will not be altogether hopeless so long as Christ, who
is our hope, still speaks His faithful promises to you,
nor will the world be lonely and dark to them who feel
that they are lapt in the sweet and all-pervading consciousness of the changeless love of the heart of Christ.
'Shall tribulation, or distress, or persecution?'—in any
of these things, 'we are more than conquerors through
Him that loved us.'  Brethren, that is the Christian
way of looking at all externals, not only at the dark
and the sorrowful, but at the bright and the gladsome.
If the withdrawal of external blessings does not touch
the central sanctities and sweetness of a life in communion with Jesus, the bestowal of external blessedness does not much brighten or gladden it.  We can
face the withdrawal of them all, we need not covet
the possession of them all, for we have all in Christ;
and the world without His love contributes less to
our blessedness and our peace than the absence of all
its joys with His love does.  So let us feel that earth,

in its givings and in its withholdings, is equally
impotent to touch the one thing that we need, the
conscious possession of the love of Christ.

All these foes, as I have said, have no power over
the fact of Christ's love to us, but they have power,
and a very terrible power, over our consciousness of
that love; and we may so kick against the pricks as to
lose, in the pain of our sorrows, the assurance of His
presence, or be so fascinated by the false and vulgar
sweetnesses and promises of the world as, in the
eagerness of our chase after them, to lose our sense of
the all-sufficing certitude of His love. Tribulation does
not strip us of His love, but tribulation may so darken
our perceptions that we cannot see the sun. Joys need
not rob us of His heart, but joys may so fill ours, as
that there shall be no longing for His presence within
us. Therefore let us not exaggerate the impotence of
these foes, but feel that there are real dangers, as in
the sorrows so in the blessings of our outward life, and
that the evil to be dreaded is that outward things,
whether in their bright or in their dark aspects, may
come between us and the home of our hearts, the love
of the loving Christ.

II. So then, note next, the abundant victory of love.

Mark how the Apostle, in his lofty and enthusiastic
way, is not content here with simply saying that he
and his fellows conquer. It would be a poor thing, he
seems to think, if the balance barely inclined to our
side, if the victory were but just won by a hair's
breadth and triumph were snatched, as it were, out of
the very jaws of defeat. There must be something
more than that to correspond to the power of the
victorious Christ that is in us. And so, he says, we
very abundantly conquer; we not only hinder these

things which he has been enumerating from doing that which it is their aim apparently to do, but we actually convert them into helpers or allies. The '*more* than conquerors' seems to mean, if there is any definite idea to be attached to it, the conversion of the enemy conquered into a friend and a helper. The American Indians had a superstition that every foe tomahawk sent fresh strength into the warrior's arm. And all afflictions and trials rightly borne, and therefore overcome, make a man stronger, and bring him nearer to Jesus Christ.

Note then, further, that not only is this victory more than bare victory, being the conversion of the enemy into allies, but that it is a victory which is won even whilst we are in the midst of the strife. It is not that we shall be conquerors in some far-off heaven, when the noise of battle has ceased and they hang the trumpet in the hall, but it is here now, in the hand-to-hand and foot-to-foot death-grapple that we do overcome. No ultimate victory, in some far-off and blessed heaven, will be ours unless moment by moment, here, to-day, 'we *are* more than conquerors through Him that loved us.'

So, then, about this abundant victory there are these things to say:—You conquer the world only, then, when you make it contribute to your conscious possession of the love of Christ. That is the real victory, the only real victory in life. Men talk about overcoming here on earth, and they mean thereby the accomplishment of their designs. A man has 'victory,' as it is phrased, in the world's strife, when he secures for himself the world's goods at which he has aimed, but that is not the Christian idea of the conquest of calamity. Everything that makes me feel more thrillingly in my

inmost heart the verity and the sweetness of the love
of Jesus Christ as my very own, is conquered by me
and compelled to subserve my highest good, and
everything which slips a film between me and Him,
which obscures the light of His face to me, which
makes me less desirous of, and less sure of, and less
happy in, and less satisfied with, His love, is an enemy
lost has conquered me.  And all these evils as the
world calls them, and as our bleeding hearts have
often felt them to be, are converted into allies and
friends when they drive us to Christ, and keep us close
to Him, in the conscious possession of His sweet and
changeless love.  That is the victory, and the only victory.  Has the world helped me to lay hold of Christ?
Then I have conquered it.  Has the world loosened
my grasp upon Him?  Then it has conquered me.

Note then, further, that this abundant victory depends on how we deal with the changes of our outward
lives, our sorrows or our joys.  There is nothing, *per
se*, salutary in affliction, there is nothing, *per se*,
antagonistic to Christian faith in it either.  No man is
made better by his sorrows, no man need be made
worse by them.  That depends upon how we take the
things which come storming against us.  The set of
your sails, and the firmness of your grasp upon the
tiller, determine whether the wind shall carry you to
the haven or shall blow you out, a wandering waif,
upon a shoreless and melancholy sea.  There are some
of you that have been blown away from your moorings
by sorrow.  There are some professing Christians who
have been hindered in their work, and had their peace
and their faith shattered all but irrevocably, because
they have not accepted, in the spirit in which they
were sent, the trials that have come for their good.

The worst of all afflictions is a wasted affliction, and they are all wasted unless they teach us more of the reality and the blessedness of the love of Jesus Christ.

III. Lastly, notice the love which makes us conquerors.

The Apostle, with a wonderful instinctive sense of fitness, names Christ here by a name congruous to the thoughts which occupy his mind, when he speaks of Him that loved us. His question has been, Can anything separate us from the love of Christ? And his answer is, So far from that being the case, that very love, by occasion of sorrows and afflictions, tightens its grasp upon us, and, by the communication of itself to us, makes us more than conquerors. This great love of Jesus Christ, from which nothing can separate us, will use the very things that seem to threaten our separation as a means of coming nearer to us in its depth and in its preciousness.

The Apostle says 'Him that loved us,' and the words in the original distinctly point to some one fact as being the great instance of love. That is to say they point to His death. And so we may say Christ's love helps us to conquer because in His death He interprets for us all possible sorrows. If it be true that love to each of us nailed Him there, then nothing that can come to us but must be a love-token, and a fruit of that same love. The Cross is the key to all tribulation, and shows it to be a token and an instrument of an unchanging love.

Further, that great love of Christ helps us to conquer, because in His sufferings and death He becomes the Companion of all the weary. The rough, dark, lonely road changes its look when we see His footprints there, not without specks of blood in them,

where the thorns tore His feet. We conquer our
afflictions if we recognise that 'in all our afflictions He
was afflicted,' and that Himself has drunk to its bitterest
dregs the cup which He commends to our lips. He has
left a kiss upon its margin, and we need not shrink
when He holds it out to us and says 'Drink ye
all of it.' That one thought of the companionship
of the Christ in our sorrows makes us more than
conquerors.

And lastly, this dying Lover of our souls communicates to us all, if we will, the strength whereby we
may coerce all outward things into being helps to the
fuller participation of His perfect love. Our sorrows
and all the other distracting externals do seek to drag
us away from Him. Is all that happens in counter-
action to that pull of the world, that we tighten our
grasp upon Him, and will not let Him go; as some
poor wretch might the horns of the altar that did not
respond to his grasp? Nay! what we lay hold of is no
dead thing, but a living hand, and it grasps us more
tightly than we can ever grasp it. So because He
holds us, and not because we hold Him, we shall not
be dragged away, by anything outside of our own
weak and wavering souls, and all these embattled
foes may come against us, they may shear off everything else, they cannot sever Christ from us unless we
ourselves throw Him away. 'In this thou shalt
conquer.' 'They overcame by the blood of the Lamb,
and by the word of His testimony.'

*The text seems to indicate to be conquer
is to be brought from the love of Co*

# LOVE'S TRIUMPH

'Neither death, nor life, nor angels, nor principalities, nor powers, nor things present, nor things to come, nor height, nor depth, nor any other creature, shall be able to separate us from the love of God.'—ROMANS viii. 38, 39.

THESE rapturous words are the climax of the Apostle's long demonstration that the Gospel is the revelation of 'the righteousness of God from faith to faith,' and is thereby 'the power of God unto salvation.' What a contrast there is between the beginning and the end of his argument! It started with sombre, sad words about man's sinfulness and aversion from the knowledge of God. It closes with this sunny outburst of triumph; like some stream rising among black and barren cliffs, or melancholy moorlands, and foaming through narrow rifts in gloomy ravines, it reaches at last fertile lands, and flows calm, the sunlight dancing on its broad surface, till it loses itself at last in the unfathomable ocean of the love of God.

We are told that the Biblical view of human nature is too dark. Well, the important question is not whether it is dark, but whether it is true. But, apart from that, the doctrine of Scripture about man's moral condition is not dark, if you will take the whole of it together. Certainly, a part of it is very dark. The picture, for instance, of what men are, painted at the beginning of this Epistle, is shadowed like a canvas of Rembrandt's. The Bible is 'Nature's sternest painter but her best.' But to get the whole doctrine of Scripture on the subject, we have to take its confidence as to what men may become, as well as its portrait of what they are—and then who will say that the anthropology of Scripture is gloomy? To me it seems that the unrelieved blackness of the view which, because it

o

admits no fall, can imagine no rise, which sees in all
man's sins and sorrows no token of the dominion of an
alien power, and has, therefore, no reason to believe
that they can be separated from humanity, is the true
'Gospel of despair,' and that the system which looks
steadily at all the misery and all the wickedness, and
calmly proposes to cast it all out, is really the only
doctrine of human nature which throws any gleam of
light on the darkness.  Christianity begins indeed with,
'There is none that doeth good, no, not one,' but it
ends with this victorious pæan of our text.

And what a majestic close it is to the great words
that have gone before, fitly crowning even their lofty
height!  One might well shrink from presuming to
take such words as a text, with any idea of exhausting
or of enhancing them.  My object is very much more
humble.  I simply wish to bring out the remarkable
order, in which Paul here marshals, in his passionate,
rhetorical amplification, all the enemies that can be
supposed to seek to wrench us away from the love of
God; and triumphs over them all.  We shall best
measure the fullness of the words by simply taking
these clauses as they stand in the text.

I. The love of God is unaffected by the extremest
changes of our condition.

The Apostle begins his fervid catalogue of vanquished
foes by a pair of opposites which might seem to cover
the whole ground—'neither death nor life.'  What
more can be said?  Surely, these two include everything.  From one point of view they do.  But yet, as
we shall see, there is more to be said.  And the special
reason for beginning with this pair of possible enemies
is probably to be found by remembering that they are
a pair, that between them they do cover the whole

ground and represent the *extremes* of change which can befall us. The one stands at the one pole, the other at the other. If these two stations, so far from each other, are equally near to God's love, then no intermediate point can be far from it. If the most violent change which we can experience does not in the least matter to the grasp which the love of God has on us, or to the grasp which we may have on it, then no less violent a change can be of any consequence. It is the same thought in a somewhat modified form, as we find in another word of Paul's, 'Whether we live, we live unto the Lord; and whether we die, we die unto the Lord.' Our subordination to Him is the same, and our consecration should be the same, in all varieties of condition, even in that greatest of all variations. His love to us makes no account of that mightiest of changes. How should it be affected by slighter ones?

The distance of a star is measured by the apparent change in its position, as seen from different points of the earth's surface or orbit. But this great Light stands steadfast in our heaven, nor moves a hair's-breadth, nor pours a feebler ray on us, whether we look up to it from the midsummer day of busy life, or from the midwinter of death. These opposites are parted by a distance to which the millions of miles of the world's path among the stars are but a point, and yet the love of God streams down on them alike.

Of course, the confidence in immortality is implied in this thought. Death does not, in the slightest degree, affect the essential vitality of the soul; so it does not, in the slightest degree, affect the outflow of God's love to that soul. It is a change of condition and circumstance, and no more. He does not lose us in the dust of death. The withered leaves on the pathway are

trampled into mud, and indistinguishable to human
eyes; but He sees them even as when they hung green
and sunlit on the mystic tree of life.

How beautifully this thought contrasts with the
saddest aspect of the power of death in our human
experience! He is Death the Separator, who unclasps
our hands from the closest, dearest grasp, and divides
asunder joints and marrow, and parts soul and body,
and withdraws us from all our habitude and associations and occupations, and loosens every bond of society
and concord, and hales us away into a lonely land.
But there is one bond which his 'abhorred shears'
cannot cut. Their edge is turned on *it*. One Hand
holds us in a grasp which the fleshless fingers of Death
in vain strive to loosen. The separator becomes the
uniter; he rends us apart from the world that He may
'bring us to God.' The love filtered by drops on us in
life is poured upon us in a flood in death; 'for I am
persuaded, that neither death nor life shall be able to
separate us from the love of God.'

II. The love of God is undiverted from us by any
other order of beings.

'Nor angels, nor principalities, nor powers,' says
Paul. Here we pass from conditions affecting ourselves
to living beings beyond ourselves. Now, it is important
for understanding the precise thought of the Apostle
to observe that this expression, when used without any
qualifying adjective, seems uniformly to mean good
angels, the hierarchy of blessed spirits before the
throne. So that there is no reference to 'spiritual
wickedness in high places' striving to draw men away
from God. The supposition which the Apostle makes
is, indeed, an impossible one, that these ministering
spirits, who are sent forth to minister to them who

shall be heirs of salvation, should so forget their
mission and contradict their nature as to seek to bar
us out from the love which it is their chiefest joy to
bring to us.  He knows it to be an impossible supposition, and its very impossibility gives energy to his
conclusion, just as when in the same fashion he makes
the other equally impossible supposition about an
angel from heaven preaching another gospel than that
which he had preached to them.

So we may turn the general thought of this second
category of impotent efforts in two different ways, and
suggest, first, that it implies the utter powerlessness of
any third party in regard to the relations between our
souls and God.

We alone have to do with Him alone.  The awful
fact of individuality, that solemn mystery of our personal being, has its most blessed or its most dread
manifestation in our relation to God.  There no other
Being has any power.  Counsel and stimulus, suggestion or temptation, instruction or lies, which may tend
to lead us nearer to Him or away from Him, they may
indeed give us; but after they have done their best or
their worst, all depends on the personal act of our own
innermost being.  Man or angel can affect that, but
from without.  The old mystics called prayer 'the
flight of the lonely soul to the only God.'  It is the
name for all religion.  These two, God and the soul,
have to 'transact,' as our Puritan forefathers used to
say, as if there were no other beings in the universe
but only they two.  Angels and principalities and
powers may stand beholding with sympathetic joy;
they may minister blessing and guardianship in many
ways; but the decisive act of union between God and
the soul they can neither effect nor prevent.

And as for them, so for men around us; the limits of their power to harm us are soon set. They may shut us out from human love by calumnies, and dig deep gulfs of alienation between us and dear ones; they may hurt and annoy us in a thousand ways with slanderous tongues, and arrows dipped in poisonous hatred, but one thing they cannot do. They may build a wall around us, and imprison us from many a joy and many a fair prospect, but they cannot put a roof on it to keep out the sweet influences from above, or hinder us from looking up to the heavens. Nobody can come between us and God but ourselves.

Or, we may turn this general thought in another direction, and say, These blessed spirits around the throne do not absorb and intercept His love. They gather about its steps in their 'solemn troops and sweet societies'; but close as are their ranks, and innumerable as is their multitude, they do not prevent that love from passing beyond them to us on the outskirts of the crowd. The planet nearest the sun is drenched and saturated with fiery brightness, but the rays from the centre of life pass on to each of the sister spheres in its turn, and travel away outwards to where the remotest of them all rolls in its far-off orbit, unknown for millenniums to dwellers closer to the sun, but through all the ages visited by warmth and light according to its needs. Like that poor, sickly woman who could lay her wasted fingers on the hem of Christ's garment, notwithstanding the thronging multitude, we can reach our hands through all the crowd, or rather He reaches His strong hand to us and heals and blesses us. All the guests are fed full at that great table. One's gain is not another's loss. The multitudes sit on the green grass, and the last man of the last fifty gets as much as the first. 'They did all eat, and were filled'; and more remains than fed them all. So all beings are 'nourished from the King's country,' and none jostle others out of their share. This healing fountain is not exhausted of its curative power by the early comers. 'I will give unto this last, even as unto thee.' 'Nor angels, nor principalities, nor powers, shall be able to separate us from the love of God.'

III. The love of God is raised above the power of time.

'Nor things present, nor things to come,' is the Apostle's next class of powers impotent to disunite us from the love of God. The rhythmical arrangement of the text deserves to be noticed, as bearing not only on its music and rhetorical flow, but as affecting its force. We had first a pair of opposites, and then a triplet; 'death and life: angels, principalities, and powers.' We have again a pair of opposites; 'things present, things to come,' again followed by a triplet, 'height nor depth, nor any other creature.' The effect of this is to divide the whole into two, and to throw the first and second classes more closely together, as also the third and fourth. Time and Space, these two mysterious ideas, which work so fatally on all human love, are powerless here.

The great revelation of God, on which the whole of Judaism was built, was that made to Moses of the name 'I Am that I Am.' And parallel to the verbal revelation was the symbol of the Bush, burning and unconsumed, which is so often misunderstood. It appears wholly contrary to the usage of Scriptural visions, which are ever wont to express in material form the same truth which accompanies them in words, that

the meaning of that vision should be, as it is frequently
taken as being, the continuance of Israel unharmed by
the fiery furnace of persecution.    Not the continuance
of Israel, but the eternity of Israel's God is the teaching of that flaming wonder.    The burning Bush and
the Name of the Lord proclaimed the same great truth
of self-derived, self-determined, timeless, undecaying
Being.    And what better symbol than the bush burning, and yet not burning out, could be found of that
God in whose life there is no tendency to death, whose
work digs no pit of weariness into which it falls, who
gives and is none the poorer, who fears no exhaustion
in His spending, no extinction in His continual shining ?

And this eternity of Being is no mere metaphysical
abstraction.    It is eternity of love, for God is love.
That great stream, the pouring out of His own very
inmost Being, knows no pause, nor does the deep
fountain from which it flows ever sink one hair's-
breadth in its pure basin.

We know of earthly loves which cannot die.    They
have entered so deeply into the very fabric of the
soul, that like some cloth dyed in grain, as long as the
threads hold together they will retain the tint.    re
have to thank God for such instances of love stron  n  r
than death, which make it easier for us to believ  in
the unchanging duration of His.    But we know, too, of
love that can change, and we know that all love must
part.    Few of us have reached middle life, who do not,
looking back, see our track strewed with the gaunt
skeletons of dead friendships, and dotted with 'oaks
of weeping,' waving green and mournful over graves,
and saddened by footprints striking away from the line
of march, and leaving us the more solitary for their
departure.

How blessed then to know of a love which cannot change or die! The past, the present, and the future are all the same to Him, to whom 'a thousand years,' that can corrode so much of earthly love, are in their power to change 'as one day,' and 'one day,' which can hold so few of the expressions of our love, may be 'as a thousand years' in the multitude and richness of the gifts which it can be expanded to contain. The whole of what He has been to any past, He is to us to-day. 'The God of Jacob is our refuge.' All these old-world stories of loving care and guidance may be repeated in our lives.

So we may bring the blessedness of all the past into the present, and calmly face the misty future, sure that it cannot rob us of His love.

Whatever may drop out of our vainly-clasping hands, it matters not, if only our hearts are stayed on His love, which neither things present nor things to come can alter or remove. Looking on all the flow of ceaseless change, the waste and fading, the alienation and cooling, the decrepitude and decay of earthly affection, we can lift up with gladness, heightened by the contrast, the triumphant song of the ancient Church: 'Give thanks unto the Lord: for He is good: because His mercy endureth for ever!'

IV. The love of God is present everywhere.

The Apostle ends his catalogue with a singular trio of antagonists; 'nor height, nor depth, nor any other creature,' as if he had got impatient of the enumeration of impotencies, and having named the outside boundaries in space of the created universe, flings, as it were, with one rapid toss, into that large room the whole that it can contain, and triumphs over it all.

As the former clause proclaimed the powerlessness of Time, so this proclaims the powerlessness of that other great mystery of creatural life which we call Space. Height or depth, it matters not. That diffusive love diffuses itself equally in all directions. Up or down, it is all the same. The distance from the centre is the same to Zenith or to Nadir.

Here, we have the same process applied to that idea of Omnipresence as was applied in the former clause to the idea of Eternity. That thought, so hard to grasp with vividness, and not altogether a glad one to a sinful soul, is all softened and glorified, as some solemn Alpine cliff of bare rock is when the tender morning light glows on it, when it is thought of as the Omnipresence of Love. 'Thou, God, seest me,' may be a stern word, if the God who sees be but a mighty Maker or a righteous Judge. As reasonably might we expect a prisoner in his solitary cell to be glad when he thinks that the jailer's eye is on him from some unseen spy-hole in the wall, as expect any thought of God but one to make a man read that grand one hundred and thirty-ninth Psalm with joy: 'If I ascend into heaven, Thou art there; if I make my bed in Sheol, behold, Thou art there.' So may a man say shudderingly to himself, and tremble as he asks in vain, 'Whither shall I flee from Thy Presence?' But how different it all is when we can cast over the marble whiteness of that solemn thought the warm hue of life, and change the form of our words into this of our text: 'Nor height, nor depth, shall be able to separate us from the love of God.'

In that great ocean of the divine love we live and move and have our being, floating in it like some sea flower which spreads its filmy beauty and waves its

long tresses in the depths of mid-ocean.  The sound of
its waters is ever in our ears, and above, beneath,
around us, its mighty currents run evermore.  We
need not cower before the fixed gaze of some stony
god, looking on us unmoved like those Egyptian deities
that sit pitiless with idle hands on their laps, and wide-
open lidless eyes gazing out across the sands.  We
need not fear the Omnipresence of Love, nor the
Omniscience which knows us altogether, and loves us
even as it knows.  Rather we shall be glad that we are
ever in His Presence, and desire, as the height of all
felicity and the power for all goodness, to walk all the
day long in the light of His countenance, till the day
come when we shall receive the crown of our perfecting in that we shall be 'ever with the Lord.'

   The recognition of this triumphant sovereignty of
love over all these real and supposed antagonists
makes us, too, lords over them, and delivers us from
the temptations which some of them present us to
separate ourselves from the love of God.  They all
become our servants and helpers, uniting us to that
love.  So we are set free from the dread of death and
from the distractions incident to life.  So we are
delivered from superstitious dread of an unseen world,
and from craven fear of men.  So we are emancipated
from absorption in the present and from careful
thought for the future.  So we are at home everywhere, and every corner of the universe is to us one of
the many mansions of our Father's house.  'All things
are yours, . . . and ye are Christ's; and Christ is
God's.'

   I do not forget the closing words of this great text.
I have not ventured to include them in our present
subject, because they would have introduced another

wide region of thought to be laid down on our already
too narrow canvas.

But remember, I beseech you, that this love of God is
explained by our Apostle to be 'in Christ Jesus our
Lord.' Love illimitable, all-pervasive, eternal; yes,
but a love which has a channel and a course; love
which has a method and a process by which it pours
itself over the world. It is not, as some representations would make it, a vague, nebulous light diffused
through space as in a chaotic half-made universe, but
all gathered in that great Light which rules the day—
even in Him who said: 'I am the Light of the world.'
In Christ the love of God is all centred and embodied,
that it may be imparted to all sinful and hungry
hearts, even as burning coals are gathered on a hearth
that they may give warmth to all that are in the house.
'God *so* loved the world'—not merely *so much*, but in
*such a fashion*—'that'—that what? Many people
would leap at once from the first to the last clause of
the verse, and regard eternal life for all and sundry as
the only adequate expression of the universal love of
God. Not so does Christ speak. Between that universal love and its ultimate purpose and desire for
every man He inserts two conditions, one on God's
part, one on man's. God's love reaches its end, namely,
the bestowal of eternal life, by means of a divine act
and a human response. 'God *so* loved the world, that
He *gave* His only begotten Son, that whosoever *believeth*
in Him should not perish, but have everlasting life.'
So all the universal love of God for you and me and
for all our brethren is 'in Christ Jesus our Lord,' and
faith in Him unites us to it by bonds which no foe can
break, no shock of change can snap, no time can rot,
no distance can stretch to breaking. 'For I am per-

suaded, that neither death nor life, nor angels, nor principalities, nor powers, nor things present, nor things to come, nor height, nor depth, nor any other creature, shall be able to separate us from the love of God, which is in Christ Jesus our Lord.'

## THE SACRIFICE OF THE BODY

'I beseech you, therefore, brethren, by the mercies of God, that ye present your bodies a living sacrifice, holy, acceptable unto God, which is your reasonable service.'—ROMANS xii. 1.'

IN the former part of this letter the Apostle has been building up a massive fabric of doctrine, which has stood the waste of centuries, and the assaults of enemies, and has been the home of devout souls. He now passes to speak of practice, and he binds the two halves of his letter indissolubly together by that significant 'therefore,' which does not only look back to the thing last said, but to the whole of the preceding portion of the letter. 'What God hath joined together let no man put asunder.' Christian living is inseparably connected with Christian believing. Possibly the error of our forefathers was in cutting faith too much loose from practice, and supposing that an orthodox creed was sufficient, though I think the extent to which they did suppose that has been very much exaggerated. The temptation of this day is precisely the opposite. 'Conduct is three-fourths of life,' says one of our teachers. Yes. But what about the *fourth* fourth which underlies conduct? Paul's way is the right way. Lay broad and deep the foundations of God's facts revealed to us, and then build upon that the fabric of a noble life. This generation superficially

tends to cut practice loose from faith, and so to look
for grapes from thorns and figs from thistles. Wrong
thinking will not lead to right doing. 'I beseech you,
*therefore*, brethren, that ye present your bodies a living
sacrifice.'

The Apostle, in beginning his practical exhortations,
lays as the foundations of them all two companion
precepts: one, with which we have to deal, affecting
mainly the outward life; its twin sister, which follows
in the next verse, affecting mainly the inward life.
He who has drunk in the spirit of Paul's doctrinal
teaching will present his body a living sacrifice, and be
renewed in the spirit of his mind; and thus, outwardly
and inwardly, will be approximating to God's ideal,
and all specific virtues will be his in germ. Those two
precepts lay down the broad outline, and all that
follow in the way of specific commandments is but
filling in its details.

I. We observe that we have here, first, an all-inclusive
directory for the outward life.

Now, it is to be noticed that the metaphor of sacrifice
runs through the whole of the phraseology of my text.
The word rendered 'present' is a technical expression
for the sacerdotal action of offering. A tacit contrast
is drawn between the sacrificial ritual, which was
familiar to Romans as well as Jews, and the true
Christian sacrifice and service. In the former a large
portion of the sacrifices consisted of animals which
were slain. Ours is to be 'a living sacrifice.' In the
former the offering was presented to the Deity, and
became His property. In the Christian service, the
gift passes, in like manner, from the possession of
the worshipper, and is set apart for the uses of God,
for that is the proper meaning of the word 'holy.'

The outward sacrifice gave an odour of a sweet smell, which, by a strong metaphor, was declared to be fragrant in the nostrils of Deity. In like manner, the Christian sacrifice is 'acceptable unto God.' These other sacrifices were purely outward, and derived no efficacy from the disposition of the worshipper. Our sacrifice, though the material of the offering be corporeal, is the act of the inner man, and so is called 'rational' rather than 'reasonable,' as our Version has it, or as in other parts of Scripture, 'spiritual.' And the last word of my text, 'service,' retains the sacerdotal allusion, because it does not mean the service of a slave or domestic, but that of a priest.

And so the sum of the whole is that the master-word for the outward life of a Christian is sacrifice. That, again, includes two things — self-surrender and surrender to God.

Now, Paul was not such a superficial moralist as to begin at the wrong end, and talk about the surrender of the outward life, unless as the result of the prior surrender of the inward, and that priority of the consecration of the man to his offering of the body is contained in the very metaphor. For a priest needs to be consecrated before he can offer, and we in our innermost wills, in the depths of our nature, must be surrendered and set apart to God ere any of our outward activities can be laid upon His altar. The Apostle, then, does not make the mistake of substituting external for internal surrender, but he presupposes that the latter has preceded. He puts the sequence more fully in the parallel passage in this very letter: 'Yield yourselves unto God, and your bodies as instruments of righteousness unto Him.' So, then, first of all, we must be priests by our inward consecration, and then, since 'a priest must have somewhat to offer,' we must bring the outward life and lay it upon His altar.

Now, of the two thoughts which I have said are involved in this great keyword, the former is common to Christianity, with all noble systems of morality, whether religious or irreligious. It is a commonplace, on which I do not need to dwell, that every man who will live a man's life, and not that of a beast, must sacrifice the flesh, and rigidly keep it down. But that commonplace is lifted into an altogether new region, assumes a new solemnity, and finds new power for its fulfilment when we add to the moralist's duty of control of the animal and outward nature the other thought, that the surrender must be to God.

There is no need for my dwelling at any length on the various practical directions in which this great exhortation must be wrought out. It is of more importance, by far, to have well fixed in our minds and hearts the one dominant thought that sacrifice is the keyword of the Christian life than to explain the directions in which it applies. But still, just a word or two about these. There are three ways in which we may look at the body, which the Apostle here says is to be yielded up unto God.

It is the recipient of impressions from without. *There* is a field for consecration. The eye that looks upon evil, and by the look has rebellious, lustful, sensuous, foul desires excited in the heart, breaks this solemn law. The eye that among the things seen dwells with complacency on the pure, and turns from the impure as if a hot iron had been thrust into its pupil; that in the things seen discerns shimmering behind them, and manifested through them, the things unseen and eternal, is the consecrated eye. 'Art for

Art's sake,' to quote the cant of the day, has too often
meant art for the flesh's sake. And there are pictures
and books, and sights of various sorts, flashed before
the eyes of you young men and women which it is
pollution to dwell upon, and should be pain to remember.
I beseech you all to have guard over these gates
of the heart, and to pray, 'Turn away mine eyes from
viewing vanity.' And the other senses, in like manner,
have need to be closely connected with God if they are
not to rush us down to the devil.

The body is not only the recipient of impressions.
It is the possessor of appetites and necessities. See to
it that these are indulged, with constant reference to
God. It is no small attainment of the Christian life
'to eat our meat with gladness and singleness of heart,
praising God.' In a hundred directions this characteristic
of our corporeal lives tends to lead us all away
from supreme consecration to Him. There is the
senseless luxury of this generation. There is the exaggerated
care for physical strength and completeness
amongst the young; there is the intemperance in
eating and drinking, which is the curse and the shame
of England. There is the provision for the flesh, the
absorbing care for the procuring of material comforts,
which drowns the spirit in miserable anxieties, and
makes men bond-slaves. There is the corruption which
comes from drunkenness and from lust. There is the
indolence which checks lofty aspirations and stops
a man in the middle of noble work. And there
are many other forms of evil on which I need not
dwell, all of which are swept clean out of the way
when we lay to heart this injunction: 'I beseech you
present your bodies a living sacrifice,' and let appetites
and tastes and corporeal needs be kept in rigid sub-

P

ordination and in conscious connection with Him. I
remember a quaint old saying of a German school-
master, who apostrophised his body thus: 'I go with
you three times a day to eat; you must come with me
three times a day to pray.' Subjugate the body, and
let it be the servant and companion of the devout
spirit.

It is also, besides being the recipient of impressions,
and the possessor of needs and appetites, our instrument for working in the world. And so the exhortation of my text comes to include this, that all our
activities done by means of brain and eye and tongue
and hand and foot shall be consciously devoted to Him,
and laid as a sacrifice upon His altar. That pervasive,
universally diffused reference to God, in all the details
of daily life, is the thing that Christian men and
women need most of all to try to cultivate. 'Pray
without ceasing,' says the Apostle. This exhortation
can only be obeyed if our work is indeed worship, being
done by God's help, for God's sake, in communion
with God.

So, dear friends, sacrifice is the keynote—meaning
thereby surrender, control, and stimulus of the corporeal frame, surrender to God, in regard to the impressions which we allow to be made upon our senses,
to the indulgence which we grant to our appetites,
and the satisfaction which we seek for our needs,
and to the activities which we engage in by means
of this wondrous instrument with which God has
trusted us. These are the plain principles involved in
the exhortation of my text. 'He that soweth to the
flesh, shall of the flesh reap corruption.' 'I keep under
my body, and bring it into subjection.' It is a good
servant; it is a bad master.

II. Note, secondly, the relation between this priestly service and other kinds of worship.

I need only say a word about that. Paul is not meaning to depreciate the sacrificial ritual, from which he drew his emblem. But he is meaning to assert that the devotion of a life, manifested through bodily activity, is higher in its nature than the symbolical worship of any altar and of any sacrifice. And that falls in with prevailing tendencies in this day, which has laid such a firm hold on the principle that daily conduct is better than formal worship, that it has forgotten to ask the question whether the daily conduct is likely to be satisfactory if the formal worship is altogether neglected. I believe, as profoundly as any man can, that the true worship is distinguishable from and higher than the more sensuous forms of the Catholic or other sacramentarian churches, or the more simple of the Puritan and Nonconformist, or the altogether formless of the Quaker. I believe that the best worship is the manifold activities of daily life laid upon God's altar, so that the division between things secular and things sacred is to a large extent misleading and irrelevant. But at the same time I believe that you have very little chance of getting this diffused and all-pervasive reference of all a man's doings to God unless there are, all through his life, recurring with daily regularity, reservoirs of power, stations where he may rest, kneeling-places where the attitude of service is exchanged for the attitude of supplication; times of quiet communion with God which shall feed the worshipper's activities as the white snowfields on the high summits feed the brooks that sparkle by the way, and bring fertility wherever they run. So, dear

brethren, remember that whilst life is the field of
worship there must be the inward worship within the
shrine if there is to be the outward service.

III. Lastly, note the equally comprehensive motive
and ground of this all-inclusive directory for conduct.

'I beseech you, by the mercies of God.' That plural
does not mean that the Apostle is extending his view
over the whole wide field of the divine beneficence,
but rather that he is contemplating the one all-
inclusive mercy about which the former part of his
letter has been eloquent—viz. the gift of Christ—and
contemplating it in the manifoldness of the blessings
which flow from it. The mercies of God which move
a man to yield himself as a sacrifice are not the diffused
beneficences of His providence, but the concentrated
love that lies in the person and work of His Son.

And there, as I believe, is the one motive to which
we can appeal with any prospect of its being powerful
enough to give the needful impetus all through a life.
The sacrifice of Christ is the ground on which our
sacrifices can be offered and accepted, for it was the
sacrifice of a death propitiatory and cleansing, and on
it, as the ancient ritual taught us, may be reared the
enthusiastic sacrifice of a life—a thankoffering for it.

Nor is it only the ground on which our sacrifice is
accepted, but it is the great motive by which our
sacrifice is impelled. *There* is the difference between
the Christian teaching, 'present your bodies a sacrifice,' and the highest and noblest of similar teaching
elsewhere. One of the purest and loftiest of the
ancient moralists was a contemporary of Paul's. He
would have re-echoed from his heart the Apostle's
directory, but he knew nothing of the Apostle's motive.
So his exhortations were powerless. He had no spell

to work on men's hearts, and his lofty teachings were as the voice of one crying in the wilderness. Whilst Seneca taught, Rome was a cesspool of moral putridity and Nero butchered. So it always is. There may be noble teachings about self-control, purity, and the like, but an evil and adulterous generation is slow to dance to such piping.

Our poet has bid us—

> 'Move upwards, casting out the beast,
> And let the ape and tiger die.'

But how is this heavy bulk of ours to 'move upwards'; how is the beast to be 'cast out'; how are the 'ape and tiger' in us to be slain? Paul has told us, 'By the mercies of God.' Christ's gift, meditated on, accepted, introduced into will and heart, is the one power that will melt our obstinacy, the one magnet that will draw us after it.

Nothing else, brethren, as your own experience has taught you, and as the experience of the world confirms, nothing else will bind Behemoth, and put a hook in his nose. Apart from the constraining motive of the love of Christ, all the cords of prudence, conscience, advantage, by which men try to bind their unruly passions and manacle the insisting flesh, are like the chains on the demoniac's wrists—'And he had oftentimes been bound by chains, and the chains were snapped asunder.' But the silken leash with which the fair Una in the poem leads the lion, the silken leash of love will bind the strong man, and enable us to rule ourselves. If we will open our hearts to the sacrifice of Christ, we shall be able to offer ourselves as thankofferings. If we will let His love sway our wills and consciences, He will give our wills and consciences power to master and to offer up our flesh

And the great change, according to which He will one day change the body of our humiliation into the likeness of the body of His glory, will be begun in us, if we live under the influence of the motive and the commandment which this Apostle bound together in our text and in his other great words, 'Ye are not your own; ye are bought with a price, therefore glorify God in your body and spirit, which are His.'

## TRANSFIGURATION

'Be not conformed to this world; but be ye transformed by the renewing of your mind, that ye may prove what is that good, and acceptable, and perfect will of God '—ROMANS xii. 2.

I HAD occasion to point out, in a sermon on the preceding verse, that the Apostle is, in this context, making the transition from the doctrinal to the practical part of his letter, and that he lays down broad principles, of which all his subsequent injunctions and exhortations are simply the filling up of the details.   One master word, for the whole Christian life, as we then saw, is sacrifice, self-surrender, and that to God.   In like manner, Paul here brackets, with that great conception of the Christian life, another equally dominant and equally comprehensive.   In one aspect, it is self-surrender; in another, it is growing transformation.   And, just as in the former verse we found that an inward surrender preceded the outward sacrifice, and that the inner man, having been consecrated as a priest, by this yielding of himself to God, was then called upon to manifest inward consecration by outward sacrifice, so in this further exhortation, an inward 'renewing of the mind' is regarded as the necessary antecedent of transformation of outward life.

So we have here another comprehensive view of what the Christian life ought to be, and that not only grasped, as it were, in its very centre and essence, but traced out in two directions—as to that which must precede it within, and as to that which follows it as consequence.   An outline of the possibilities, and therefore the duties, of the Christian, is set forth here, in these three thoughts of my text, the renewed mind issuing in a transfigured life, crowned and rewarded by a clearer and ever clearer insight into what we ought to be and do.

I. Note, then, that the foundation of all transformation of character and conduct is laid deep in a renewed mind.

Now it is a matter of world-wide experience, verified by each of us in our own case, if we have ever been honest in the attempt, that the power of self-improvement is limited by very narrow bounds.   Any man that has ever tried to cure himself of the most trivial habit which he desires to get rid of, or to alter in the slightest degree the set of some strong taste or current of his being, knows how little he can do, even by the most determined effort.   Something may be effected, but, alas! as the proverbs of all nations and all lands have taught us, it is very little indeed.   'You cannot expel nature with a fork,' said the Roman. 'What's bred in the bone won't come out of the flesh,' says the Englishman.   'Can the Ethiopian change his skin or the leopard his spots?' says the Hebrew.   And we all know what the answer to that question is. The problem that is set before a man when you tell him to effect self-improvement is something like that

which confronted that poor paralytic lying in the porch
at the pool: 'If you can walk you will be able to get to
the pool that will make you able to walk. But you
have got to be cured before you can do what you need
to do in order to be cured.' Only one knife can cut
the knot. The Gospel of Jesus Christ presents itself,
not as a mere republication of morality, not as merely
a new stimulus and motive to do what is right, but as
an actual communication to men of a new power to
work in them, a strong hand laid upon our poor, feeble
hand with which we try to put on the brake or to apply
the stimulus. It is a new gift of a life which will
unfold itself after its own nature, as the bud into
flower, and the flower into fruit; giving new desires,
tastes, directions, and renewing the whole nature.
And so, says Paul, the beginning of transformation
of character is the renovation in the very centre of
the being, and the communication of a new impulse
and power to the inward self.

Now, I suppose that in my text the word 'mind' is
not so much employed in the widest sense, including
all the affections and will, and the other faculties of
our nature, as in the narrower sense of the perceptive
power, or that faculty in our nature by which we
recognise, and make our own, certain truths. 'The
renewing of the mind,' then, is only, in such an interpretation, a theological way of putting the simpler
English thought, a change of estimates, a new set of
views; or if that word be too shallow, as indeed it is,
a new set of convictions. It is profoundly true that
'As a man thinketh, so is he.' Our characters are
largely made by our estimates of what is good or bad,
desirable or undesirable. And what the Apostle is
thinking about here is, as I take it, principally how

the body of Christian truth, if it effects a lodgment in, not merely the brain of a man, but his whole nature, will modify and alter it all. Why, we all know how often a whole life has been revolutionised by the sudden dawning or rising in its sky, of some starry new truth, formerly hidden and undreamed of. And if we should translate the somewhat archaic phraseology of our text into the plainest of modern English, it just comes to this: If you want to change your characters, and God knows they all need it, change the deep convictions of your mind; and get hold, as living realities, of the great truths of Christ's Gospel. If you and I really believed what we say we believe, that Jesus Christ has died for us, and lives for us, and is ready to pour out upon us the gift of His Divine Spirit, and wills that we should be like Him, and holds out to us the great and wonderful hopes and prospects of an absolutely eternal life of supreme and serene blessedness at His right hand, should we be, could we be, the sort of people that most of us are? It is not the much that you say you believe that shapes your character; it is the little that you habitually realise. Truth professed has no transforming power; truth received and fed upon can revolutionise a man's whole character.

So, dear brethren, remember that my text, though it is an analysis of the methods of Christian progress, and though it is a wonderful setting forth of the possibilities open to the poorest, dwarfed, blinded, corrupted nature, is also all commandment. And if it is true that the principles of the Gospel exercise transforming power upon men's lives, and that in order for these principles to effect their natural results there must be honest dealing with them, on our parts, take

this as the practical outcome of all this first part of
my sermon—let us all see to it that we keep ourselves
in touch with the truths which we say we believe;
and that we thorough-goingly apply these truths
in all their searching, revealing, quickening, curbing
power, to every action of our daily lives. If for one
day we could bring everything that we do into touch
with the creed that we profess, we should be different
men and women. Make of your every thought an
action; link every action with a thought. Or, to put
it more Christianlike, let there be nothing in your
creed which is not in your commandments; and let
nothing be in your life which is not moulded by these.
The beginning of all transformation is the revolutionised conviction of a mind that has accepted the
truths of the Gospel.

II. Well then, secondly, note the transfigured life.

The Apostle uses in his positive commandment, ' Be
ye transformed,' the same word which is employed by
two of the Evangelists in their account of our Lord's
transfiguration. And although I suppose it would be
going too far to assert that there is a distinct reference
intended to that event, it may be permissible to look
back to it as being a lovely illustration of the possibilities that open to an honest Christian life—the
possibility of a change, coming from within upwards,
and shedding a strange radiance on the face, whilst
yet the identity remains. So by the rippling up from
within of the renewed mind will come into our lives
a transformation not altogether unlike that which
passed on Him when His garments did shine 'so as
no fuller on earth could white them'; and His face was
as the sun in his strength.

The life is to be transfigured, yet it remains the

same, not only in the consciousness of personal identity, but in the main trend and drift of the character.
There is nothing in the Gospel of Jesus Christ which
is meant to obliterate the lines of the strongly marked
individuality which each of us receives by nature.
Rather the Gospel is meant to heighten and deepen
these, and to make each man more intensely himself,
more thoroughly individual and unlike anybody else.
The perfection of our nature is found in the pursuit,
to the furthest point, of the characteristics of our
nature, and so, by reason of diversity, there is the
greater harmony, and, all taken together, will reflect
less inadequately the infinite glories of which they are
all partakers. But whilst the individuality remains,
and ought to be heightened by Christian consecration,
yet a change should pass over our lives, like the change
that passes over the winter landscape when the
summer sun draws out the green leaves from the hard
black boughs, and flashes a fresh colour over all the
brown pastures. There should be such a change as
when a drop or two of ruby wine falls into a cup, and
so diffuses a gradual warmth of tint over all the
whiteness of the water. Christ in us, if we are true
to Him, will make us more ourselves, and yet new
creatures in Christ Jesus.

And the transformation is to be into His likeness
who is the pattern of all perfection. We must be
moulded after the same type. There are two types
possible for us: this world; Jesus Christ. We have
to make our choice which is to be the headline after
which we are to try to write. 'They that make them
are like unto them.' Men resemble their gods; men
become more or less like their idols. What you conceive to be desirable you will more and more assimi-

late yourselves to. Christ is the Christian man's
pattern; is He not better than the blind, corrupt
world?

That transformation is no sudden thing, though the
revolution which underlies it may be instantaneous.
The working *out* of the new motives, the working *in*
of the new power, is no mere work of a moment. It
is a lifelong task till the lump be leavened. Michael
Angelo, in his mystical way, used to say that sculpture
effected its aim by the removal of parts; as if the
statue lay somehow hid in the marble block. We
have, day by day, to work at the task of removing
the superfluities that mask its outlines. Sometimes
with a heavy mallet, and a hard blow, and a broad
chisel, we have to take away huge masses; sometimes,
with fine tools and delicate touches, to remove a
grain or two of powdered dust from the sparkling
block, but always to seek more and more, by slow,
patient toil, to conform ourselves to that serene type
of all perfectness that we have learned to love in
Jesus Christ.

And remember, brethren, this transformation is
no magic change effected whilst men sleep. It is a
commandment which we have to brace ourselves to
perform, day by day to set ourselves to the task of
more completely assimilating ourselves to our Lord.
It comes to be a solemn question for each of us
whether we can say, 'To-day I am liker Jesus Christ
than I was yesterday; to-day the truth which renews
the mind has a deeper hold upon me than it ever had
before.'

But this positive commandment is only one side of
the transfiguration that is to be effected. It is clear
enough that if a new likeness is being stamped upon

a man, the process may be looked at from the other
side; and that in proportion as we become liker Jesus
Christ, we shall become more unlike the old type to
which we were previously conformed. And so, says
Paul, 'Be not conformed to this world, but be ye
transformed.' He does not mean to say that the non-
conformity precedes the transformation. They are two
sides of one process; both arising from the renewing of
the mind within.

Now, I do not wish to do more than just touch
most lightly upon the thoughts that are here, but I
dare not pass them by altogether. 'This world' here,
in my text, is more properly 'this age,' which means
substantially the same thing as John's favourite word
'world,' viz. the sum total of godless men and things
conceived of as separated from God, only that by this
expression the essentially fleeting nature of that type
is more distinctly set forth. Now the world is the
world to-day just as much as it was in Paul's time.
No doubt the Gospel has sweetened society; no doubt
the average of godless life in England is a better
thing than the average of godless life in the Roman
Empire. No doubt there is a great deal of Christianity
diffused through the average opinion and ways of
looking at things, that prevail around us. But the
world is the world still. There are maxims and ways
of living, and so on, characteristic of the Christian
life, which are in as complete antagonism to the ideas
and maxims and practices that prevail amongst men
who are outside of the influences of this Christian
truth in their own hearts, as ever they were.

And although it can only be a word, I want to put
in here a very earnest word which the tendencies of
this generation do very specially require. It seems to

be thought, by a great many people, who call themselves Christians nowadays, that the nearer they can
come in life, in ways of looking at things, in estimates
of literature, for instance, in customs of society, in
politics, in trade, and especially in amusements—the
nearer they can come to the un-Christian world, the
more 'broad' (save the mark!) and 'superior to prejudice' they are.  'Puritanism,' not only in theology,
but in life and conduct, has come to be at a discount in
these days.  And it seems to be by a great many professing Christians thought to be a great feat to walk
as the mules on the Alps do, with one foot over the
path and the precipice down below.  Keep away from
the edge.  You are safer so.  Although, of course, I
am not talking about mere conventional dissimilar-
ities ; and though I know and believe and feel all that
can be said about the insufficiency, and even in-
sincerity, of such, yet there is a broad gulf between
the man who believes in Jesus Christ and His Gospel
and the man who does not, and the resulting con-
ducts cannot be the same unless the Christian man is
insincere.

III. And now lastly, and only a word, note the great
reward and crown of this transfigured life.

Paul puts it in words which, if I had time, would
require some commenting upon.  The issue of such
a life is, to put it into plain English, an increased
power of perceiving, instinctively and surely, what it
is God's will that we should do.  And that is the
reward.  Just as when you take away disturbing
masses of metal from near a compass, it trembles
to its true point, so when, by the discipline of
which I have been speaking, there are swept away
from either side of us the things that would perturb

our judgment, there comes, as blessing and reward,
a clear insight into that which it is our duty
to do.

There may be many difficulties left, many perplexities. There is no promise here, nor is there anything in the tendencies of Christ-like living, to lead us
to anticipate that guidance in regard to matters of
prudence or expediency or temporal advantage will
follow from such a transfigured life. All such matters
are still to be determined in the proper fashion, by
the exercise of our own best judgment and common-
sense. But in the higher region, the knowledge of
good and evil, surely it is a blessed reward, and one of
the highest that can be given to a man, that there
shall be in him so complete a harmony with God that,
like God's Son, he 'does always the things that please
Him,' and that the Father will show him whatsoever
things Himself doeth; and that these also will the son
do likewise. To know beyond doubt what I ought to
do, and knowing, to have no hesitation or reluctance
in doing it, seems to me to be heaven upon earth, and
the man that has it needs but little more. This, then,
is the reward. Each peak we climb opens wider
and clearer prospects into the untravelled land
before us.

And so, brethren, here is the way, the only way, by
which we can change ourselves, first let us have our
minds renewed by contact with the truth, then we
shall be able to transform our lives into the likeness
of Jesus Christ, and our faces too will shine, and our
lives will be ennobled, by a serene beauty which men
cannot but admire, though it may rebuke them. And
as the issue of all we shall have clearer and deeper
insight into that will, which to know is life, in keeping

of which there is great reward. And thus our apostle's promise may be fulfilled for each of us. 'We all with unveiled faces reflecting'—as a mirror does—'the glory of the Lord, are changed . . . into the same image.'

## SOBER THINKING

'For I say, through the grace that is given unto me, to every man that is among you, not to think of himself more highly than he ought to think; but to think soberly, according as God hath dealt to every man the measure of faith.'—ROMANS xii. 3.

IT is hard to give advice without seeming to assume superiority; it is hard to take it, unless the giver identifies himself with the receiver, and shows that his counsel to others is a law for himself. Paul does so here, led by the delicate perception which comes from a loving heart, compared with which deliberate 'tact' is cold and clumsy. He wishes, as the first of the specific duties to which he invites the Roman Christians, an estimate of themselves based upon the recognition of God as the Giver of all capacities and graces, and leading to a faithful use for the general good of the 'gifts differing according to the grace given to us.' In the first words of our text, he enforces his counsel by an appeal to his apostolic authority; but he so presents it that, instead of separating himself from the Roman Christians by it, he unites himself with them. He speaks of 'the grace given to *me*,' and in verse 6 of 'the grace given to *us*.' He was made an Apostle by the same giving God who has bestowed varying gifts on each of *them*. He knows what is the grace which he possesses as he would have them know; and in these counsels he is assuming no superiority, but is

simply using the special gift bestowed on him for the
good of all. With this delicate turn of what might
else have sounded harshly authoritative, putting pro-
minently forward the divine gift and letting the man
Paul to whom it was given fall into the background,
he counsels as the first of the social duties which
Christian men owe to one another, a sober and just
estimate of themselves. This sober estimate is here
regarded as being important chiefly as an aid to right
service. It is immediately followed by counsels to
the patient and faithful exercise of differing gifts.
For thus we may know what our gifts are; and the
acquisition of such knowledge is the aim of our
text.

I. What determines our gifts.

Paul here gives a precise standard, or 'measure' as
he calls it, according to which we are to estimate
ourselves. 'Faith' is the measure of our gifts, and is
itself a gift from God. The strength of a Christian
man's faith determines his whole Christian character.
Faith is trust, the attitude of receptivity. There are
in it a consciousness of need, a yearning desire and a
confidence of expectation. It is the open empty hand
held up with the assurance that it will be filled; it is
the empty pitcher let down into the well with the assurance that it will be drawn up filled. It is the precise
opposite of the self-dependent isolation which shuts us
out from God. The law of the Christian life is ever,
'according to your faith be it unto you'; 'believe that
ye receive and ye have them.' So then the more faith
a man exercises the more of God and Christ he has.
It is the measure of our capacity, hence there may be
indefinite increase in the gifts which God bestows on
faithful souls. Each of us will have as much as he

desires and is capable of containing. The walls of the
heart are elastic, and desire expands them.

The grace given by faith works in the line of its
possessor's natural faculties; but these are superna-
turally reinforced and strengthened while, at the same
time, they are curbed and controlled, by the divine gift,
and the natural gifts thus dealt with become what
Paul calls *charisms*. The whole nature of a Christian
should be ennobled, elevated, made more delicate and
intense, when the 'Spirit of life that is in Christ
Jesus' abides in and inspires it. Just as a sunless
landscape is smitten into sudden beauty by a burst of
sunshine which heightens the colouring of the flowers on
the river's bank, and is flashed back from every silvery
ripple on the stream, so the faith which brings the life
of Christ into the life of the Christian makes him more
of a man than he was before. So, there will be infinite
variety in the resulting characters. It is the same
force in various forms that rolls in the thunder or
gleams in the dewdrops, that paints the butterfly's
feathers or flashes in a star. All individual idiosyncrasies should be developed in the Christian Church,
and will be when its members yield themselves fully to
the indwelling Spirit, and can truly declare that the
lives which they live in the flesh they live by the faith
of the Son of God.

But Paul here regards the measure of faith as itself
'dealt to every man'; and however we may construe
the grammar of this sentence there is a deep sense in
which our faith is God's gift to us. We have to give
equal emphasis to the two conceptions of faith as a
human act and as a divine bestowal, which have so
often been pitted against each other as contradictory
when really they are complementary. The apparent

antagonism between them is but one instance of the great antithesis to which we come to at last in reference to all human thought on the relations of man to God. 'It is He that worketh in us both to will and to do of His own good pleasure'; and all our goodness is God-given goodness, and yet it is our goodness. Every devout heart-has a consciousness that the faith which knits it to God is God's work in it, and that left to itself it would have remained alienated and faithless. The consciousness that his faith was his own act blended in full harmony with the twin consciousness that it was Christ's gift, in the agonised father's prayer, 'Lord, I believe, help Thou mine unbelief.'

II. What is a just estimate of our gifts.

The Apostle tells us, negatively, that we are not to think more highly than we ought to think, and positively that we are to 'think soberly.'

To arrive at a just estimate of ourselves the estimate must ever be accompanied with a distinct consciousness that all is God's gift. That will keep us from anything in the nature of pride or over-weening self-importance. It will lead to true humility, which is not ignorance of what we can do, but recognition that we, the doers, are of ourselves but poor creatures. We are less likely to fancy that we are greater than we are when we feel that, whatever we are, God made us so. 'What hast thou that thou didst not receive? Now, if thou didst receive it, why dost thou glory, as if thou hadst not received it?'

Further, it is to be noted that the estimate of gifts which Paul enjoins is an estimate with a view to service. Much self-investigation is morbid, because it is self-absorbed; and much is morbid because it is undertaken only for the purpose of ascertaining one's 'spiritual condition.' Such self-examination is good enough in its way, and may sometimes be very necessary; but a testing of one's own capacities for the purpose of ascertaining what we are fit for, and what therefore it is our duty to do, is far more wholesome. Gifts are God's summons to work, and our first response to the summons should be our scrutiny of our gifts with a distinct purpose of using them for the great end for which we received them. It is well to take stock of the loaves that we have, if the result be that we bring our poor provisions to Him, and put them in His hands, that He may give them back to us so multiplied as to be more than adequate to the needs of the thousands. Such just estimate of our gifts is to be attained mainly by noting ourselves at work. Patient self-observation may be important, but is apt to be mistaken; and the true test of what we can do is what we *do* do.

The just estimate of our gifts which Paul enjoins is needful in order that we may ascertain what God has meant us to be and do, and may neither waste our strength in trying to be some one else, nor hide our talent in the napkin of ignorance or false humility. There is quite as much harm done to Christian character and Christian service by our failure to recognise what is in our power, as by ambitious or ostentatious attempts at what is above our power. We have to be ourselves as God has made us in our natural faculties, and as the new life of Christ operating on these has made us new creatures in Him not by changing but by enlarging our old natures. It matters nothing what the special form of a Christian man's service may be; the smallest and the greatest are alike to the Lord of all, and He appoints His servants' work. Whether the servant be a cup-bearer or a counsellor is of little moment. 'He that is faithful in that which is least, is faithful also in much.'

The positive aspect of this right estimate of one's gifts is, if we fully render the Apostle's words, as the Revised Version does, 'so to think as to think soberly.' There is to be self-knowledge in order to 'sobriety;' which includes not only what we mean by sober-mind-edness, but self-government; and this aspect of the apostolic exhortation opens out into the thought that the gifts, which a just estimate of ourselves pronounces us to possess, need to be kept bright by the continual suppression of the mind of the flesh, by putting down earthly desires, by guarding against a selfish use of them, by preventing them by rigid control from becoming disproportioned and our masters. All the gifts which Christ bestows upon His people He bestows on condition that they bind them together by the golden chain of self-control.

## MANY AND ONE

'For we have many members in one body, and all members have not the same office: 5 So we, being many, are one body in Christ, and every one members one of another.'—ROMANS xii. 4, 5.

To Paul there was the closest and most vital connection between the profoundest experiences of the Christian life and its plainest and most superficial duties. Here he lays one of his most mystical conceptions as the very foundation on which to rear the great structure of Christian conduct, and links on to one of his pro-foundest thoughts, the unity of all Christians in Christ,

a comprehensive series of practical exhortations. We
are accustomed to hear from many lips : 'I have no use
for these dogmas that Paul delights in. Give me his
practical teaching. You may keep the Epistle to the
Romans, I hold by the thirteenth of First Corinthians.'
But such an unnatural severance between the doctrine
and the ethics of the Epistle cannot be effected without
the destruction of both. The very principle of this
Epistle to the Romans is that the difference between the
law and the Gospel is, that the one preaches conduct
without a basis for it, and that the other says, First
believe in Christ, and in the strength of that belief, do
the right and be like Him. Here, then, in the very
laying of the foundation for conduct in these verses we
have in concrete example the secret of the Christian
way of making good men.

I. The first point to notice here is, the unity of the
derived life. Many are one, because they are each in
Christ, and the individual relationship and derivation
of life from Him makes them one whilst continuing to
be many. That great metaphor, and nowadays much
forgotten and neglected truth, is to Paul's mind the
fact which ought to mould the whole life and conduct
of individual Christians and to be manifested therein.
There are three most significant and instructive symbols
by which the unity of believers in Christ Jesus is set
forth in the New Testament. Our Lord Himself gives
us the one of the vine and its branches, and that
symbol suggests the silent, effortless process by which
the life-giving sap rises and finds its way from the
deep root to the furthest tendril and the far-extended
growth. The same symbol loses indeed in one respect
its value if we transfer it to growths more congenial to
our northern climate, and instead of the vine with its

rich clusters, think of some great elm, deeply rooted,
and with its firm bole and massive branches, through
all of which the mystery of a common life penetrates
and makes every leaf in the cloud of foliage through
which we look up participant of itself.  But, profound
and beautiful as our Lord's metaphor is, the vegetative
uniformity of parts and the absence of individual characteristics make it, if taken alone, insufficient.  In the
tree one leaf is like another; it 'grows green and broad
and takes no care.'  Hence, to express the whole truth
of the union between Christ and us we must bring in
other figures.  Thus we find the Apostle adducing the
marriage tie, the highest earthly example of union,
founded on choice and affection.  But even that sacred
bond leaves a gap between those who are knit together
by it; and so we have the conception of our text, the
unity of the body as representing for us the unity of
believers with Jesus.  This is a unity of life.  He is not
only head as chief and sovereign, but He is soul or life,
which has its seat, not in this or that organ as old
physics teach, but pervades the whole and 'filleth all in
all.'  The mystery which concerns the union of soul and
body, and enshrouds the nature of physical life, is part
of the felicity of this symbol in its Christian application.  That commonest of all things, the mysterious
force which makes matter live and glow under spiritual
emotion, and changes the vibrations of a nerve, or the
undulations of the grey brain, into hope and love and
faith, eludes the scalpel and the microscope.  Of man
in his complex nature it is true that ' clouds and darkness are round about him,' and we may expect an
equally solemn mystery to rest upon that which makes
out of separate individuals one living body, animated
with the life and moved by the Spirit of the indwelling

Christ. We can get no further back, and dig no deeper down, than His own words, 'I am . . . the life.' .

But, though this unity is mysterious, it is most real. Every Christian soul receives from Christ the life of Christ. There is a real implantation of a higher nature which has nothing to do with sin and is alien from death. There is a true regeneration which is supernatural, and which makes all who possess it one, in the measure of their possession, as truly as all the leaves on a tree are one because fed by the same sap, or all the members in the natural body are one, because nourished by the same blood. So the true bond of Christian unity lies in the common participation of the one Lord, and the real Christian unity is a unity of derived life.

The misery and sin of the Christian Church have been, and are, that it has sought to substitute other bonds of unity. The whole weary history of the divisions and alienations between Christians has surely sufficiently, and more than sufficiently, shown the failure of the attempts to base Christian oneness upon uniformity of opinion, or of ritual, or of purpose. The difference between the real unity, and these spurious attempts after it, is the difference between bundles of faggots, dead and held together by a cord, and a living tree lifting its multitudinous foliage towards the heavens. The bundle of faggots may be held together in some sort of imperfect union, but is no exhibition of unity. If visible churches must be based on some kind of agreement, they can never cover the same ground as that of 'the body of Christ.'

That oneness is independent of our organisations, and even of our will, since it comes from the common possession of a common life. Its enemies are not

divergent opinions or forms, but the evil tempers and
dispositions which impede, or prevent, the flow into
each Christian soul of the uniting 'Spirit of life in
Christ Jesus' which makes the many who may be
gathered into separate folds one flock clustered around
the one Shepherd.  And if that unity be thus a fundamental fact in the Christian life and entirely apart from
external organisation, the true way to increase it in
each individual is, plainly, the drawing nearer to Him,
and the opening of our spirits so as to receive fuller,
deeper, and more continuous inflows from His own
inexhaustible fullness.  In the old Temple stood the
seven-branched candlestick, an emblem of a formal
unity; in the new the seven candlesticks are one, because Christ stands in the midst.  He makes the body
one; without Him it is a carcase.

II. The diversity.

'We have many members in one body, but all
members have not the same office.'  Life has different
functions in different organs.   It is light in the eye,
force in the arm, music on the tongue, swiftness in the
foot; so also is Christ.  The higher a creature rises in
the scale of life, the more are the parts differentiated.
The lowest is a mere sac, which performs all the functions that the creature requires; the highest is a man
with a multitude of organs, each of which is definitely
limited to one office.  In like manner the division of
labour in society measures its advance; and in like
manner in the Church there is to be the widest diversity.  What the Apostle designates as 'gifts' are
natural characteristics heightened by the Spirit of
Christ; the effect of the common life in each ought to
be the intensifying and manifestation of individuality
of character.  In the Christian ideal of humanity there

is place for every variety of gifts. The flora of the Mountain of God yields an endless multiplicity of growths on its ascending slopes which pass through every climate. There ought to be a richer diversity in the Church than anywhere besides; that tree should 'bear twelve manner of fruits, yielding its fruit every month for the healing of the nations.' 'All flesh is not the same flesh.' 'Star differeth from star in glory.'

The average Christian life of to-day sorely fails in two things: in being true to itself, and in tolerance of diversities. We are all so afraid of being ticketed as 'eccentric,' 'odd,' that we oftentimes stifle the genuine impulses of the Spirit of Christ leading us to the development of unfamiliar types of goodness, and the undertaking of unrecognised forms of service. If we trusted in Christ in ourselves more, and took our laws from His whispers, we should often reach heights of goodness which tower above us now, and discover in ourselves capacities which slumber undiscerned. There is a dreary monotony and uniformity amongst us which impoverishes us, and weakens the testimony that we bear to the quickening influence of the Spirit that is in Christ Jesus; and we all tend to look very suspiciously at any man who 'puts all the others out' by being himself, and letting the life that he draws from the Lord dictate its own manner of expression. It would breathe a new life into all our Christian communities if we allowed full scope to the diversities of operation, and realised that in them all there was the one Spirit. The world condemns originality: the Church should have learned to prize it. 'One after this fashion, and one after that,' is the only wholesome law of the development of the manifold graces of the Christian life.

III. The harmony.

'We being many are one body in Christ, and every
one members one of another.' That expression is
remarkable, for we might have expected to read rather
members *of the body*, than *of each other*; but the bringing in of such an idea suggests most emphatically that
thought of the mutual relation of each part of the
great whole, and that each has offices to discharge
for the benefit of each. In the Christian community,
as in an organised body, the active co-operation of all
the parts is the condition of health. All the rays into
which the spectrum breaks up the pure white light
must be gathered together again in order to produce
it; just as every instrument in the great orchestra
contributes to the volume of sound. The Lancashire
hand-bell ringers may illustrate this point for us.
Each man picks up his own bell from the table and
sounds his own note at the moment prescribed by the
score, and so the whole of the composer's idea is reproduced. To suppress diversities results in monotony;
to combine them is the only sure way to secure harmony. Nor must we forget that the indwelling life of
the Church can only be manifested by the full exhibition and freest possible play of all the forms which
that life assumes in individual character. It needs all,
and more than all, the types of mental characteristics
that can be found in humanity to mirror the infinite
beauty of the indwelling Lord. 'There are diversities
of operations,' and all those diversities but partially
represent that same Lord 'who worketh all in all,' and
Himself is more than all, and, after all manifestation
through human characters, remains hinted at rather
than declared, suggested but not revealed.

Still further, only by the exercise of possible
diversities is the one body nourished, for each member,

drawing life directly and without the intervention of
any other from Christ the Source, draws also from his
fellow-Christian some form of the common life that
to himself is unfamiliar, and needs human intervention in order to its reception. Such dependence upon
one's brethren is not inconsistent with a primal dependence on Christ alone, and is a safeguard against the
cultivating of one's own idiosyncrasies till they become
diseased and disproportionate. The most slenderly
endowed Christian soul has the double charge of giving
to, and receiving from, its brethren. We have all
something which we can contribute to the general
stock. We have all need to supplement our own
peculiar gifts by brotherly ministration. The prime
condition of Christian vitality has been set forth for
ever by the gracious invitation, which is also an
imperative command, ' Abide in Me and I in you '; but
they who by such abiding are recipients of a communicated life are not thereby isolated, but united to all
who like them have received ' the manifestation of the
Spirit to do good with.'

## GRACE AND GRACES

'Having then gifts, differing according to the grace that is given to us, whether
prophecy, let us prophesy according to the proportion of faith; 7. Or ministry, let
us wait on our ministering ; or he that teacheth, on teaching ; 8. Or he that ex-
horteth, on exhortation ; he that giveth, let him do it with simplicity ; he that
ruleth, with diligence ; he that showeth mercy, with cheerfulness.'—ROMANS
xii. 6-8.

THE Apostle here proceeds to build upon the great
thought of the unity of believers in the one body a
series of practical exhortations. In the first words of
our text, he, with characteristic delicacy, identifies
himself with the Roman Christians as a recipient, like

them, of 'the grace that is given to us,' and as, therefore, subject to the same precepts which he commends
to them.  He does not stand isolated by the grace that
is given to him ; nor does he look down as from the
height of his apostleship on the multitude below, saying to them,—Go.  As one of themselves he stands
amongst them, and with brotherly exhortation says,—
Come.  If that had been the spirit in which all
Christian teachers had besought men, their exhortations would less frequently have been breath spent
in vain.

We may note

I. The grace that gives the gifts.

The connection between these two is more emphatically suggested by the original Greek, in which the
word for 'gifts' is a derivative of that for 'grace.'  The
relation between these two can scarcely be verbally
reproduced in English ; but it may be, though imperfectly, suggested by reading 'graces' instead of 'gifts.'
The gifts are represented as being the direct product
of, and cognate with, the grace bestowed.  As we
have had already occasion to remark, they are in
Paul's language a designation of natural capacities
strengthened by the access of the life of the Spirit of
Christ.  As a candle plunged in a vase of oxygen leaps
up into more brilliant flame, so all the faculties of
the human soul are made a hundred times themselves
when the quickening power of the life of Christ
enters into them.

It is to be observed that the Apostle here assumes
that every Christian possesses, in some form, that
grace which gives graces.  To him a believing soul
without Christ-given gifts is a monstrosity.  No one is
without some graces, and therefore no one is without

some duties. No one who considers the multitude of professing Christians who hamper all our churches to-day, and reflects on the modern need to urge on the multitude of idlers forms of Christian activity, will fail to recognise signs of terribly weakened vitality. The humility, which in response to all invitations to work for Christ pleads unfitness is, if true, more tragical than it at first seems, for it is a confession that the man who alleges it has no real hold of the Christ in whom he professes to trust. If a Christian man is fit for no Christian work, it is time that he gravely ask himself whether he has any Christian life. 'Having gifts' is the basis of all the Apostle's exhortations. It is to him inconceivable that any Christian should not possess, and be conscious of possessing, some endowment from the life of Christ which will fit him for, and bind him to, a course of active service.

The universality of this possession is affirmed, if we note that, according to the Greek, it was 'given' at a special time in the experience of each of these Roman Christians. The rendering 'was given' might be more accurately exchanged for 'has been given,' and that expression is best taken as referring to a definite moment in the history of each believer namely, his conversion. When we 'yield ourselves to God,' as Paul exhorts us to do in the beginning of this chapter, as the commencement of all true life of conformity to His will, Christ yields Himself to us. The possession of these gifts of grace is no prerogative of officials; and, indeed, in all the exhortations which follow there is no reference to officials, though of course such were in existence in the Roman Church. They had their special functions and

special qualifications for these.  But what Paul is
dealing with now is the grace that is inseparable from
individual surrender to Christ, and has been bestowed
upon all who are His.  To limit the gifts to officials,
and to suppose that the universal gifts in any degree
militate against the recognition of officials in the
Church, are equally mistakes, and confound essentially
different subjects.

II. The graces that flow from the grace.

The Apostle's catalogue of these is not exhaustive,
nor logically arranged; but yet a certain loose order
may be noted, which may be profitable for us to trace.
They are in number seven—the sacred number; and
are capable of being divided, as so many of the series
of sevens are, into two portions, one containing four
and the other three.  The former include more public
works, to each of which a man might be specially
devoted as his life work for and in the Church.  Three
are more private, and may be conceived to have a
wider relation to the world.  There are some difficulties of construction and rendering in the list, which
need not concern us here; and we may substantially
follow the Authorised Version.

The first group of four seems to fall into two pairs,
the first of which, 'prophecy' and 'ministry,' seem
to be bracketed together by reason of the difference
between them.  Prophecy is a very high form of
special inspiration, and implies a direct reception of
special revelation, but not necessarily of future events.
The prophet is usually coupled in Paul's writings with
the apostle, and was obviously amongst those to whom
was given one of the highest forms of the gifts of
Christ. It is very beautiful to note that by natural contrast the Apostle at once passes to one of the forms of

service which a vulgar estimate would regard as remotest from the special revelation of the prophet, and is confined to lowly service. Side by side with the exalted gift of prophecy Paul puts the lowly gift of ministry. Very significant is the juxtaposition of these two extremes. It teaches us that the lowliest office is as truly allotted by Jesus as the most sacred, and that His highest gifts find an adequate field for manifestation in him who is servant of all. Ministry to be rightly discharged needs spiritual character. The original seven were men 'full of faith and of the Holy Ghost,' though all they had to do was to hand their pittances to poor widows. It may be difficult to decide for what reason other than the emphasising of this contrast the Apostle links together ministry and prophecy, and so breaks a natural sequence which would have connected the second pair of graces with the first member of the first pair. We should have expected that here, as elsewhere, 'prophet,' 'teacher,' 'exhorter,' would have been closely connected, and there seems no reason why they should not have been so, except that which we have suggested, namely, the wish to bring together the highest and the lowest forms of service.

The second pair seem to be linked together by likeness. The 'teacher' probably had for his function, primarily, the narration of the facts of the Gospel, and the setting forth in a form addressed chiefly to the understanding the truths thereby revealed; whilst the 'exhorter' rather addressed himself to the will, presenting the same truth, but in forms more intended to influence the emotions. The word here rendered 'exhort' is found in Paul's writings as bearing special meanings, such as consoling, stimulating, encouraging,

rebuking and others. Of course these two forms of
service would often be associated, and each would be
imperfect when alone; but it would appear that in
the early Church there were persons in whom the one
or the other of these two elements was so pre-
ponderant that their office was thereby designated.
Each received a special gift from the one Source. The
man who could only say to his brother, 'Be of good
cheer,' was as much the recipient of the Spirit as the
man who could connect and elaborate a systematic
presentation of the truths of the Gospel.

These four graces are followed by a group of three,
which may be regarded as being more private, as not
pointing to permanent offices so much as to individual
acts. They are 'giving,' 'ruling,' 'showing pity,' concerning which we need only note that the second of
these can hardly be the ecclesiastical office, and that it
stands between two which are closely related, as if it
were of the same kind. The gifts of money, or of
direction, or of pity, are one in kind. The right use of
wealth comes from the gift of God's grace; so does the
right use of any sway which any of us have over any
of our brethren; and so does the glow of compassion,
the exercise of the natural human sympathy which
belongs to all, and is deepened and made tenderer and
intenser by the gift of the Spirit. It would be a very
different Church, and a very different world, if Christians, who were not conscious of possessing gifts which
made them fit to be either prophets, or teachers, or
exhorters, and were scarcely endowed even for any
special form of ministry, felt that a gift from their
hands, or a wave of pity from their hearts, was a true
token of the movement of God's Spirit on their spirits.
The fruit of the Spirit is to be found in the wide

R

fields of everyday life, and the vine bears many clusters
for the thirsty lips of wearied men who may little
know what gives them their bloom and sweetness.
It would be better for both giver and receiver if
Christian beneficence were more clearly recognised as
one of the manifestations of spiritual life.

III. The exercise of the graces.

There are some difficulties in reference to the grammatical construction of the words of our text, into
which it is not necessary that we should enter here.
We may substantially follow the Authorised and
Revised Versions in supplying verbs in the various
clauses, so as to make of the text a series of exhortations. The first of these is to 'prophesy according to
the proportion of faith'; a commandment which is
best explained by remembering that in the preceding
verse 'the measure of faith' has been stated as being
the measure of the gifts. The prophet then is to
exercise his gifts in proportion to his faith. He is to
speak his convictions fully and openly, and to let his
utterances be shaped by the indwelling life. This
exhortation may well sink into the heart of preachers
in this day. It is but the echo of Jeremiah's strong
words: 'He that hath my word, let him speak my
word faithfully. What is the chaff to the wheat?
saith the Lord. Is not my word like as fire, saith the
Lord, and like a hammer that breaketh the rock in
pieces?' The ancient prophet's woe falls with double
weight on those who use their words as a veil to
obscure their real beliefs, and who prophesy, not
'according to the proportion of faith,' but according to
the expectations of the hearers, whose faith is as
vague as theirs.

In the original, the next three exhortations are alike

in grammatical construction, which is represented in
the Authorised Version by the supplement 'let us wait
on,' and in the Revised Version by 'let us give ourselves
to'; we might with advantage substitute for either
the still more simple form 'be in,' after the example of
Paul's exhortation to Timothy 'be in these things';
that is, as our Version has it, 'give thyself wholly to
them.'   The various gifts are each represented as a
sphere within which its possessor is to move, for the
opportunities for the exercise of which he is carefully
to watch, and within the limits of which he is humbly
to keep.   That general law applies equally to ministry,
and teaching and exhorting.   We are to seek to discern
our spheres; we are to be occupied with, if not
absorbed in, them.   At the least we are diligently to
use the gift which we discover ourselves to possess,
and thus filling our several spheres, we are to keep
within them, recognising that each is sacred as the
manifestation of God's will for each of us.   The
divergence of forms is unimportant, and it matters
nothing whether 'the Giver of all' grants less or more.
The main thing is that each be faithful in the administration of what he has received, and not seek to
imitate his brother who is diversely endowed, or to
monopolise for himself another's gifts.   To insist that
our brethren's gifts should be like ours, and to try to
make ours like theirs, are equally sins against the
great truth, of which the Church as a whole is the
example, that there are 'diversities of operations but
the same Spirit.'

The remaining three exhortations are in like manner
thrown together by a similarity of construction in
which the personality of the doer is put in the fore-
affend, and the emphasis of the commandment is

rested on the manner in which the grace is exercised.
The reason for that may be that in these three especially
the manner will show the grace. 'Giving' is to be
'with simplicity.' There are to be no sidelong looks to
self-interest; no flinging of a gift from a height, as a
bone might be flung to a dog; no seeking for gratitude;
no ostentation in the gift. Any taint of such mixed
motives as these infuses poison into our gifts, and
makes them taste bitter to the receiver, and recoil
in hurt upon ourselves. To 'give with simplicity' is
to give as God gives.

'Diligence' is the characteristic prescribed for the
man that rules. We have already pointed out that
this exhortation includes a much wider area than that
of any ecclesiastical officials. It points to another
kind of rule, and the natural gifts needed for any kind
of rule are diligence and zeal. Slackly-held reins make
stumbling steeds; and any man on whose shoulders is
laid the weight of government is bound to feel it as a
weight. The history of many a nation, and of many a
family, teaches that where the rule is slothful all evils
grow apace; and it is that natural energy and earnestness, deepened and hallowed by the Christian life
which here is enjoined as the true Christian way of
discharging the function of ruling, which, in some form
or another, devolves on almost all of us.

'He that showeth mercy with cheerfulness.' The
glow of natural human sympathy is heightened so as to
become a 'gift,' and the way in which it is exercised is
defined as being 'with cheerfulness.' That injunction is
but partially understood if it is taken to mean no more
than that sympathy is not to be rendered grudgingly,
or as by necessity. No sympathy is indeed possible
on such terms; unless the heart is in it, it is not at

And that it should thus flow forth spontaneously wherever sorrow and desolation evoke it, there must be a continual repression of self, and a heart disengaged from the entanglements of its own circumstances, and at leisure to make a brother's burden its very own. But the exhortation may, perhaps, rather mean that the truest sympathy carries a bright face into darkness, and comes like sunshine in a shady place.

## LOVE THAT CAN HATE

'Let love be without hypocrisy. Abhor that which is evil; cleave to that which is good. 10. In love of the brethren be tenderly affectioned one to another; in honour preferring one another.'—ROMANS xii. 9-10 (R.V.).

THUS far the Apostle has been laying down very general precepts and principles of Christian morals. Starting with the one all-comprehensive thought of self-sacrifice as the very foundation of all goodness, of transformation as its method, and of the clear knowledge of our several powers and faithful stewardship of these, as its conditions, he here proceeds to a series of more specific exhortations, which at first sight seem to be very unconnected, but through which there may be discerned a sequence of thought.

The clauses of our text seem at first sight strangely disconnected. The first and the last belong to the same subject, but the intervening clause strikes a careless reader as out of place and heterogeneous. I think that we shall see it is not so; but for the present we but note that here are three sets of precepts which enjoin, first, honest love; then, next, a healthy vehemence against evil and for good; and finally, a brotherly affection and mutual respect.

I. Let love be honest.

Love stands at the head, and is the fontal source of all separate individualised duties. Here Paul is not so much prescribing love as describing the kind of love which he recognises as genuine, and the main point on which he insists is sincerity. The 'dissimulation' of the Authorised Version only covers half the ground. It means, hiding what one is; but there is simulation, or pretending to be what one is not. There are words of love which are like the iridescent scum on the surface veiling the black depths of a pool of hatred. A Psalmist complains of having to meet men whose words were 'smoother than butter' and whose true feelings were as 'drawn swords'; but, short of such consciously lying love, we must all recognise as a real danger besetting us all, and especially those of us who are naturally inclined to kindly relations with our fellows, the tendency to use language just a little in excess of our feelings. The glove is slightly stretched, and the hand in it is not quite large enough to fill it. There is such a thing, not altogether unknown in Christian circles, as benevolence, which is largely cant, and words of conventional love about individuals which do not represent any corresponding emotion. Such effusive love pours itself in words, and is most generally the token of intense selfishness. Any man who seeks to make his words a true picture of his emotions must be aware that few harder precepts have ever been given than this brief one of the Apostle's, 'Let love be without hypocrisy.'

But the place where this exhortation comes in the apostolic sequence here may suggest to us the discipline through which obedience to it is made possible. There is little to be done by the way of directly in-

creasing either the fervour of love or the honesty of
its expression. The true method of securing both is
to be growingly transformed by 'the renewing of our
minds,' and growingly to bring our whole old selves
under the melting and softening influence of 'the
mercies of God.' It is swollen self-love, 'thinking more
highly of ourselves than we ought to think,' which
impedes the flow of love to others, and it is in the
measure in which we receive into our minds 'the
mind that was in Christ Jesus,' and look at men as He
did, that we shall come to love them all honestly and
purely. When we are delivered from the monstrous
oppression and tyranny of self, we have hearts capable of a Christlike and Christ-giving love to all men,
and only they who have cleansed their hearts by union
with Him, and by receiving into them the purging
influence of His own Spirit, will be able to love without
hypocrisy.

II. Let love abhor what is evil, and cleave to what is
good.

If we carefully consider this apparently irrelevant
interruption in the sequence of the apostolic exhortations, we shall, I think, see at once that the irrelevance
is only apparent, and that the healthy vehemence
against evil and resolute clinging to good is as
essential to the noblest forms of Christian love as
is the sincerity enjoined in the previous clause. To
detest the one and hold fast by the other are essential
to the purity and depth of our love. Evil is to be
loathed, and good to be clung to in our own moral
conduct, and wherever we see them. These two precepts are not mere tautology, but the second of them
is the ground of the first. The force of our recoil from
the bad will be measured by the firmness of our grasp

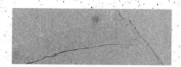

of the good; and yet, though inseparably connected, the one is apt to be easier to obey than is the other. There are types of Christian men to whom it is more natural to abhor the evil than to cleave to the good; and there are types of character of which the converse is true. We often see men very earnest and entirely sincere in their detestation of meanness and wickedness, but very tepid in their appreciation of goodness. To hate is, unfortunately, more congenial with ordinary characters than to love; and it is more facile to look down on badness than to look up at goodness.

But it needs ever to be insisted upon, and never more than in this day of spurious charity and unprincipled toleration, that a healthy hatred of moral evil and of sin, wherever found and however garbed, ought to be the continual accompaniment of all vigorous and manly cleaving to that which is good. Unless we shudderingly recoil from contact with the bad in our own lives, and refuse to christen it with deceptive euphemisms when we meet it in social and civil life, we shall but feebly grasp, and slackly hold, that which is good. Such energy of moral recoil from evil is perfectly consistent with honest love, for it is things, not men, that we are to hate; and it is needful as the completion and guardian of love itself. There is always danger that love shall weaken the condemnation of wrong, and modern liberality, both in the field of opinion and in regard to practical life, has so far condoned evil as largely to have lost its hold upon good. The criminal is pitied rather than blamed, and a multitude of agencies are so occupied in elevating the wrong-doers that they lose sight of the need of punishing.

Nor is it only in reference to society that this tendency works harm. The effect of it is abundantly manifest in the fashionable ideas of God and His character.  There are whole schools of opinion which practically strike out of their ideal of the Divine Nature abhorrence of evil, and, little as they think it, are thereby fatally impoverishing their ideal of God, and making it impossible to understand His government of the world. As always, so in this matter, the authentic revelation of the Divine Nature, and the perfect pattern for the human are to be found in Jesus Christ.  We recall that wonderful incident, when on His last approach to Jerusalem, rounding the shoulder of the Mount of Olives, He beheld the city, gleaming in the morning sunshine across the valley, and forgetting His own sorrow, shed tears over its approaching desolation, which yet He steadfastly pronounced.  His loathing of evil was whole-souled and absolute, and equally intense and complete was His cleaving to that which is good. In both, and in the harmony between them, He makes God known, and prescribes and holds forth the ideal of perfect humanity to men.

III. Let sincere and discriminating love be concentrated on Christian men.

In the final exhortation of our text 'the love of the brethren' takes the place of the more diffused and general love enjoined in the first clause.  The expression 'kindly affectioned' is the rendering of a very eloquent word in the original in which the instinctive love of a mother to her child, or the strange mystical ties which unite members of a family together, irrespective of their differences of character and temperament, are taken as an example after which Christian men are to mould their relations to one another.  The love which is without hypocrisy, and is to be diffused on all sides, is also to be gathered together

and concentrated with special energy on all who 'call
upon Jesus Christ as Lord, both their Lord and ours.'
The more general precept and the more particular are
in perfect harmony, however our human weakness
sometimes confuses them. It is obvious that this
final precept of our text will be the direct result of
the two preceding, for the love which has learned to
be moral, hating evil, and clinging to good as necessary,
when directed to possessors of like precious faith will
thrill with the consciousness of a deep mystical bond
of union, and will effloresce in all brotherly love and
kindly affections. They who are like one another in
the depths of their moral life, who are touched by like
aspirations after like holy things, and who instinctively recoil with similar revulsion from like abominations, will necessarily feel the drawing of a unity far
deeper and sacreder than any superficial likenesses of
race, or circumstance, or opinion. Two men who
share, however imperfectly, in Christ's Spirit are
more akin in the realities of their nature, however
they may differ on the surface, than either of them is
to another, however like he may seem, who is not a
partaker in the life of Christ.

This instinctive, Christian love, like all true and pure
love, is to manifest itself by 'preferring one another
in honour'; or as the word might possibly be rendered,
'anticipating one another.' We are not to wait to
have our place assigned before we give our brother
his. There will be no squabbling for the chief seat in
the synagogue, or the uppermost rooms at the feast,
where brotherly love marshals the guests. The one
cure for petty jealousies and the miserable strife for
recognition, which we are all tempted to engage in,
lies in a heart filled with love of the brethren because

of its love to the Elder Brother of them all, and to the
Father who is His Father as well as ours.  What a
contrast is presented between the practice of Christians
and these precepts of Paul!  We may well bow ourselves in shame and contrition when we read these
clear-drawn lines indicating what we ought to be,
and set by the side of them the blurred and blotted
pictures of what we are.   It is a painful but profitable task to measure ourselves against Paul's ideal of
Christ's commandment; but it will only be profitable
if it brings us to remember that Christ gives
before He commands, and that conformity with His
ideal must begin, not with details of conduct, or with
emotion, however pure, but with yielding ourselves to
the God who moves us by His mercies, and being
'transformed by the renewing of our minds' and 'the
indwelling of Christ in our hearts by faith.'

## A TRIPLET OF GRACES

'Not slothful in business; fervent in spirit; serving the Lord.'—ROMANS xii. 11.

PAUL believed that Christian doctrine was meant to
influence Christian practice; and therefore, after the
fundamental and profound exhibition of the central
truths of Christianity which occupies the earlier portion of this great Epistle, he tacks on, with a 'therefore' to his theological exposition, a series of plain,
practical teachings.  The place where conduct comes
in in the letter is profoundly significant, and, if the
significance of it had been observed and the spirit of it
carried into practice, there would have been less of a
barren orthodoxy, and fewer attempts at producing
righteous conduct without faith.

. But not only is the place where this series of exhortations occur very significant, but the order in which
they appear is also instructive. The great principle
which covers all conduct, and may be broken up into
all the minutenesses of practical directions is self-surrender. Give yourselves up to God ; that is the Alpha
and the Omega of all goodness, and wherever that
foundation is really laid, bn it will rise the fair building of a life which is a temple, adorned with whatever
things are lovely and of good report. So after Paul
has laid deep and broad the foundation of all Christian
virtue in his exhortation to present ourselves as living
sacrifices, he goes on to point out the several virtues
in which such self-surrender will manifest itself. There
runs through the most of these exhortations an arrangement in triplets—three sister Graces linked together
hand-in-hand as it were—and my text presents an
example of that threefoldness in grouping. 'Not
slothful in business; fervent in spirit; serving the Lord.'

I. We have, first, the prime grace of Christian
diligence.

'Not slothful in business' suggests, by reason of our
modern restriction of that word 'business' to a man's
daily occupation, a much more limited range to this
exhortation than the Apostle meant to give it. The
idea which is generally drawn from these words by
English readers is that they are to do their ordinary
work diligently, and, all the while, notwithstanding
the cooling or distracting influences of their daily
av cations, are to keep themselves 'fervent in spirit.'
That is a noble and needful conception of the command,
but it does not express what is in the Apostle's mind.
He does not mean by 'business' a trade or profession,
or daily occupation. But the word means 'zeal' or

'earnestness.' And what Paul says is just this—'In regard to your earnestness in all directions, see that you are not slothful.'

The force and drift of the whole precept is just the exhortation to exercise the very homely virtue of diligence, which is as much a condition of growth and maturity in the Christian as it is in any other life. The very homeliness and obviousness of the duty causes us often to lose sight of its imperativeness and necessity.

Many of us, if we would sit quietly down and think of how we go about our 'business,' as we call it, and of how we go about our Christian life, which ought to be our highest business, would have great cause for being ashamed. We begin the one early in the morning, we keep hard at it all day, our eyes are wide open to see any opening where money is to be made; that is all right. We give our whole selves to our work whilst we are at it; that is as it should be. But why are there not the same concentration, the same wide-awakeness, the same open-eyed eagerness to find out ways of advancement, the same resolved and continuous and all-comprehending and dominating enthusiasm about our Christianity as there is about our shop, or our mill, or our success as students? Why are we all fire in the one case and all ice in the other? Why do we think that it is enough to lift the burden that Christ lays upon us with one languid finger, and to put our whole hand, or rather, as the prophet says, 'both hands earnestly,' to the task of lifting the load of daily work? 'In your earnestness be not slothful.'

Brethren, that is a very homely exhortation. I wonder how many of us can say, 'Lord! I have heard, and I have obeyed Thy precept.'

II. Diligence must be fed by a fervent spirit.

The word translated 'fervent' is literally boiling. The metaphor is very plain and intelligible. The spirit brought into contact with Christian truth and with the fire of the Holy Spirit will naturally have its temperature raised, and will be moved by the warm touch as heat makes water in a pot hung above a fire boil. Such emotion, produced by the touch of the fiery Spirit of God, is what Paul desires for, and enjoins on, all Christians; for such emotion is the only way by which the diligence, without which no Christian progress will be made, can be kept up.

No man will work long at a task that his heart is not in; or if he does, because he is obliged, the work will be slavery. In order, then, that diligence may neither languish and become slothfulness, nor be felt to be a heavy weight and an unwelcome necessity, Paul here bids us see to it that our hearts are moved because there is a fire below which makes 'the soul's depths boil in earnest.'

Now, of course, I know that, as a great teacher has told us, 'The gods approve the depth and not the tumult of the soul,' and I know that there is a great deal of emotional Christianity which is worth nothing. But it is not that kind of fervour that the Apostle is enjoining here. Whilst it is perfectly true that mere emotion often does co-exist with, and very often leads to, entire negligence as to possessing and manifesting practical excellence, the true relation between these is just the opposite—viz. that this fervour of which I speak, this wide-awakeness and enthusiasm of a spirit all quickened into rapidity of action by the warmth which it has felt from God in Christ, should drive the wheels of life. Boiling water makes steam, does it

not? And what is to be done with the steam
comes off the 'boiling' spirit? You may either let it
go roaring through a waste-pipe and do nothing but
make a noise and be idly dissipated in the air, or you
may lead it into a cylinder and make it lift a piston,
and then you will get work out of it. That is what the
Apostle desires us to do with our emotion. The lightning goes careering through the sky, but we have
harnessed it to tram-cars nowadays, and made it 'work
for its living,' to carry our letters and light our rooms.
Fervour of a Christian spirit is all right when it is
yoked to Christian work, and made to draw what else
is a heavy chariot. It is not emotion, but it is indolent
emotion, that is the curse of much of our 'fervent'
Christianity.

There cannot be too much fervour. There may be
too little outlet provided for the fervour to work in.
It may all go off in comfortable feeling, in enthusiastic
prayers and 'Amens!' and 'So be it, Lords!' and the
like, or it may come with us into our daily tasks,
and make us buckle to with more earnestness, and
more continuity. Diligence driven by earnestness,
and fervour that works, are the true things.

And surely, surely there cannot be any genuine
Christianity — certainly there cannot be any deep
Christianity—which is not fervent.

We hear from certain quarters of the Church a great
deal about the virtue of moderation. But it seems to
me that, if you take into account what Christianity
tells us, the 'sober' feeling is fervent feeling, and tepid
feeling is imperfect feeling. I cannot understand any
man believing as plain matter-of-fact the truths on
which the whole New Testament insists, and keeping
himself 'cool,' or, as our friends call it, 'moderate.'

...thren, enthusiasm—which properly means the condition of being dwelt in by a god—is the wise, the reasonable attitude of Christian men, if they believe their own Christianity and are really serving Jesus Christ. They should be 'diligent in business, fervent' —boiling—in spirit.

III. The diligence and the fervency are both to be animated by the thought, 'Serving the Lord!'

Some critics, as many of you know, no doubt, would prefer to read this verse in its last clause 'serving the time.' But that seems to me a very lame and incomplete climax for the Apostle's thought, and it breaks entirely the sequence which, as I think, is discernible in it. Much rather, he here, in the closing member of the triplet, suggests a thought which will be stimulus to the diligence and fuel to the fire that makes the spirit boil.

In effect he says, 'Think, when your hands begin to droop, and when your spirits begin to be cold and indifferent, and languor to steal over you, and the paralysing influences of the commonplace and the familiar, and the small begin to assert themselves— think that you are serving the Lord.' Will that not freshen you up? Will that not set you boiling again? Will it not be easy to be diligent when we feel that we are 'ever in the great Taskmaster's eye'? There are many reasons for diligence—the greatness of the work, for it is no small matter for us to get the whole lump of our nature leavened with the good leaven; the continual operation of antagonistic forces which are all round us, and are working night-shifts as well as day ones, whether we as Christians are on short time or not, the brevity of the period during which we have to work, and the tremendous issues which depend upon the completeness of our service here—all these things are reasons for our diligence. But *the* reason is : 'Thou Christ hast died for me, and livest for me; truly I am Thy slave.' That is the thought that will make a man bend his back to his work, whatever it be, and bend his will to his work, too, however unwelcome it may be; and that is the thought that will stir his whole spirit to fervour and earnestness, and thus will deliver him from the temptations to languid and perfunctory work that ever creep over us.

You can carry that motive—as we all know, and as we all forget when the pinch comes—into your shop, your study, your office, your mill, your kitchen, or wherever you go. 'On the bells of the horses there shall be written, Holiness to the Lord,' said the prophet, and 'every bowl in Jerusalem' may be sacred as the vessels of the altar. All life may flash into beauty, and tower into greatness, and be smoothed out into easiness, and the crooked things may be made straight and the rough places plain, and the familiar and the trite be invested with freshness and wonder as of a dream, if only we write over them, 'For the sake of the Master.' Then, whatever we do or bear, be it common, insignificant, or unpleasant, will change its aspect, and all will be sweet. Here is the secret of diligence and of fervency, 'I set the Lord always before me.'

## ANOTHER TRIPLET OF GRACES

'Rejoicing in hope; patient in tribulation; continuing instant in prayer.'
ROMANS xii. 12.

THESE three closely connected clauses occur, as you all know, in the midst of that outline of the Christian life with which the Apostle begins the practical part of

S

this Epistle.  Now, what he omits in this sketch of
Christian duty seems to me quite as significant as what
he inserts.  It is very remarkable that in the twenty
verses devoted to this subject, this is the only one which
refers to the inner secrets of the Christian life.  Paul's
notion of 'deepening the spiritual life' was 'Behave
yourself better in your relation to other people.'  So
all the rest of this chapter is devoted to inculcating our
duties to one another.  Conduct is all-important.  An
orthodox creed is valuable if it influences action, but
not otherwise.  Devout emotion is valuable, if it drives
the wheels of life, but not otherwise.  Christians should
make efforts to attain to clear views and warm feelings, but the outcome and final test of both is a daily
life of visible imitation of Jesus.  The deepening of
spiritual life should be manifested by completer, practical righteousness in the market-place and the street
and the house, which non-Christians will acknowledge.

But now, with regard to these three specific exhortations here, I wish to try to bring out their connection
as well as the force of each of them.

I. So I remark first, that the Christian life ought to
be joyful because it is hopeful.

Now, I do not suppose that many of us habitually
recognise it as a Christian duty to be joyful.  We think
that it is a matter of temperament and partly a matter
of circumstance.  We are glad when things go well
with us.  If we have a sunny disposition, and are
naturally light-hearted, all the better; if we have a
melancholy or morose one, all the worse.  But do we
recognise this, that a Christian who is not joyful is not
living up to his duty; and that there is no excuse,
either in temperament or in circumstances, for our not
being so, and always being so?  'Rejoice in the Lord

alway,' says Paul; and then, as if he thought, 'Some
of you will be thinking that that is a very rash commandment, to aim at a condition quite impossible to
make constant,' he goes on—'and, to convince you that
I do not say it hastily, I will repeat it—"and again I
say, rejoice."' Brethren, we shall have to alter our
conceptions of what true gladness is before we can
come to understand the full depth of the great thought
that joy is a Christian duty. The true joy is not the
kind of joy that a saying in the Old Testament com-
pares to the 'crackling of thorns under a pot,' but
something very much calmer, with no crackle in it;
and very much deeper, and very much more in alliance
with 'whatsoever things are lovely and of good report,'
than that foolish, short-lived, and empty mirth that
burns down so soon into black ashes.

To be glad is a Christian duty. Many of us have as
much religion as makes us sombre, and impels us often
to look upon the more solemn and awful aspects of
Christian truth, but we have not enough to make us
glad. I do not need to dwell upon all the sources in
Christian faith and belief, of that lofty and imperatively
obligatory gladness, but I confine myself to the one in
my text, 'Rejoicing in hope.'

Now, we all know—from the boy that is expecting to
go home for his holidays in a week, up to the old man
to whose eye the time-veil is wearing thin—that hope,
if it is certain, is a source of gladness. How lightly
one's bosom's lord sits upon its throne, when a great
hope comes to animate us! how everybody is pleasant,
and all things are easy, and the world looks different!
Hope, if it is certain, will gladden, and if our Christianity grasps, as it ought to do, the only hope that is
absolutely certain, and as sure as if it were in the past

and had been experienced, then our hearts, too, will
sing for joy.  True joy is *not* a matter of temperament,
so much as a matter of faith.  It is *not* a matter of circumstances.  All the surface drainage may be dry, but
there is a well in the courtyard deep and cool and full
and exhaustless, and a Christian who rightly under-
stands and cherishes the Christian hope is lifted above
temperament, and is not dependent upon conditions for
his joys.

The Apostle, in an earlier part of this same letter,
defines for us what that hope is, which thus is the
secret of perpetual gladness, when he speaks about
'rejoicing in hope of the glory of God.'  Yes, it is that
great, supreme, calm, far off, absolutely certain prospect of being gathered into the divine glory, and
walking there, like the three in the fiery furnace, unconsumed and at ease; it is that hope that will triumph
over temperament, and over all occasions for melancholy, and will breathe into our life a perpetual gladness.   Brethren, is it not strange and sad that with
such a treasure by our sides we should consent to live
such poor lives as we do?

But remember, although I cannot say to myself,
'Now I will be glad,' and cannot attain to joy by a
movement of the will or direct effort, although it is of
no use to say to a man—which is all that the world can
ever say to him—'Cheer up and be glad,' whilst you do
not alter the facts that make him sad, there is a way
by which we can bring about feelings of gladness or of
gloom.  It is just this—we can choose what we will
look at.  If you prefer to occupy your mind with the
troubles, losses, disappointments, hard work, blighted
hopes of this poor sin-ridden world, of course sadness
will come over you often, and a general grey tone will

be the usual tone of your lives, as it is of the lives of many of us, broken only by occasional bursts of foolish mirth and empty laughter. But if you choose to turn away from all these, and instead of the dim, dismal, hard present, to sun yourselves in the light of the yet unrisen sun, which you can do, then, having rightly chosen the subjects to think about, the feeling will come as a matter of course. You cannot make yourselves glad by, as it were, laying hold of yourselves and lifting yourselves into gladness, but you can rule the direction of your thoughts, and so can bring around you summer in the midst of winter, by steadily contemplating the facts—and they are present facts, though we talk about them collectively as 'the future' —the facts on which all Christian gladness ought to be based. We can carry our own atmosphere with us; like the people in Italy, who in frosty weather will be seen sitting in the market-place by their stalls with a dish of embers, which they grasp in their hands, and so make themselves comfortably warm on the bitterest day. You can bring a reasonable degree of warmth into the coldest weather, if you will lay hold of the vessel in which the fire is, and keep it in your hand and close to your heart. Choose what you think about, and feelings will follow thoughts.

But it needs very distinct and continuous effort for a man to keep this great source of Christian joy clear before him. We are like the dwellers in some island of the sea, who, in some conditions of the atmosphere, can catch sight of the gleaming mountain-tops on the mainland across the stormy channel between. But thick days, with a heavy atmosphere and much mist, are very frequent in our latitude, and then all the distant hills are blotted out, and we see nothing but the cold, grey sea, breaking on the cold, grey stones. Still, you can scatter the mist if you will. You can make the atmosphere bright; and it is worth an effort to bring clear before us, and to keep high above the mists that cling to the low levels, the great vision which will make us glad. Brethren, I believe that one great source of the weakness of average Christianity amongst us to-day is the dimness into which so many of us have let the hope of the glory of God pass in our hearts. So I beg you to lay to heart this first commandment, and to rejoice in hope.

II. Now, secondly, here is the thought that life, if full of joyful hope, will be patient.

I have been saying that the gladness of which my text speaks is independent of circumstances, and may persist and be continuous even when externals occasion sadness. It is possible—I do not say it is easy, God knows it is hard—I do not say it is frequently attained, but I do say it is possible—to realise that wonderful ideal of the Apostle's 'As sorrowful, yet always rejoicing.' The surface of the ocean may be tossed and fretted by the winds, and churned into foam, but the great central depths 'hear not the loud winds when they call,' and are still in the midst of tempest. And we, dear brethren, ought to have an inner depth of spirit, down to the disturbance of which no surface-trouble can ever reach. That is the height of attainment of Christian faith, but it is a possible attainment for every one of us.

And if there be that burning of the light under the water, like 'Greek fire,' as it was called, which many waters could not quench—if there be that persistence of gladness beneath the surface-sorrow, as you find a running stream coming out below a glacier, then the joy and the hope, which co-exist with the sorrow, will make life patient.

Now, the Apostle means by these great words, 'patient' and 'patience,' which are often upon his lips, something more than simple endurance.  That endurance is as much as many of us can often muster up strength to exercise.  It sometimes takes all our faith and all our submission simply to say, 'I opened not my mouth, because thou didst it; and I will bear what thine hand lays upon me.'  But that is not all that the idea of Christian 'patience' includes, for it also takes in the thought of active work, and it is *perseverance* as much as *patience*.

Now, if my heart is filled with a calm gladness because my eye is fixed upon a celestial hope, then both the passive and active sides of Christian 'patience' will be realised by me.  If my hope burns bright, and occupies a large space in my thoughts, then it will not be hard to take the homely consolation of good John Newton's hymn and say—

> 'Though painful at present,
>   'Twill cease before long;
> And then, oh, how pleasant
>   The conqueror's song!'

A man who is sailing to America, and knows that he will be in New York in a week, does not mind, although his cabin is contracted, and he has a great many discomforts, and though he has a bout of sea-sickness. The disagreeables are only going to last for a day or two.  So our hope will make us bear trouble, and not make much of it.

And our hope will strengthen us, if it is strong, for all the work that is to be done.  Persistence in the path of duty, though my heart be beating like a

smith's hammer on the anvil, is what, Christian men
should aim at, and possess. If we have within. our
hearts that fire of a certain hope, it will impel us to
diligence in doing the humblest duty, whether circumstances be for or against us; as some great steamer is
driven right on its course, through the ocean, whatever
storms may blow in the teeth of its progress, because,.
deep down in it, there are furnaces and boilers which
supply the steam that drives the engines. So a life
that is joyful because it is hopeful will be full of calm
endurance and strenuous work. 'Rejoicing in hope;
patient,' persevering in tribulation.

III. Lastly, our lives will be joyful, hopeful, and
patient, in proportion as they are prayerful. .

'Continuing. instant'—which, of course, just means
steadfast—'in prayer.' Paul uttered a paradox when he
said, 'Rejoice in the Lord alway,' as he said long before
this verse, in the very first letter that he ever wrote, or
at least the first which has come down to us. There he
bracketed it along with two other equally paradoxical
sayings. 'Rejoice evermore; pray without ceasing; in
everything give thanks.' If you pray without ceasing .
you can rejoice without ceasing.

But can I pray without ceasing? Not if by prayer
you mean only words of supplication and petition, but
if by prayer you mean also a mental attitude of devotion, and a kind of sub-conscious reference to God in
all that you do, such unceasing prayer is possible. Do
not let us blunt the edge of this commandment, and
weaken our own consciousness of having failed to
obey it, by getting entangled in the cobwebs of mere
curious discussions as to whether the absolute ideal of
perfectly unbroken communion with God is possible in
this life. At all events it is possible to us to approxi-

mate to that ideal a great deal more closely than our
consciences tell us that we ever yet have done.  If we
are trying to keep our hearts in the midst of daily duty
in contact with God, and if, ever and anon in the press
of our work, we cast a thought towards Him and a
prayer, then joy and hope and patience will come to
us, in a degree that we do not know much about yet,
but might have known all about long, long ago.

There is a verse in the Old Testament which we may
well lay to heart: 'They cried unto God in the battle,
and He was entreated of them.'  Well, what sort of a
prayer do you think that would be?  Suppose that you
were standing in the thick of battle with the sword of
an enemy at your throat, there would not be much
time for many words of prayer, would there?  But the
cry could go up, and the thought could go up, and as
they went up, down would come the strong buckler
which God puts between His servants and all evil.
That is the sort of prayer that you, in the battle of
business, in your shops and counting-houses and warehouses and mills, we students in our studies, and you
mothers in your families and your kitchens, can send
up to heaven.  If thus we 'pray without ceasing,' then
we shall 'rejoice evermore,' and our souls will be kept
in patience and filled with the peace of God.


## STILL ANOTHER TRIPLET

'Distributing to the necessity of saints; given to hospitality.  14. Bless them
which persecute you: bless, and curse not.  15 Rejoice with them that do rejoice,
and weep with them that weep.'—ROMANS xii. 13-15.

IN these verses we pass from the innermost region of
communion with God into the wide field of duties in
relation to men.  The solitary secrecies of rejoicing

hope, endurance, and prayer unbroken, are exchanged
for the publicities of benevolence and sympathy. In
the former verses the Christian soul is in 'the secret
place of the Most High'; in those of our text he comes
forth with the light of God on his face, and hands
laden with blessings. The juxtaposition of the two
suggests the great principles to which the morality of
the New Testament is ever true—that devotion to God
is the basis of all practical helpfulness to man, and that
practical helpfulness to man is the expression and
manifestation of devotion to God.

The three sets of injunctions in our text, dissimilar
though they appear, have a common basis. They are
varying forms of one fundamental disposition—love;
which varies in its forms according to the necessities
of its objects, bringing temporal help to the needy,
meeting hostility with blessing, and rendering sympathy to both the glad and the sorrowful. There is,
further, a noteworthy connection, not in sense but
in sound, between the first and second clauses of
our text, which is lost in our English Version. 'Given
to hospitality' is, as the Revised margin shows,
literally, pursuing hospitality. Now the Greek, like
the English word, has the special meaning of following
with a hostile intent, and the use of it in the one sense
suggests its other meaning to Paul, whose habit of
'going off at a word,' as it has been called, is a notable
feature of his style. Hence, this second injunction, of
blessing the persecutors, comes as a kind of play upon
words, and is obviously occasioned by the verbal
association. It would come more appropriately at a
later part of the chapter, but its occurrence here is
characteristic of Paul's idiosyncrasy. We may represent the connection of these two clauses by such a

rendering as: Pursue hospitality, and as for those who pursue you, bless, and curse not.

We may look at these three flowers from the one root of love.

I. Love that speaks in material help.

We have here two special applications of that love which Paul regards as 'the bond of perfectness,' knitting all Christians together. The former of these two is love that expresses itself by tangible material aid. The persons to be helped are 'saints,' and it is their 'needs' that are to be aided. There is no trace in the Pauline Epistles of the community of goods which for a short time prevailed in the Church of Jerusalem and which was one of the causes that led to the need for the contribution for the poor saints in that city which occupied so much of Paul's attention at Corinth and elsewhere. But, whilst Christian love leaves the rights of property intact, it charges them with the duty of supplying the needs of the brethren. They are not absolute and unconditioned rights, but are subject to the highest principles of stewardship for God, trusteeship for men, and sacrifice for Christ. These three great thoughts condition and limit the Christian man's possession of the wealth, which, in a modified sense, it is allowable for him to call his own. His brother's need constitutes a first charge on all that belongs to him, and ought to precede the gratification of his own desires for superfluities and luxuries. If we 'see our brother have need and shut up our bowels of compassion against him' and use our possessions for the gratification of our own whims and fancies, 'how dwelleth the love of God in us?' There are few things in which Christian men of this day have more need for the vigorous exercise of conscience, and for enlightenment, than in their getting, and spending, and keeping money. In that region lies the main sphere of usefulness for many of us; and if we have not been 'faithful in that which is least,' our unfaithfulness there makes it all but impossible that we should be faithful in that which is greatest. The honest and rigid contemplation of our own faults in the administration of our worldly goods, might well invest with a terrible meaning the Lord's tremendous question, 'If ye have not been faithful in that which is another's, who shall give you that which is your own?'

The hospitality which is here enjoined is another shape which Christian love naturally took in the early days. When believers were a body of aliens, dispersed through the world, and when, as they went from one place to another, they could find homes only amongst their own brethren, the special circumstances of the time necessarily attached special importance to this duty; and as a matter of fact, we find it recognised in all the Epistles of the New Testament as one of the most imperative of Christian duties. 'It was the unity and strength which this intercourse gave that formed one of the great forces which supported Christianity.' But whilst hospitality was a special duty for the early Christians, it still remains a duty for us, and its habitual exercise would go far to break down the frowning walls which diversities of social position and of culture have reared between Christians.

II. The love that meets hostility with blessing.

There are perhaps few words in Scripture which have been more fruitful of the highest graces than this commandment. What a train of martyrs, from primitive times to the Chinese Christians in recent years,

have remembered these words, and left their legacy of
blessing as they laid their heads on the block or stood
circled by fire at the stake! For us, in our quieter
generation, actual persecution is rare, but hostility of
ill-will more or less may well dog our steps, and the
great principle here commended to us is that we are to
meet enmity with its opposite, and to conquer by love.
The diamond is cut with sharp knives, and each stroke
brings out flashing beauty. There are kinds of wood
which are fragrant when they burn; and there are
kinds which show their veining under the plane. It is
a poor thing if a Christian character only gives back
like a mirror the expression of the face that looks at it.
To meet hate with hate, and scorn with scorn, is not
the way to turn hate into love and scorn into sympathy.
Indifferent equilibrium in the presence of active antagonism is not possible for us. As long as we are sensitive we shall wince from a blow, or a sarcasm, or a
sneer. We must bless in order to keep ourselves from
cursing. The lesson is very hard, and the only way of
obeying it fully is to keep near Christ and drink in His
spirit who prayed 'Father, forgive them, for they
know not what they do.'

III. Love that flows in wide sympathy.

Of the two forms of sympathy which are here
enjoined, the former is the harder. To 'rejoice with
them that do rejoice' makes a greater demand on
unselfish love than to 'weep with them that weep.'
Those who are glad feel less need of sympathy than do
the sorrowful, and envy is apt to creep in and mar the
completeness of sympathetic joy. But even the latter
of the two injunctions is not altogether easy. The
cynic has said that there is 'something not wholly
displeasing in the misfortunes of our best friends';

and, though that is an utterly worldly and unchristian remark, it must be confessed not to be altogether wanting in truth.

But for obedience to both of these injunctions, a heart at leisure from itself is needed to sympathise; and not less needed is a sedulous cultivation of the power of sympathy. No doubt temperament has much to do with the degree of our obedience; but this whole context goes on the assumption that the grace of God working on temperament strengthens natural endowments by turning them into 'gifts differing according to the grace that is given to us.' Though we live in that awful individuality of ours, and are each, as it were, islanded in ourselves 'with echoing straits between us thrown,' it is possible for us, as the result of close communion with Jesus Christ, to bridge the chasms, and to enter into the joy of a brother's joy. He who groaned in Himself as He drew near to the grave of Lazarus, and was moved to weep with the weeping sisters, will help us, in the measure in which we dwell in Him and He in us, that we too may look 'not every man on his own things, but every man also on the things of others.'

On the whole, love to Jesus is the basis of love to man, and love to man is the practical worship of Christianity. As in all things, so in the exhortations which we have now been considering, Jesus is our pattern and power. He Himself communicates with our necessities, and opens His heart to give us hospitable welcome there. He Himself has shown us how to meet and overcome hatred with love, and hurt with blessing. He shares our griefs, and by sharing lessens them. He shares our joys, and by sharing hallows them. The summing up of all these specific injunctions is, 'Let that mind be in you which was also in Christ Jesus.'

## STILL ANOTHER TRIPLET

'Be of the same mind one toward another. Set not your mind on high things, but condescend to things that are lowly. Be not wise in your own conceits.'—Romans xii. 16 (R.V.).

WE have here again the same triple arrangement which has prevailed through a considerable portion of the context. These three exhortations are linked together by a verbal resemblance which can scarcely be preserved in translation. In the two former the same verb is employed: and in the third the word for 'wise' is cognate with the verb found in the other two clauses. If we are to seek for any closer connection of thought we may find it first in this—that all the three clauses deal with mental attitudes, whilst the preceding ones dealt with the expression of such; and second in this —that the first of the three is a general precept, and the second and third are warnings against faults which are most likely to interfere with it.

I. We note, the bond of peace.

'Be of the same mind one toward another.' It is interesting to notice how frequently the Apostle in many of his letters exhorts to mutual harmonious relations. For instance, in this very Epistle he invokes 'the God of patience and of comfort' to grant to the Roman Christians 'to be of the same mind with one another according to Christ Jesus,' and to the Corinthians, who had their full share of Greek divisiveness, he writes, 'Be of the same mind, live in peace,' and assures them that, if so, 'the God of love and peace

will be with them'; to his beloved Philippians he pours
out his heart in beseeching them by 'the consolation
that is in Christ Jesus, and the comfort of love, and the
fellowship of the Spirit—' that they would 'fulfil his
joy, that they be of the same mind, having the same
love, being of one accord, of one mind'; whilst to the
two women in that Church who were at variance with
one another he sends the earnest exhortation 'to be of
the same mind in the Lord,' and prays one whom we
only know by his loving designation of 'a true yoke-
fellow,' to help them in what would apparently put
a strain upon their Christian principle. For communities and for individuals the cherishing of the
spirit of amity and concord is a condition without
which there will be little progress in the Christian life.

But it is to be carefully noted that such a spirit may
co-exist with great differences about other matters. It
is not opposed to wide divergence of opinion, though
in our imperfect sanctification it is hard for us to
differ and yet to be in concord. We all know the
hopelessness of attempting to make half a dozen good
men think alike on any of the greater themes of the
Christian religion; and if we could succeed in such a
vain attempt, there would still be many an unguarded
door through which could come the spirit of discord,
and the half-dozen might have divergence of heart
even whilst they profess identity of opinion. The true
hindrances to our having 'the same mind one toward
another' lie very much deeper in our nature than the
region in which we keep our creeds. The self-regard
and self-absorption, petulant dislike of fellow-
Christians' peculiarities, the indifference which comes
from lack of imaginative sympathy, and which
ministers to the ignorance which causes it, and a

thousand other weaknesses in Christian character
bring about the deplorable alienation which but too
plainly marks the relation of Christian communities
and of individual Christians to one another in this
day.   When one thinks of the actual facts in every
corner of Christendom, and probes one's own feelings,
the contrast between the apostolic ideal and the
Church's realisation of it presents a contradiction so
glaring that one wonders if Christian people at all
believe that it is their duty 'to be of the same mind
one toward another.'

The attainment of this spirit of amity and concord
ought to be a distinct object of effort, and especially
in times like ours, when there is no hostile pressure
driving Christian people together, but when our great
social differences are free to produce a certain inevitable divergence and to check the flow of our sympathy, and when there are deep clefts of opinion, growing deeper every day, and seeming to part off Christians
into camps which have little understanding of, and
less sympathy with, one another.  Even the strong
individualism, which it is the glory of true Christian
faith to foster in character, and which some forms of
Christian fellowship do distinctly promote, works
harm in this matter; and those who pride themselves
on belonging to 'Free churches,' and standing apart
from creed-bound and clergy-led communities, are
specially called upon to see to it that they keep this
exhortation, and cultivate 'the unity of the Spirit in
the bond of peace.'

It should not be necessary to insist that the closest
mutual concord amongst all believers is but an
imperfect manifestation, as all manifestations in life
of the deepest principles must be, of the true oneness

T

which binds together in the most sacred unity, and should bind together in closest friendship, all partakers of the one life. And assuredly the more that one life flows into our spirits, the less power will all the enemies of Christian concord have over us. It is the Christ in us which makes us kindred with all others in whom He is. It is self, in some form or other, that separates us from the possessors of like precious faith. When the tide is out, the little rock-pools on the shore lie separated by stretches of slimy weeds, but the great sea, when it rushes up, buries the divisions, and unites them all. Our Christian unity is unity in Christ, and the only sure way 'to be of the same mind one toward another' is, that 'the mind which was in Christ Jesus be in us also.'

II. The divisive power of selfish ambition.

'Set not your mind on high things, but condescend to things that are lowly.' The contrast here drawn between the high and the lowly makes it probable that the latter as well as the former is to be taken as referring to 'things' rather than persons. The margin of the Revised Version gives the literal rendering of the word translated 'condescend.' 'To be carried away with,' is metaphorically equivalent to surrendering one's self to; and the two clauses present two sides of one disposition, which seeks not for personal advancement or conspicuous work which may minister to self-gratulation, but contentedly fills the lowly sphere, and 'the humblest duties on herself doth lay.' We need not pause to point out that such an ideal is dead against the fashionable maxims of this generation. Personal ambition is glorified as an element in progress, and to a world which believes in such a proverb as 'devil take the hindmost,' these two exhortations can only seem fanatical absurdity. And yet, perhaps, if we fairly take into account how the seeking after personal advancement and conspicuous work festers the soul, and how the flower of heart's-ease grows, as Bunyan's shepherd-boy found out, in the lowly valley, these exhortations to a quiet performance of lowly duties and a contented filling of lowly spheres, may seem touched with a higher wisdom than is to be found in the arenas where men trample over each other in their pursuit of a fame 'which appeareth for a little time, and then vanisheth away.' What a peaceful world it would be, and what peaceful souls they would have, if Christian people really adopted as their own these two simple maxims. They are easy to understand, but how hard they are to follow.

It needs scarcely be noted that the temper condemned here destroys all the concord and amity which the Apostle has been urging in the previous clause. Where every man is eagerly seeking to force himself in front of his neighbour, any community will become a struggling mob; and they who are trying to outrun one another and who grasp at 'high things,' will never be 'of the same mind one toward another.' But, we may observe that the surest way to keep in check the natural selfish tendency to desire conspicuous things for ourselves is honestly, and with rigid self-control, to let ourselves be carried away by enthusiasm for humble tasks. If we would not disturb our lives and fret our hearts by ambitions that, even when gratified, bring no satisfaction, we must yield ourselves to the impulse of the continuous stream of lowly duties which runs through every life.

But, plainly as this exhortation is needful, it is too

heavy a strain to be ever carried out except by the
power of Christ formed in the heart.   It is in His
earthly life that we find the great example of the
highest stooping to the lowest duties, and elevating
them by taking them upon Himself.  He did not 'strive
nor cry, nor cause His voice to be heard in the streets.'
Thirty years of that perfect life were spent in a little
village folded away in the Galilean hills, with rude
peasants for the only spectators, and the narrow
sphere of a carpenter's shop for its theatre.  For the
rest, the publicity possible would have been obscurity
to an ambitious soul.  To speak comforting words to
a few weeping hearts; to lay His hands on a few
sick folk and heal them; to go about in a despised land
doing good, loved indeed by outcasts and sinners,
unknown by all the dispensers of renown, and consciously despised by all whom the world honoured—
that was the perfect life of the Incarnate God.  And
that is an example which His followers seem with one
consent to set aside in their eager race after distinction and work that may glorify their names.  The
difficulty of a faithful following of these precepts,
and the only means by which that difficulty can be
overcome, are touchingly taught us in another of
Paul's Epistles by the accumulation of motives which
he brings to bear upon his commandment, when he exhorts by the tender motives of ' comfort in Christ, consolation of love, fellowship of the Spirit, and tender
mercies and compassions, that ye fulfil my joy, being
of the same mind, of one accord; doing nothing
through faction or vainglory, but in lowliness of mind
each counting other better than himself.'  As the
pattern for each of us in our narrow sphere, he holds
forth the mind that was in Christ Jesus, and the great

self-emptying which he shrank not from, 'but being
in the form of God counted it not a prize to be on
an equality with God; but, being found in fashion as
a man, He humbled Himself, becoming obedient even
unto death.'

III. The divisive power of intellectual self-conceit.

In this final clause the Apostle, in some sense,
repeats the maxim with which he began the series of
special exhortations in this chapter. He there enjoined 'every one among you not to think of himself
more highly than he ought to think'; here he deals
with one especial form of such too lofty thinking,
viz. intellectual conceit. He is possibly quoting the
Book of Proverbs (iii. 7), where we read, 'Be not wise
in thine own eyes,' which is preceded by, 'Lean not to
thine own understanding; in all thy ways acknowledge
Him'; and is followed by, 'Fear the Lord and depart
from evil'; thus pointing to the acknowledgment and
fear of the Lord as the great antagonist of such
over-estimate of one's own wisdom as of all other
faults of mind and life. It needs not to point out
how such a disposition breaks Christian unity of spirit.
There is something especially isolating in that form
of self-conceit. There are few greater curses in the
Church than little coteries of superior persons who
cannot feed on ordinary food, whose enlightened
intelligence makes them too fastidious to soil their
dainty fingers with rough, vulgar work, and whose
supercilious criticism of the unenlightened souls that
are content to condescend to lowly Christian duties,
is like an iceberg that brings down the temperature
wherever it floats. That temper indulged in, breaks the
unity, reduces to inactivity the work, and puts an end
to the progress, of any Christian community in which

it is found; and just as its predominance is harmful,
so the obedience to the exhortation against it is inseparable from the fulfilling of its sister precepts.  To
know ourselves for the foolish creatures that we are,
is a mighty help to being 'of the same mind one
toward another.' Who thinks of himself soberly and
according to the measure of faith which God hath
dealt to him will not hunger after high things, but
rather prefer the lowly ones that are on a level with
his lowly self.

The exhortations of our text were preceded with
injunctions to distribute material help, and to bestow
helpful sympathy.  The tempers enjoined in our
present text are the inward source and fountain of
such external bestowments.  The rendering of
material help and of sympathetic emotion are right
and valuable only as they are the outcome of this
unanimity and lowliness.  It is possible to 'distribute
to the necessity of saints' in such a way as that the
gift pains more than a blow; it is possible to proffer
sympathy so that the sensitive heart shrinks from it.
It was 'when the multitude of them that believed
were of one heart and one soul' that it became natural
to have all things common.  As in the aurora borealis,
quivering beams from different centres stream out
and at each throb approach each other till they touch
and make an arch of light that glorifies the winter's
night, so, if Christian men were 'of the same mind
toward one another,' did not 'set their minds on high
things, but condescended to things that were lowly,
and were not wise in their own conceits,' the Church of
Christ would shine forth in the darkness of a selfish
world and would witness to Him who came down
'from the highest throne in glory' to the lowliest

place in this lowly world, that He might lift us to His own height of glory everlasting.

## STILL ANOTHER TRIPLET

'Render to no man evil for evil. Take thought for things honourable in the sight of all men. 18 If it be possible, as much as in you lieth, be at peace with all men.'—ROMANS xii. 17, 18 (R.V.).

THE closing words of this chapter have a certain unity in that they deal principally with a Christian's duty in the face of hostility and antagonism. A previous injunction touched on the same subject in the exhortation to bless the persecutors; but with that exception, all the preceding verses have dealt with duties owing to those with whom we stand in friendly relations. Such exhortations take no cognisance of the special circumstances of the primitive Christians as 'lambs in the midst of wolves'; and a large tract of Christian duty would be undealt with, if we had not such directions for feelings and actions in the face of hate and hurt. The general precept in our text is expanded in a more complete form in the verses which follow the text, and we may postpone its consideration until we have to deal with them. It is one form of the application of the 'love without hypocrisy' which has been previously recommended. The second of these three precepts seems, quite heterogeneous, but it may be noticed that the word for 'evil' in the former and that for 'honourable,' in these closely resemble each other in sound, and the connection of the two clauses may be partially owing to that verbal resemblance; whilst we may also discern a real link between the thoughts in the consideration that we owe even to our enemies

the exhibition of a life which a prejudiced hostility
will be forced to recognise as good.  The third of these
exhortations prescribes unmoved persistence in friendly
regard to all men.

Dealing then, in this sermon only, with the second
and third of these precepts, and postponing the consideration of the first to the following discourse, we
have here the counsel that

I. Hostility is to be met with a holy and beautiful
life.

The Authorised Version inadequately translates the
significant word in this exhortation by 'honest.'  The
Apostle is not simply enjoining honesty in our modern,
narrow sense of the word, which limits it to the rendering to every man his own.  It is a remarkable thing that
'honest,' like many other words expressing various
types of goodness, has steadily narrowed in significa-
tion, and it is very characteristic of England that
probity as to money and material goods should be its
main meaning.  Here the word is used in the full
breadth of its ancient use, and is equivalent to that
which is fair with the moral beauty of goodness.

A Christian man then is bound to live a life which all
men will acknowledge to be good.  In that precept is
implied the recognition of even bad men's notions of
morality as correct.  The Gospel is not a new system
of ethics, though in some points it brings old virtues
into new prominence, and alters their perspective.  It
is further implied that the world's standard of what
Christians ought to be may be roughly taken as a true
one.  Christian men would learn a great deal about
themselves, and might in many respects heighten their
ideal, if they would try to satisfy the expectations of
the most degraded among them as to what they ought

to be. The worst of men has a rude sense of duty
which tops the attainments of the best. Christian
people ought to seek for the good opinion of those
around them. They are not to take that opinion as
the motive for their conduct, nor should they do good
in order to be praised or admired for it; but they are
to 'adorn the doctrine,' and to let their light shine
that men seeing their good may be led to think more
loftily of its source, and so to 'glorify their Father
which is in heaven.' That is one way of preaching the
Gospel. The world knows goodness when it sees it,
though it often hates it, and has no better ground for
its dislike of a man than that his purity and beauty of
character make the lives of others seem base indeed.
Bats feel the light to be light, though they flap against
it, and the winnowing of their leathery wings and
their blundering flight are witnesses to that against
which they strike. Jesus had to say, 'The world
hateth Me because I testify of it that the deeds
thereof are evil.' That witness was the result of His
being 'the Light of the world'; and if His followers
are illuminated from Him, they will have the same
effect, and must be prepared for the same response.
But none the less is it incumbent upon them to 'take
thought for things honourable in the sight of all
men.'

This duty involves the others of taking care that we
have goodness to show, and that we do not make our
goodness repulsive by our additions to it. There are
good people who comfort themselves when men dislike
them, or scoff at them, by thinking that their religion
is the cause, when it is only their own roughness and
harshness of character. It is not enough that we
present an austere and repellent virtue; the fair food

should be set on a fair platter. This duty is especially .
owing to our enemies. They are our keenest critics.
They watch for our halting. The thought of their
hostile scrutiny should ever stimulate us, and the
consciousness that Argus-eyes are watching us, with a
keenness sharpened by dislike, should lead us not only
to vigilance over our own steps, but also to the prayer,
'Lead me in a plain path, because of those who watch
me.' To 'provide things honest in the sight of all
men' is a possible way of disarming some hostility,
conciliating some prejudice, and commending to some
hearts the Lord whom we seek to imitate.

II. Be sure that, if there is to be enmity, it is all on
one side.

' As much as in you lieth, be at peace with all.'

These words are, I think, unduly limited when they
are supposed to imply that there are circumstances in
which a Christian has a right to be at strife. As if
they meant: Be peaceable as far as you can; but if it
be impossible, then quarrel. The real meaning goes
far deeper than that. 'It takes two to make a
quarrel,' says the old proverb; it takes two to make
peace also, does it not? We cannot determine whether
our relations with men will be peaceful or no; we are
only answerable for our part, and for that we are
answerable. 'As much as lieth in you' is the explanation
of 'if it be possible.' Your part is to be at peace; it is
not your part up to a certain point and no further, but
always, and in all circumstances, it is your part. It
may not be possible to be at peace with all men; there
may be some who *will* quarrel with you. You are not
to blame for that, but their part and yours are separate,
and your part is the same whatever they do. Be you
at peace with all men whether they are at peace with

you or not. Don't you quarrel with them even if they
will quarrel with you. That seems to me to be plainly
the meaning of the words. It would be contrary to
the tenor of the context and the teaching of the New
Testament to suppose that here we had that favourite
principle, 'There is a point beyond which forbearance
cannot go,' where it becomes right to cherish hostile
sentiments or to try to injure a man. If there be such
a point, it is very remarkable that there is no attempt
made in the New Testament to define it. The nearest
approach to such definition is 'till seventy times seven,'
the two perfect numbers multiplied into themselves.
So I think that this injunction absolutely prescribes per-
sistent, patient peacefulness, and absolutely proscribes
our taking up the position of antagonism, and under
no circumstances meeting hate with hate. It does not
follow that there is never to be opposition. It may be
necessary for the good of the opponent himself, and
for the good of society, that he should be hindered in
his actions of hostility, but there is never to be bitterness; and we must take care that none of the devil's
leaven mingles with our zeal against evil.

There is no need for enlarging on the enormous
difficulty of carrying out such a commandment in our
daily lives. We all know too well how hard it is; but
we may reflect for a moment on the absolute necessity
of obeying this precept to the full. For their own
souls' sakes Christian men are to avoid all bitterness,
strife, and malice. Let us try to remember, and to
bring to bear on our daily lives, the solemn things
which Jesus said about God's forgiveness being
measured by our forgiveness. The faithful, even
though imperfect, following of this exhortation would
revolutionise our lives. Nothing that we can only win

.by fighting with our fellows is worth fighting for. Men will weary of antagonism which is met only by the imperturbable calm of a heart at peace with God; and seeking peace with all men. The hot fire of hatred dies down, like burning coals scattered on a glacier, when laid against the crystal coldness of a patient, peaceful spirit. Watch-dogs in farmhouses will bark half the night through because they hear another barking a mile off. It takes two to make a quarrel; let me be sure that I am never one of the two!

## STILL ANOTHER TRIPLET

'Dearly beloved, avenge not yourselves, but rather give place unto wrath: for it is written, Vengeance is mine; I will repay, saith the Lord. 20 Therefore if thine enemy hunger, feed him: if he thirst, give him drink; for in so doing thou shalt heap coals of fire on his head 21. Be not overcome of evil, but overcome evil with good.'—ROMANS xii. 19-21.

THE natural instinct is to answer enmity with enmity, and kindliness with kindliness. There are many people of whom we think well and like, for no other reason than because we believe that they think well of and like us. Such a love is really selfishness. In the same fashion, dislike, and alienation on the part of another naturally reproduce themselves in our own minds. A dog will stretch its neck to be patted, and snap at a stick raised to strike it. It requires a strong effort to master this instinctive tendency, and that effort the plainest principles of Christian morality require from us all. The precepts in our text are in twofold form, negative and positive; and they are closed with a general principle, which includes both these forms, and much more besides. There are two pillars, and a great lintel coping them, like the trilithons of Stonehenge.

I. We deal with the negative precept.

'Avenge not yourselves, beloved, but give place unto wrath.' Do not take the law into your own hands, but leave God's way of retribution to work itself out. By avenging, the Apostle means a passionate redress of private wrongs at the bidding of personal resentment. We must note how deep this precept goes. It prohibits not merely external acts which, in civilised times are restrained by law, but, as with Christian morality, it deals with thoughts and feelings, and not only with deeds. It forbids such natural and common thoughts as 'I owe him an ill turn for that'; 'I should like to pay him off.' A great deal of what is popularly called 'a proper spirit' becomes extremely improper if tested by this precept. There is an eloquent word in German which we can only clumsily reproduce, which christens the ugly pleasure at seeing misfortune and calls it 'joy in others' disasters.' We have not the word; would that we had not the thing!

A solemn reason is added for the difficult precept, in that frequently misunderstood saying, 'Give place unto wrath.' The question is, Whose wrath? And, plainly, the subsequent words of the section show that it is God's. That quotation comes from Deuteronomy xxxii. 35. It is possibly unfortunate that 'vengeance' is ascribed to God; for hasty readers lay hold of the idea of passionate resentment, and transfer it to Him, whereas His retributive action has in it no resentment and no passion. Nor are we to suppose that the thought here is only the base one, *they are sure to be punished, so we need not trouble.* The Apostle points to the solemn fact of retribution as an element in the Divine government. It is not merely automatically working laws which recompense evil by evil, but it is the face of the Lord which is inexorably and inevitably set 'against them that do evil.' That recompense is not hidden away in the future behind the curtain of death, but is realised in the present, as every evil-doer too surely and bitterly experiences.

'Vengeance is mine, I will repay, saith the Lord.' God only has the right to recompense the ungodly and the sinner as well as the righteous. Dwelling in such a system as we do, how dares any one take that work into his hands? It requires perfect knowledge of the true evil of an action, which no one has who cannot read the heart; it requires perfect freedom from passion; it requires perfect immunity from evil desert on the part of the avenger; in a word, it belongs to God, and to Him alone. We have nothing to do with apportioning retribution to desert, either in private actions or in the treatment of so-called criminals. In the latter our objects should be reformation and the safety of society. If we add to these retribution, we transcend our functions.

II. Take the positive,—Follow God's way of meeting hostility with beneficence.

The hungry enemy is to be fed, the thirsty to be given drink; and the reason is, that such beneficence will 'heap coals of fire upon his head.' The negative is not enough. To abstain from vengeance will leave the heart unaffected, and may simply issue in the cessation of all intercourse. The reason assigned sounds at first strange. It is clear that the 'coals of fire' which are to be heaped on the head are meant to melt and soften the heart, and cause it to glow with love. There may be also included the burning pangs of shame felt by a man whose evil is answered by good. But these are secondary and auxiliary to the

true end of kindling the fire of love in his alienated
heart. The great object which every Christian man is
bound to have in view is to win over the enemy and
melt away misconceptions and hostility. It is not
from any selfish regard to one's own personal ease that
we are so to act, but because of the sacred regard
which Christ has taught us to cherish for the blessing
of peace amongst men, and in order that we may
deliver a brother from the snare, and make him share
in the joys of fellowship with God. The only way
to burn up the evil in his heart is by heaping coals of
kindness and beneficence on his head. And for such
an end it becomes us to watch for opportunities. We
have to mark the right moment, and make sure that
we time our offer for food when he is hungry and of
drink when he thirsts; for often *mal-a-propos* offers of
kindness make things worse. Such is God's way. His
thunderbolts we cannot grasp, His love we can copy.
Of the two weapons mercy and judgment which He
holds in His hand, the latter is emphatically His own;
the former should be ours too.

III. In all life meet and conquer evil with good.

This last precept, 'Be not overcome of evil, but
overcome evil with good,' is cast into a form which
covers not only relations to enemies, but all contact
with evil of every kind. It involves many great
thoughts which can here be only touched. It implies
that in all our lives we have to fight evil, and that it
conquers, and we are beaten when we are led to do it.
It is only conquered by being transformed into good.
We overcome our foes when we win them to be lovers.
We overcome our temptations to doing wrong when
we make them occasions for developing virtues; we
overcome the evil of sorrow when we use it to bring

us nearer to God; we overcome the men around us when we are not seduced by their example to evil, but attract them to goodness by ours.

Evil is only thus transformed by the positive exercise of goodness on our part. We have seen this in regard to enemies in the preceding remarks. In regard to other forms of evil, it is often better not to fight them directly, but to occupy the mind and heart with positive truth and goodness, and the will and hands with active service. A rusty knife will not be cleaned so effectually by much scouring as by strenuous use. Our lives are to be moulded after the great example of Him, who at almost the last moment of His earthly course said, ' Be of good cheer: I have overcome the world.' Jesus seeks to conquer evil in us all, and counts that He has conquered it when He has changed it into love.

## LOVE AND THE DAY

'Owe no man anything, but to love one another: for he that loveth another hath fulfilled the law. 9. For this, Thou shalt not commit adultery, Thou shalt not kill, Thou shalt not steal, Thou shalt not bear false witness, Thou shalt not covet; and if there be any other commandment it is briefly comprehended in this saying, namely, Thou shalt love thy neighbour as thyself. 10. Love worketh no ill to his neighbour: therefore love is the fulfilling of the law. 11. And that, knowing the time, that now it is high time to awake out of sleep: for now is our salvation nearer than when we believed. 12. The night is far spent, the day is at hand: let us therefore cast off the works of darkness, and let us put on the armour of light. 13. Let us walk honestly, as in the day; not in rioting and drunkenness, not in chambering and wantonness, not in strife and envying: 14. But put ye on the Lord Jesus Christ, and make not provision for the flesh, to fulfil the lusts thereof.' —ROMANS XIII. 8-14.

THE two paragraphs of this passage are but slightly connected. The first inculcates the obligation of universal love; and the second begins by suggesting, as a motive for the discharge of that duty, the near

approach of 'the day.' The light of that dawn draws
Paul's eyes and leads him to wider exhortations on
Christian purity as befitting the children of light.

I. Verses 8-10 set forth the obligation of a love which
embraces all men, and comprehends all duties to them.
The Apostle has just been laying down the general
exhortation, 'Pay every man his due,' and applying it
especially to the Christian's relation to civic rulers.  He
repeats it in a negative form, and bases on it the
obligation of loving every man.  That love is further
represented as the sum and substance of the law.
Thus Paul brings together two thoughts which are
often dealt with as mutually exclusive,—namely, love
and law.  He does not talk sentimentalisms about the
beauty of charity and the like, but lays it down, as a
'hard and fast rule,' that we are bound to love every
man with whom we come in contact ; or, as the Greek
has it, 'the other.'

That is the first plain truth taught here.  Love is
not an emotion which we may indulge or not, as we
please.  It is not to select its objects according to our
estimate of their lovableness or goodness.  But we are
bound to love, and that all round, without distinction
of beautiful or ugly, good or bad.   'A hard saying;
who can hear it?'  Every man is our creditor for that
debt.  He does not get his due from us unless he gets
love.  Note, further, that the debt of love is never
discharged.  After all payments it still remains owing.
There is no paying in full of all demands, and, as Bengel
says, it is an undying debt.  We are apt to weary of
expending love, especially on unworthy recipients, and
to think that we have wiped off all claims, and it may
often be true that our obligations to others compel us
to cease helping one; but if we laid Paul's words to

U

heart, our patience would be longer-breathed, and we should not be so soon ready to shut hearts and purses against even unthankful suitors.

Further, Paul here teaches us that this debt (*debitum*, 'duty') of love includes all duties. It is the fulfilling of the law, inasmuch as it will secure the conduct which the law prescribes. The Mosaic law itself indicates this, since it recapitulates the various commandments of the second table, in the one precept of love to our neighbour (Lev. xix. 18). Law enjoins but has no power to get its injunctions executed. Love enables and inclines to do all that law prescribes, and to avoid all that it prohibits. The multiplicity of duties is melted into unity; and that unity, when it comes into act, unfolds into whatsoever things are lovely and of good report. Love is the mother tincture which, variously diluted and manipulated, yields all potent and fragrant draughts. It is the white light which the prism of daily life resolves into its component colours.

But Paul seems to limit the action of love here to negative doing no ill. That is simply because the commandments are mostly negative, and that they are is a sad token of the lovelessness natural to us all. But do we love ourselves only negatively, or are we satisfied with doing ourselves no harm? That stringent pattern of love to others not only prescribes degree, but manner. It teaches that true love to men is not weak indulgence, but must sometimes chastise, and thwart, and always must seek their good, and not merely their gratification.

Whoever will honestly seek to apply that negative precept of working no ill to others, will find it positive enough. We harm men when we fail to help them.

If we can do them a kindness, and do it not, we do them ill. Non-activity for good is activity for evil. Surely, nothing can be plainer than the bearing of this teaching on the Christian duty as to intoxicants. If by using these a Christian puts a stumbling-block in the way of a weak will, then he is working ill to his neighbour, and that argues absence of love, and that is dishonest, shirking payment of a plain debt.

II. The great stimulus to love and to all purity is set forth as being the near approach of the day (verses 11-14). 'The day,' in Paul's writing, has usually the sense of the great day of 'the Lord's return, and may have that meaning here; for, as Jesus has told us, 'it is not for' even inspired Apostles 'to know the times or the seasons,' and it is no dishonour to apostolic inspiration to assign to it the limits which the Lord has assigned.

But, whether we take this as the meaning of the phrase, or regard it simply as pointing to the time of death as the dawning of heaven's day, the weight of the motive is unaffected. The language is vividly picturesque. The darkness is thinning, and the blackness turning grey. Light begins to stir and whisper. A band of soldiers lies asleep, and, as the twilight begins to dawn, the bugle call summons them to awake, to throw off their night-gear,—namely, the works congenial to darkness,—and to brace on their armour of light. Light may here be regarded as the material of which the glistering armour is made; but, more probably, the expression means weapons appropriate to the light.

Such being the general picture, we note the fact which underlies the whole representation; namely, that every life is a definite whole which has a fixed end. Jesus said, 'We must work the works of Him that sent Me, while it is day: the night cometh.' Paul uses the opposite metaphors in these verses. But, though the two sayings are opposite in form, they are identical in substance.  In both, the predominant thought is that of the rapidly diminishing space of earthly life, and the complete unlikeness to it of the future. We stand like men on a sandbank with an incoming tide, and every wash of the waves eats away its edges, and presently it will yield below our feet. We forget this for the most part, and perhaps it is not well that it should be ever present; but that it should never be present is madness and sore loss.

Paul, in his intense moral earnestness, in verse 13, bids us regard ourselves as already in 'the day,' and shape our conduct as if it shone around us and all things were made manifest by its light. The sins to be put off are very gross and palpable. They are for the most part sins of flesh, such as even these Roman Christians had to be warned against, and such as need to be manifested by the light even now among many professing Christian communities.

But Paul has one more word to say. If he stopped without it, he would have said little to help men who are crying out, 'How am I to strip off this clinging evil, which seems my skin rather than my clothing? How am I to put on that flashing panoply?' There is but one way,—put on the Lord Jesus Christ. If we commit ourselves to Him by faith, and front our temptations in His strength, and thus, as it were, wrap ourselves in Him, He will be to us dress and armour, strength and righteousness. Our old self will fall away, and we shall take no forethought for the flesh, to fulfil the lusts thereof.

# SALVATION NEARER

THERE is no doubt, I supppse, that the Apóstle, in common with the whole of the early Church, entertained more or less consistently the expectation of living to witness the second coming of Jesus Christ. There are in Paul's letters passages which look both in the direction of that anticipation, and in the other one of expecting to taste death. 'We which are alive and remain unto the coming of the Lord,' he says twice in one chapter. 'I am ready to be offered, and the hour of my departure is at hand,' he says in his last letter.

Now this contrariety of anticipation is but the natural result of what our Lord Himself said, 'It is not for you to know the times and the seasons,' and no one, who is content to form his doctrine of the knowledge resulting from inspiration from the words of Jesus Christ Himself, need stumble in the least degree in recognising the plain fact that Paul and his brother Apostles did not know when the Master was to come. Christ Himself had told them that there was a chamber locked against their entrance, and therefore we do not need to think that it militates against the authoritative inspiration of these early teachers of the Church, if they, too, searched 'what manner of time the Spirit which was in them did signify when it testified beforehand . . . the glory that should follow.'

Now, my text is evidently the result of the former of these two anticipations, viz. that Paul and his generation were probably to see the coming of the Lord from heaven. And to him the thought that 'the night was far spent,' as the context says, 'and the day was at hand,' underlay his most buoyant hope, and was the inspiration and motive-spring of his most strenuous effort.

Now, our relation to the closing moments of our own earthly lives, to the fact of death, is precisely the same as that of the Apostle and his brethren to the coming of the Lord. We, too, stand in that position of partial ignorance, and for us practically the words of my text, and all their parallel words, point to how we should think of, and how we should be affected by, the end to which we are coming. And this is the grand characteristic of the Christian view of that last solemn moment. 'Now is our salvation nearer than when we believed.' So I would note, first of all, what these words teach us should be the Christian view of our own end; and, second, to what conduct that view should lead us.

I. The Christian view of death.

'Now is our salvation nearer.' We have to think away by faith and hope all the grim externals of death, and to get to the heart of the thing. And then everything that is repulsive, everything that makes flesh and blood shrink, disappears and is evaporated, and beneath the folds of his black garment, there is revealed God's last, sweetest, most triumphant angel-messenger to Christian souls, the great, strong, silent Angel of Death, and he carries in his hand the gift of a full salvation. That is what our Apostle rose to the rapture of beholding, when he knew that the thought of his surviving till Christ came again must be put away, and when close to the last moment of his life, he said, 'The Lord shall deliver me, and save me into His everlasting kingdom.' What was the deliverance and being saved that he expected and expresses in these

words? Immunity from punishment? Escape from
the headsman's axe? Being 'delivered from the mouth
of the lion,' the persecuting fangs of the bloody Nero?
By no means. He knew that death was at hand, and
he said, 'He will save me'—not from it, but through it
—'into His everlasting kingdom.' And so in the words
of my text we may say—though Paul did not mean
them so—as we see the distance between us, and that
certain close, dwindling, dwindling, dwindling: 'Now,'
as moment after moment ticks itself into the past,
'now is our salvation nearer than when we believed.'
Children, when they are getting near their holidays,
take strips of paper, and tear off a piece as each day
passes. And as we tear off the days let us feel that we
are drawing closer to our home, and that the blessedness laid up for us in it is drawing nearer to us. 'Our
salvation,' not our destruction, our fuller life, not in
any true sense of the word our 'death,' is 'nearer than
when we believed.'

But some one may say, 'Is a man not saved till after
he is dead?' Is salvation future, not coming till after
the grave? No, certainly not. There are three aspects
of that word in Scripture. Sometimes the New Testament writers treat salvation as past, and represent a
Christian as being invested with the possession of it
all at the very moment of his first faith. That is true,
that whatever is yet to be evolved from what is given
to the poorest and foulest sinner, in the moment of his
initial faith in Christ, there is nothing to be added to
it. The salvation which the penitent thief received on
the cross is all the salvation that he was ever to get.
But out of it there came welling and welling and welling, when he had passed into the region 'where beyond
these voices there is peace'—there came welling out

from that inexhaustible fountain which was opened in
him all the fullnesses of an eternal progress in the
heavens. And so it is with us. Salvation is a past
gift which we received when we believed.

But in another aspect, which is also emphatically
stated in Scripture, it is a progressive process, and not
merely a gift bestowed once for all in the past. I
do not dwell upon that thought, but just remind you
of a turn of expression which occurs in various connec-
tions more than once. 'The Lord added to the Church
daily such as were being saved,' says Luke. Still more
emphatically in the Epistle to the Corinthians, the
Apostle puts into antithesis the two progressive processes, and speaks of the Gospel as being preached, and
being a savour of life unto life ' to them that are being
saved,' and a savour of destruction 'to them that are
being lost.' No moral or spiritual condition is stereo-
typed or stagnant. It is all progressive. And so the
salvation that is given once for all is ever being unfolded, and the Christian life on earth is the unfolding
of it.

But in another aspect still, such as is presented in my
text, and in other parallel passages, that salvation is
regarded as lying on the other side of the flood, because
the manifestations of it there, the evolving there of
what is in it, and the great gifts that come then, are so
transcendently above all even of our selectest experiences here, that they are, as it were, new, though still
their roots are in the old. The salvation which cul-
minates in the absolute removal from our whole being
of all manner of evil, whether it be sorrow or sin, and
in the conclusive bestowal upon us of all manner of
good, whether it be righteousness or joy, and which has
for its seal ' the adoption, to wit, the redemption of the

body,' so that body, soul, and spirit 'make one music as
before, but vaster,' is so far beyond the germs of itself
which here we experience that my text and its like are
amply vindicated.  And the man who is most fully
persuaded and conscious that he possesses the salvation of God, and most fully and blessedly aware that
that salvation is gradually gaining power in his life, is
the very man who will most feel that between its
highest manifestation on earth, and its lowest in the
heavens there is such a gulf as that the wine that he
will drink there at the Father's table is indeed new
wine.  And so 'is our salvation nearer,' though we
already possess it, 'than when we believed.'

Dear brethren, if these things be true, and if to die is
to be saved into the kingdom, do not two thoughts
result?  The one is that that blessed consummation
should occupy more of our thoughts than I am afraid
it does.  As life goes on, and the space dwindles
between us and it, we older people naturally fall into
the way, unless we are fools, of more seriously and
frequently turning our thoughts to the end.  I suppose
the last week of a voyage to Australia has far more
thoughts in it about the landing next week than the
two or three first days of beating down the English
Channel had.  I do not want to put old heads on young
shoulders in this or in any other respect.  But sure I
am that it does belong very intimately to the strength
of our Christian characters that we should, as the
Psalmist says, be 'wise' to 'consider our latter end.'

The other thought that follows is as plain, viz. that
that anticipation should always be buoyant, hopeful,
joyous.  We have nothing to do with the sad aspects
of parting from earth.  They are all but non-existent
for the Christian consciousness, when it is as vigorous

and God-directed as it, ought to be. They drop into
the background, and sometimes are lost to sight altogether. Remember how this Apostle, when he does
think about death, looks at it with—I was going to quote
words which may strike you as being inappropriate—'a
frolic welcome'; how, at all events, he is neither a bit
afraid of it, nor does he see in it anything from which to
shrink. He speaks of being with Christ, which is far
better; 'absent from the body, present with the Lord';
'the dissolution of the earthly house of this tabernacle'—
the tumbling down of the old clay cottage in order that
a stately palace of marble and precious stones may be
reared upon its site; 'the hour of my departure is at
hand; I have finished the fight.' Peter, too, chimes in
with his words: 'My exodus; my departure,' and both
of the two are looking, if not longingly, at all events
without a tremor of the eyelid, into the very eyeballs
of the messenger whom most men feel so hideous. Is
it not a wonderful gift to Christian souls that by faith
in Jesus Christ, the realm in which their hope can
expatiate is more than doubled, and annexes the dim
lands beyond the frontier of death? Dear friends, if
we are living in Christ, the thought of the end and that
here we are absent from home, ought to be infinitely
sweet, of whatever superficial terrors this poor, shrinking flesh may still be conscious. And I am sure that
the nearer we get to our Saviour, and the more we
realise the joyous possession of salvation as already
ours, and the more we are conscious of the expanding
of that gift in our hearts, the more we shall be delivered
from that fear of death which makes men all their
'lifetime subject to bondage.' So I beseech you to aim
at this, that, when you look forward, the furthest thing
you see on the horizon of earth may be that great

Angel of Death coming to save you into the everlasting kingdom.

Now, just a word about

II. The conduct to which such a hope should incite.

The Apostle puts it very plainly in the context, and we need but expand in a word or two what he teaches us there. 'And that knowing the time, that now it is high time to awake out of sleep, for now is our salvation nearer than when we believed.' To what does he refer by 'that'? The whole of the practical exhortations to a Christian life which have been given before. Everything that is duty becomes tenfold more stringent and imperative when we apprehend the true meaning of that last moment. They tell us that it is unwholesome to be thinking about death and the beyond, because to do so takes away interest from much of our present occupations and weakens energy. If there is anything from which a man is wrenched away because he steadily contemplates the fact of being wrenched away altogether from everything before long, it is something that he had better be wrenched from. And if there be any occupations which dwindle into nothingness, and into which a man cannot for the life of him fling himself with any thoroughgoing enthusiasm or interest, if once the thought of death stirs in him, depend upon it they are occupations which are in themselves contemptible and unworthy. All good aims will gain greater power over us; we shall have a saner estimate of what is worth living for; we shall have a new standard of what is the relative importance of things; and if some that looked very great turn out to be very small when we let that searching light in upon them, and others which seemed very insignificant spring suddenly up into dominating magni-

tude—that new and truer perspective will be all clear
gain. The more we feel that our salvation is sweeping
towards us, as it were, from the throne of God through
the blue abysses, the more diligently we shall 'work
while it is called day,' and the more earnestly we shall
seek, when the Saviour and His salvation come, to be
found with loins girt for all strenuous work, and lamps
burning in all the brightness of the light of a Christian
character.

Further, says Paul, this hopeful, cheerful contemplation of approaching salvation should lead us to cast off
the evil, and to put on the good. You will remember
the heart-stirring imagery which the Apostle employs
in the context, where he says, 'The day is at hand; let
us therefore fling off the works of darkness'—as men
in the morning, when the daylight comes through the
window, and makes them lift their eyelids, fling off
their night-gear—'and let us put on the armour of
light.' We are soldiers, and must be clad in what will
be bullet-proof, and will turn a sword's edge. And
where shall steel of celestial temper be found that can
resist the fiery darts shot at the Christian soldier? His
armour must be 'of light.' Clad in the radiance of
Christian character he will be invulnerable. And how
can we, who have robed ourselves in the works of
darkness, either cast them off or array ourselves in
sparkling armour of light? Paul tells us, 'Put ye on
the Lord Jesus Christ, and make not provision for the
flesh.' The picture is of a camp of sleeping soldiers; the
night wears thin, the streaks of saffron are coming in
the dawning east. One after another the sleepers
awake; they cast aside their night-gear, and they
brace on the armour that sparkles in the beams of the
morning sun. So they are ready when the trumpet

sounds the reveille, and with the morning comes the
Captain of the Lord's host, and with the Captain comes
the perfecting of the salvation which is drawing nearer
and nearer to us, as our moments glide through our
fingers like the beads of a rosary. Many men think of
death and fear; the Christian should think of death—
and hope.

## THE SOLDIER'S MORNING-CALL

'Let us put on the armour of light.'—ROMANS xiii. 12.

IT is interesting to notice that the metaphor of the
Christian armour occurs in Paul's letters throughout
his whole course. It first appears, in a very rudimentary form, in the earliest of the Epistles, that to
the Thessalonians. It appears here in a letter which
belongs to the middle of his career, and it appears
finally in the Epistle to the Ephesians, in its fully
developed and drawn-out shape, at almost the end of
his work. So we may fairly suppose that it was one
of his familiar thoughts. Here it has a very picturesque
addition, for the picture that is floating before his vivid
imagination is that of a company of soldiers, roused
by the morning bugle, casting off their night-gear
because the day is beginning to dawn, and bracing on
the armour that sparkles in the light of the rising sun.
'That,' says Paul, 'is what you Christian people ought
to be. Can you not hear the notes of the reveille?
The night is far spent; the day is at hand; therefore
let us put off the works of darkness—the night-gear
that was fit for those hours of slumber. Toss it away,
and put on the armour that belongs to the day.'

Now, I am not going to ask or try to answer the

question of how far this Apostolic exhortation is based
upon the Apostle's expectation that the world was
drawing near its end.  That does not matter at all for
us at present, for the fact which he expresses as the
foundation of this exhortation is true about us all,
and about our position in the midst of these fleeting
shadows round us.  We are hastening to the dawning
of the true day.  And so let me try to emphasise the
exhortation here, old and threadbare and commonplace
as it is, because we all need it, at whatever point of
life's journey we have arrived.

Now, the first thing that strikes me is that the garb
for the man expectant of the day is armour.

We might have anticipated something very different
in accordance with the thoughts that Paul's imagery
here suggests, about the difference between the night
which is so swiftly passing, and is full of enemies and
dangers, and the day which is going to dawn, and
is full of light and peace and joy.  We might have
expected that he would have said, 'Let us put on the
festal robes.'  But no!  'The night is far spent; the
day is at hand.'  But the dress that befits the expectant of the day is not yet the robe of the feast, but it
is 'the armour' which, put into plain words, means just
this, that there is fighting, always fighting, to be done.
If you are ever to belong to the day, you have to
equip yourselves *now* with armour and weapons.  I do
not need to dwell upon that, but I do wish to insist
upon this fact, that after all that may be truly said
about growth in grace, and the peaceful approximation towards perfection in the Christian character,
we cannot dispense with the other element in progress,
and that is fighting.  We have to struggle for every
step.  *Growth* is not enough to define completely the

process by which men become conformed to the image of
the Father, and are 'made meet to be partakers of the
inheritance of the saints in light.' Growth does express part of it, but only a part. Conflict is needed
to come in, before you have the whole aspect of
Christian progress before your minds. For there will
always be antagonism without and traitors within.
There will always be recalcitrant horses that need to
be whipped up, and jibbing horses that need to be
dragged forward, and shying ones that need to be
violently coerced and kept in the traces. Conflict is
the law, because of the enemies, and because of the
conspiracy between the weakness within and the things
without that appeal to it.

We hear a great deal to-day about being 'sanctified
by faith.' I believe that as much as any man, but the
office of faith is to bring us the power that cleanses,
and the application of that power requires our work,
and it requires our fighting. So it is not enough to
say, 'Trust for your sanctifying as you have trusted for
your justifying and acceptance,' but you have to work
out what you get by your faith, and you will never
work it out unless you fight against your unworthy
self, and the temptations of the world. The garb of
the candidate for the day is armour.

And there is another side to that same thought, and
that is, the more vivid our expectations of that blessed
dawn the more complete should be our bracing on of
the armour. The anticipation of that future, in very
many instances, in the Christian Church, has led to
precisely the opposite state of mind. It has induced
people to drop into mere fantastic sentiment, or to
ignore this contemptible present, and think that they
have nothing to do with it, and are only 'waiting for

the coming of the Lord,' and the like.  Paul says, 'Just because, on your eastern horizon, you can see the pink flush that tells that the night is gone, and the day is coming, therefore do not be a sentimentalist, do not be idle, do not be negligent or contemptuous of the daily tasks; but *because* you see it, put on the armour of light, and whether the time between the rising of the whole orb of the sun on the horizon be long or short, fill the hours with triumphant conflict.  Put on the whole armour of light.'

Again, note here what the armour is.  Of course that phrase, 'the armour of light,' may be nothing more than a little bit of colour put in by a picturesque imagination, and may suggest simply how the burnished steel would shine and glitter when the sunbeams smote it, and the glistening armour, like that of Spenser's Red Cross Knight, would make a kind of light in the dark cave, into which he went.  Or it may mean 'the armour that befits the light'; as is perhaps suggested by the antithesis 'the works of darkness,' which are to be 'put off.'  These are works that match the darkness, and similarly the armour is to be the armour that befits the light, and that can flash back its beams.  But I think there is more than that in the expression.  I would rather take the phrase to be parallel to another of this Apostle's, who speaks in 2nd Corinthians of the 'armour of righteousness on the right hand and on the left.'  'Light' makes the armour, 'righteousness' makes the armour.  The two phrases say the same thing, the one in plain English, the other in figure, which being brought down to daily life is just this, that the true armour and weapon of a Christian man is Christian character.  'Whatsoever things are true, whatsoever things are lovely, whatsoever things are of good report,' these are the pieces of armour, and these are the weapons which we are to wield. A Christian man fights against evil in himself by putting on good. The true way tó empty the heart of sin is to fill the heart with righteousness. The lances of the light, according to the significant old Greek myth, slew pythons. The armour is 'righteousness on the right hand and on the left.' Stick to plain, simple, homely duties, and you will find that they will defend your heart against many a temptation. A flask that is full of rich wine may be plunged into the saltest ocean, and not a drop will find its way in. Fill your heart with righteousness; your lives—let them glisten in the light, and the light will be your armour. God is light, wherefore God cannot be tempted with evil. 'Walk in the light, as He is in the light' . . . and 'the blood of Jesus Christ cleanseth from all sin.'

But there is another side to that thought, for if you will look, at your leisure, to the closing words of the chapter, you will find the Apostle's own exposition of what putting on the armour of light means. 'Put ye on the Lord Jesus Christ'—that is his explanation of putting on 'the armour of light.' For 'once ye were darkness, but now are ye light in the Lord,' and it is in the measure in which we are united to Him, by the faith which binds us to Him, and by the love which works obedience and conformity, that we wear the invulnerable armour of light. Christ Himself is, and He supplies to all, the separate graces which Christian men can wear. We may say that He is 'the panoply of God,' as Paul calls it in Ephesians, and when we wear Him, and only in the measure in which we do wear Him, in that measure are we clothed with it. And so the last thing that I would point out here is

x

that the obedience to these commands requires continual effort.

The Christians in Rome, to whom Paul was writing,
were no novices in the Christian life. Long ago many
of them had been brought to Him. But the oldest
Christian amongst them needed the exhortation as
much as the rawest recruit in the ranks. Continual
renewal day by day is what we need, and it will not
be secured without a great deal of work. Seeing that
there is a 'putting off' to go along with the 'putting
on,' the process is a very long one. ' 'Tis a lifelong task
till the lump be leavened.' It is a lifelong task till we
strip off all the rags of this old self; and 'being
clothed,' are not 'found naked.' It takes a lifetime
to fathom Jesus; it takes a lifetime to appropriate
Jesus, it takes a lifetime to be clothed with Jesus.
And the question comes to each of us, have we 'put
off the old man with his deeds'? Are we daily, as sure
as we put on our clothes in the morning, putting on
Christ the Lord?

For notice with what solemnity the Apostle gives
the master His full, official, formal title here, 'put
ye on the *Lord Jesus Christ.*' Do we put Him on as
*Lord*; bowing our whole wills to Him, and accepting
Him, His commandments, promises, providences, with
glad submission? Do we put on *Jesus*, recognising in
His manhood as our Brother not only the pattern of
our lives, but the pledge that the pattern, by His help
and love, is capable of reproduction in ourselves? Do
we put Him on as 'the Lord Jesus *Christ*,' who was
anointed with the Divine Spirit, that from the head it
might flow, even to the skirts of the garments, and
every one of us might partake of that unction and be
made pure and clean thereby? 'Put ye on the Lord

Jesus Christ,' and do it day by day, and then you have 'put on the whole armour of God.'

And when the day that is dawning has risen to its full, then, not till then, may we put off the armour and put on the white robe, lay aside the helmet, and have our brows wreathed with the laurel, sheathe the sword, and grasp the palm, being 'more than conquerors through Him who loved us,' and fights in us, as well as for us.

## THE LIMITS OF LIBERTY

'So then every one of us shall give account of himself to God. 13. Let us not therefore judge one another any more: but judge this rather, that no man put a stumblingblock, or an occasion to fall, in his brother's way. 14. I know, and am persuaded by the Lord Jesus, that there is nothing unclean of itself · but to him that esteemeth any thing to be unclean, to him it is unclean. 15. But if thy brother be grieved with thy meat, now walkest thou not charitably. Destroy not him with thy meat, for whom Christ died. 16. Let not then your good be evil spoken of: 17. For the kingdom of God is not meat and drink, but righteousness, and peace, and joy in the Holy Ghost. 18. For he that in these things serveth Christ is acceptable to God, and approved of men. 19. Let us therefore follow after the things which make for peace, and things wherewith one may edify another. 20. For meat destroy not the work of God. All things indeed are pure; but it is evil for that man who eateth with offence. 21. It is good neither to eat flesh, nor to drink wine, nor any thing whereby thy brother stumbleth, or is offended, or is made weak. 22 Hast thou faith? have it to thyself before God. Happy is he that condemneth not himself in that thing which he alloweth. 23 And he that doubteth is damned if he eat, because he eateth not of faith: for whatsoever is not of faith is sin.'—ROMANS xiv. 12 23.

THE special case in view, in the section of which this passage is part, is the difference of opinion as to the lawfulness of eating certain meats.  It is of little consequence, so far as the principles involved are concerned, whether these were the food which the Mosaic ordinances made unclean, or, as in Corinth, meats offered to idols. The latter is the more probable, and would be the more important in Rome.  The two opinions on the point represented two tendencies of mind, which always exist; one more scrupulous, and one more liberal. Paul has been giving the former class the lesson they needed in the former part of this chapter; and he now turns to the 'stronger' brethren, and lays down the law for. their conduct. We may, perhaps, best simply follow him, verse by verse.

We note then, first, the great thought with which he starts, that of the final judgment, in which each man shall. give account of himself. What has that to do with the question in hand? This, that it ought to keep us from premature and censorious judging. We have something more pressing to do than to criticise each other. Ourselves are enough to keep our hands full, without taking a lift of our fellows' conduct. And this, further, that, in view of the final judgment, we should hold a preliminary investigation on our own principles of action, and 'decide' to adopt as the overruling law for ourselves, that we shall do nothing which will make duty harder for our brethren. Paul habitually settled small matters on large principles, and brought the solemnities of the final account to bear on the market-place and the meal.

In verse 13 he lays down the supreme principle for settling the case in hand. No Christian is blameless if he voluntarily acts so as to lay a stumbling-block or an occasion to fall in another's path. Are these two things the same? Possibly, but a man may stumble, and not fall, and that which makes him stumble may possibly indicate a temptation to a less grave evil than that which makes him fall does. It may be noticed that in the sequel we hear of a brother's being 'grieved' first, and then of his being 'overthrown.' In any case, there is no mistake about the principle laid down and repeated in verse 21. It is a hard saying for some of us. Is my liberty to be restricted by the narrow

scruples of 'strait-laced' Christians? Yes. Does not
that make them masters, and attach too much importance to their narrowness? No. It recognises Christ
as Master, and all His servants as brethren.   If the
scrupulous ones go so far as to say to the more liberal,
'You cannot be Christians if you do not do as we do,'
then the limits of concession have been reached, and
we are to do as Paul did, when he flatly refused to yield
one hair's-breadth to the Judaisers.   If a man says,
You must adopt this, that, or the other limitation in
conduct, or else you shall be unchurched, the only
answer is, I will not.  We are to be flexible as long as
possible, and let weak brethren's scruples restrain our
action.   But if they insist on things indifferent as
essential, a yet higher duty than that of regard to their
weak consciences comes in, and faithfulness to Christ
limits concession to His servants.

But, short of that extreme case, Paul lays down the
law of curbing liberty in deference to 'narrowness.'
In verse 14 he states with equal breadth the extreme
principle of the liberal party, that nothing is unclean
of itself.   He has learned that 'in the Lord Jesus.'
Before he was 'in. Him,' he had been entangled in
cobwebs of legal cleanness and uncleanness; but now
he is free.   But he adds an exception, which must be
kept in mind by the liberal-minded section—namely,
that a clean thing is unclean to a man who thinks it
is.   Of course, these principles do not affect the eternal
distinctions of right and wrong.   Paul is not playing
fast and loose with the solemn, divine law which makes
sin and righteousness independent of men's notions.
He. is speaking of things indifferent — ceremonial
observances and the like; and the modern analogies of
these are conventional pieces of conduct, in regard to

amusements and the like, which, in themselves, a
Christian man can do or abstain from without sin.

Verse 15 is difficult to understand, if the 'for' at the
beginning is taken strictly. Some commentators would
read instead of it a simple 'but,' which smooths the flow
of thought. But possibly the verse assigns a reason
for the law in verse 13, rather than for the statements
in verse 14. And surely there is no stronger reason
for tender consideration for even the narrowest scruples
of Christians than the obligation to walk in love. Our
common brotherhood binds us to do nothing that would
even grieve one of the family. For instance, Christian
men have different views of the obligations of Sunday
observance. It is conceivable that a very 'broad'
Christian might see no harm in playing lawn-tennis in
his garden on a Sunday; but if his doing so scandalised,
or, as Paul says, 'grieved' Christian people of less
advanced views, he would be sinning against the law
of love if he did it.

There are many other applications of the principle
readily suggested. The principle is the thing to keep
clearly in view. It has a wide field for its exercise in
our times, and when the Christian brotherhood includes
such diversities of culture and social condition. And
that is a solemn deepening of it, 'Destroy not with
thy meat him for whom Christ died.' Note the almost
bitter emphasis on 'thy,' which brings out not only the
smallness of the gratification for which the mischief is
done, but the selfishness of the man who will not yield
up so small a thing to shield from evil which may prove
fatal, a brother for whom Christ did not shrink from
yielding up life. If He is our pattern, any sacrifice of
tastes and liberties for our brother's sake is plain duty,
and cannot be neglected without selfish sin. One great

reason, then, for the conduct enjoined, is set forth in verse 15. It is the clear dictate of Christian love.

Another reason is urged in verses 16 to 18. It displays the true character of Christianity, and so reflects honour on the doer. 'Your good' is an expression for the whole sum of the blessings obtained by becoming Christians, and is closely connected with what is here meant by the 'kingdom of God.' That latter phrase seems here to be substantially equivalent to the inward condition in which they are who have submitted to the dominion of the will of God. It is 'the kingdom within us' which is 'righteousness, peace, and joy in the Holy Ghost.' What have you won by your Christianity? the Apostle in effect says, Do you think that its purpose is mainly to give you greater licence in regard to these matters in question? If the most obvious thing in your conduct' is your 'eating and drinking,' your whole Christian standing will be misconceived, and men will fancy that your religion permits laxity of life. But if, on the other hand, you show that you are Christ's servants by righteousness, peace, and joy, you will be pleasing to God, and men will recognise that your religion is from Him, and that you are consistent professors of it.

Modern liberal-minded brethren can easily translate all this for to-day's use. Take care that you do not give the impression that your Christianity has its main operation in permitting you to do what your weaker brethren have scruples about. If you do not yield to them, but flaunt your liberty in their and the world's faces, your advanced enlightenment will be taken by rough-and-ready observers as mainly cherished because it procures you these immunities. Show by your life that you have the true spiritual gifts. Think more

about them than about your 'breadth,' and superiority
to 'narrow prejudices.'    Realise the purpose of the
Gospel as concerns your own moral perfecting, and the
questions in hand will fall into their right place.

In verses 19 and 20 two more reasons are given for
restricting liberty in deference to others' scruples.
Such conduct contributes to peace.    If truth is im-
perilled, or Christ's name in danger of being tarnished,
counsels of peace are counsels of treachery; but there
are not many things worth buying at the price of
Christian concord.   Such conduct tends to build up our
own and others' Christian character.   Concessions to
the 'weak' may help them to become strong, but flying
in the face of their scruples is sure to hurt them, in one
way or another.

In verse 15, the case was supposed of a brother's being
grieved by what he felt to be laxity.    That case corre-
sponded to the stumbling-block of verse 13.    A worse
result seems contemplated in verse 20,—that of the
weak brother, still believing that laxity was wrong,
and yet being tempted by the example of the stronger
to indulge in it.    In that event, the responsibility of
overthrowing what God had built lies at the door of
the tempter.    The metaphor of 'overthrowing' is
suggested by the previous one of 'edifying.'   Christian
duty is mutual building up of character; inconsiderate
exercise of 'liberty' may lead to pulling down, by
inducing to imitation which conscience condemns.

From this point onwards, the Apostle first reiterates
in inverse order his two broad principles, that clean
things are unclean to the man who thinks them so,
and that Christian obligation requires abstinence from
permitted things if our indulgence tends to a brother's
hurt.    The application of the latter principle to the

duty of total abstinence from intoxicants for the sake
of others is perfectly legitimate, but it is an application,
not the direct purpose of the Apostle's injunctions.

In verses 22 and 23, the section is closed by two
exhortations, in which both parties, the strong and the
weak, are addressed. The former is spoken to in
verse 22, the latter in verse 23. The strong brother is
bid to be content with having his wider views, or
'faith'—that is, certainty that his liberty is in accordance with Christ's will. It is enough that he should
enjoy that conviction, only let him make sure that he
can hold it as in God's sight, and do not let him flourish
it in the faces of brethren whom it would grieve, or
might lead to imitating his practice, without having
risen to his conviction. And let him be quite sure that
his conscience is entirely convinced, and not bribed by
inclination; for many a man condemns himself by
letting wishes dictate to conscience.

On the other hand, there is a danger that those who
have scruples should, by the example of those who
have not, be tempted to do what they are not quite
sure is right. If you have any doubts, says Paul, the
safe course is to abstain from the conduct in question.
Perhaps a brother can go to the theatre without harm,
if he believes it right to do so; but if you have any
hesitation as to the propriety of going, you will be
condemned as sinning if you do. You must not measure
your corn by another man's bushel. Your convictions,
not his, are to be your guides. 'Faith' is used here in
a somewhat unusual sense. It means certitude of
judgment. The last words of verse 23 have no such
meaning as is sometimes extracted from them; namely,
that actions, however pure and good, done by unbe-
lievers, are of the nature of sin. They simply mean

that whatever a Christian man does without clear warrant of his judgment and conscience is sin to him, whatever it is to others.

## TWO FOUNTAINS, ONE STREAM

'That we, through patience and comfort of the Scriptures, might have hope. . . . 13. The God of hope fill you with all joy and peace in believing, that ye may abound in hope.'—ROMANS xv. 4, 13.

THERE is a river in Switzerland fed by two uniting streams, bearing the same name, one of them called the 'white,' one of them the 'grey,' or dark. One comes down from the glaciers, and bears half-melted snow in its white ripple; the other flows through a lovely valley, and is discoloured by its earth. They unite in one common current. So in these two verses we have two streams, a white and a black, and they both blend together and flow out into a common hope. In the former of them we have the dark stream—'through patience and comfort,' which implies affliction and effort. The issue and outcome of all difficulty, trial, sorrow, ought to be hope. And in the other verse we have the other valley, down which the light stream comes: 'The God of hope fill you with all joy and peace in believing, that ye may abound in hope.'

So both halves of the possible human experience are meant to end in the same blessed result; and whether you go round on the one side of the sphere of human life, or whether you take the other hemisphere, you come to the same point, if you have travelled with God's hand in yours, and with Him for your Guide.

Let us look, then, at these two contrasted origins of the same blessed gift, the Christian hope.

I. We have, first of all, the hope that is the child of the night, and born in the dark.

'Whatsoever things,' says the Apostle, 'were written aforetime, were written for our learning, that we, through patience,'—or rather *the brave perseverance*—'and consolation'—or rather perhaps *encouragement*—'of the Scriptures might have hope.' The written word is conceived as the source of patient endurance which acts as well as suffers. This grace Scripture works in us through the encouragement which it ministers in manifold ways, and the result of both is hope.

So, you see, our sorrows and difficulties are not connected with, nor do they issue in, bright hopefulness, except by reason of this connecting link. There is nothing in a man's troubles to make him hopeful. Sometimes, rather, they drive him into despair; but at all events, they seldom drive him to hopefulness, except where this link comes in. We cannot pass from the black frowning cliffs on one side of the gorge to the sunny tablelands on the other without a bridge —and the bridge for a poor soul from the blackness of sorrow, and the sharp grim rocks of despair, to the smiling pastures of hope, with all their half-open blossoms, is builded in that Book, which tells us the meaning and purpose of them all; and is full of the histories of those who have fought and overcome, have hoped and not been ashamed.

Scripture is given for this among other reasons, that it may encourage us, and so may produce in us this great grace of active patience, if we may call it so.

The first thing to notice is, how Scripture gives encouragement—for such rather than consolation is the meaning of the word. It is much to dry tears, but it is more to stir the heart as with a trumpet call. Consolation is precious, but we need more for well-being than only to be comforted. And, surely, the whole tone of Scripture in its dealing with the great mystery of pain and sorrow, has a loftier scope than even to minister assuagement to grief, and to stay our weeping. It seeks to make us strong and brave to face and to master our sorrows, and to infuse into us a high-hearted courage, which shall not merely be able to accept the biting blasts, but shall feel that they bring a glow to the cheek and oxygen to the blood, while wrestling with them builds up our strength, and trains us for higher service. It would be a poor aim to comfort only; but to encourage—to make strong in heart, resolved in will, and incapable of being overborne or crushed in spirit by any sorrows— that is a purpose worthy of the Book, and of the God who speaks through it.

This purpose, we may say, is effected by Scripture in two ways. It encourages us by its records, and by its revelation of principles.

Who can tell how many struggling souls have taken heart again, as they pondered over the sweet stories of sorrow subdued which stud its pages, like stars in its firmament? The tears shed long ago which God has put 'in His bottle,' and recorded in ' His book,' have truly been turned into pearls. That long gallery of portraits of sufferers, who have all trodden the same rough road, and been sustained by the same hand, and reached the same home, speaks cheer to all who follow them. Hearts wrung by cruel partings from those dearer to them than their own souls, turn to the pages which tell how Abraham, with calm sorrow, laid his

Sarah in the cave at Macpelah; or how, when Jacob's eyes were dim that he could not see, his memory still turned to the hour of agony when Rachael died by him, and he sees clear in its light her lonely grave, where so much of himself was laid; or to the still more sacred page which records the struggle of grief and faith in the hearts of the sisters of Bethany. All who are anyways afflicted in mind, body, or estate find in the Psalms men speaking their deepest experiences before them; and the grand majesty of sorrow that marks 'the patience of Job,' and the flood of sunshine that bathes him, revealing the 'end of the Lord,' have strengthened countless sufferers to bear and to hold fast, and to hope. We are all enough of children to be more affected by living examples than by dissertations, however true, and so Scripture is mainly history, revealing God by the record of His acts, and disclosing the secret of human life by telling us the experiences of living men.

But Scripture has another method of ministering encouragement to our often fainting and faithless hearts. It cuts down through all the complications of human affairs, and lays bare the innermost motive power. It not only shows us in its narratives the working of sorrow, and the power of faith, but it distinctly lays down the source and the purpose, the whence and the whither of all suffering. No man need quail or faint before the most torturing pains or most disastrous strokes of evil, who holds firmly the plain teaching of Scripture on these two points. They all come *from* my Father, and they all come *for* my good. It is a short and simple creed, easily apprehended. It pretends to no recondite wisdom. It is a homely philosophy which common

intellects can grasp, which children can understand,
and hearts half paralysed by sorrow can take in. So
much the better. Grief and pain are so common that
their cure had need to be easily obtained. Ignorant
and stupid people have to writhe in agony as well as
wise and clever ones, and until grief is the portion
only of the cultivated classes, its healing must come
from something more universal than philosophy; or
else the nettle would be more plentiful than the dock;
and many a poor heart would be stung to death.
Blessed be God! the Christian view of sorrow, while
it leaves much unexplained, focuses a steady light on
these two points; its origin and its end. 'He for our
profit, that we may be partakers of His holiness,' is
enough to calm all agitation, and to make the faintest
heart take fresh courage. With that double certitude
clear before us, we can face anything. The slings and
arrows which strike are no more flung blindly by an
'outrageous fortune,' but each bears an inscription,
like the fabled bolts, which tells what hand drew the
bow, and they come with His love.

Then, further, the courage thus born of the Scriptures produces another grand thing—patience, or
rather perseverance. By that word is meant more
than simply the passive endurance which is the main
element in patience, properly so called. Such passive
endurance is a large part of our duty in regard to
difficulties and sorrows, but is never the whole of it.
It is something to endure and even while the heart is
breaking, to submit unmurmuring, but, transcendent
as that is, it is but half of the lesson which we have to
learn and to put in practice. For if all our sorrows
have a disciplinary and educational purpose, we shall
not have received them aright, unless we have tried

to make that purpose effectual, by appropriating whatsoever moral and spiritual teaching they each have for us. Nor does our duty stop there. For while one high purpose of sorrow is to deaden our hearts to earthly objects, and to lift us above earthly affections, no sorrow can ever relax the bonds which oblige us to duty. The solemn pressure of 'I ought,' is as heavy on the sorrowful as on the happy heart. We have still to toil, to press forward, in the sweat of our brow, to gain our bread, whether it be food for our bodies, or sustenance for our hearts and minds. Our responsibilities to others do not cease because our lives are darkened. Therefore, heavy or light of heart, we have still to stick to our work, and though we may never more be able to do it with the old buoyancy, still to do it with our might.

It is that dogged persistence in plain duty, that tenacious continuance in our course, which is here set forth as the result of the encouragement which Scripture gives. Many of us have all our strength exhausted in mere endurance, and have let obvious duties slip from our hands, as if we had done all that we could do when we had forced ourselves to submit. Submission would come easier if you took up some of those neglected duties, and you would be stronger for patience, if you used more of your strength for service. You do well if you do not sink under your burden, but you would do better if, with it on your shoulders, you would plod steadily along the road; and if you did, you would feel the weight less. It seems heaviest when you stand still doing nothing. Do not cease to toil because you suffer. You will feel your pain more if you do. Take the encouragement which Scripture gives, that it may animate you to bate no jot of heart or hope, but still bear up and steer right onward.

And let the Scripture directly minister to you perseverance as well as indirectly supply it through the encouragement which it gives. It abounds with exhortations, patterns, and motives of such patient continuance in well-doing. It teaches us a solemn scorn of ills. It, angel-like, bears us up on soft, strong hands, lest we bruise ourselves on, or stumble over, the rough places on our roads. It summons us to diligence by the visions of the prize, and glimpses of the dread fate of the slothful, by all that is blessed in hope, and terrible in foreboding, by appeals to an enlightened self-regard, and by authoritative commands to conscience, by the pattern of the Master, and by the tender motives of love to Him to which He, Himself, has given voice. All these call on us to be followers of them who, through faith and perseverance, inherit the promises.

But we have yet another step to take. These two, the encouragement and perseverance produced by the right use of Scripture, will lead to hope.

It depends on how sorrow and trial are borne, whether they produce a dreary hopelessness which sometimes darkens into despair, or a brighter, firmer hope than more joyous days knew. We cannot say that sorrow produces hope. It does not, unless we have this connecting link—the experience in sorrow of a God-given courage which falters not in the onward course, nor shrinks from any duty. But if, in the very press and agony, I am able, by God's grace, to endure nor cease to toil, I have, in myself, a living proof of His power, which entitles me to look forward with the sure confidence that, through all the uproar of the storm, He will bring me to my harbour of rest where there is peace. The lion once slain houses a swarm of bees who lay up honey in its carcase. The trial borne with brave persistence yields a store of sweet hopes. If we can look back and say, 'Thou hast been with me in six troubles,' it is good logic to look forward and say, 'and in seven Thou wilt not forsake me.' When the first wave breaks over the ship, as she clears the heads and heels over before the full power of the open sea, inexperienced lands-men think they are all going to the bottom, but they soon learn that there is a long way between rolling and foundering, and get to watch the highest waves towering above the bows in full confidence that these also will slip quietly beneath the keel as the others have done, and be left harmless astern.

The Apostle, in this very same letter, has another word parallel to this, in which he describes the issues of rightly-borne suffering when he says, 'Tribulation worketh perseverance'—the same word that is used here—'and perseverance worketh' the proof in our experience of a sustaining God; and the proof in our experience of a sustaining God works hope. We know that of ourselves we could not have met tribulation, and therefore the fact that we have been able to meet and overcome it is demonstration of a mightier power than our own, working in us, which we know to be from God, and therefore inexhaustible and ever ready to help. That is foundation firm enough to build solid fabrics of hope upon, whose bases go down to the centre of all things, the purpose of God, and whose summits, like the upward shooting spire of some cathedral, aspire to, and seem almost to touch, the heavens.

Y

So hope is born of sorrow, when these other things come between. The darkness gives birth to the light, and every grief blazes up a witness to a future glory. Each drop that hangs on the wet leaves twinkles into rainbow light that proclaims the sun. The garish splendours of the prosperous day hide the stars, and through the night of our sorrow there shine, thickly sown and steadfast, the constellations of eternal hopes. The darker the midnight, the surer, and perhaps the nearer, the coming of the day. Sorrow has not had its perfect work unless it has led us by the way of courage and perseverance to a stable hope. Hope has not pierced to the rock, and builds only 'things that can be shaken,' unless it rests on sorrows borne by God's help.

II. So much then for the genealogy of one form of the Christian hope. But we have also a hope that is born of the day, the child of sunshine and gladness; and that is set before us in the second of the two verses which we are considering, 'The God of hope fill you with all joy and peace in believing, that ye may abound in hope.'

So then, 'the darkness and the light are both alike' to our hope, in so far as each may become the occasion for its exercise. It is not only to be the sweet juice expressed from our hearts by the winepress of calamities, but that which flows of itself from hearts ripened and mellowed under the sunshine of God-given blessedness.

We have seen that the bridge by which sorrow led to hope, is perseverance and courage; in this second analysis of the origin of hope, joy and peace are the bridge by which Faith passes over into it. Observe the difference: there is no direct connection between affliction and hope, but there is between joy and hope. We have no right to say, 'Because I suffer, I shall possess good in the future'; but we have a right to say, 'Because I rejoice'—of course with a joy in God— 'I shall never cease to rejoice in Him.' Such joy is the prophet of its own immortality and completion. And, on the other hand, the joy and peace which are naturally the direct progenitors of Christian hope, are the children of faith. So that we have here two generations, as it were, of hope's ancestors;—Faith produces joy and peace, and these again produce hope.

Faith leads to joy and peace. Paul has found, and if we only put it to the proof, we shall also find, that the simple exercise of simple faith fills the soul with '*all* joy and peace.' Gladness in all its variety and in full measure, calm repose in every kind and abundant in its still depth, will pour into my heart as water does into a vessel, on condition of my taking away the barrier and opening my heart through faith. Trust and thou shalt be glad. Trust, and thou shalt be calm. In the measure of thy trust shall be the measure of thy joy and peace.

Notice, further, how indissolubly connected the present exercise of faith is with the present experience of joy and peace. The exuberant language of this text seems a world too wide for anything that many professing Christians ever know even in the moments of highest elevation, and certainly far beyond the ordinary tenor of their lives. But it is no wonder that these should have so little joy, when they have so little faith. It is only while we are looking to Jesus that we can expect to have joy and peace. There is no flashing light on the surface of the mirror, but when it is turned full to the sun. Any interruption in the electric current is registered accurately by an interruption in the continuous line perforated on the telegraph ribbon; and so every diversion of heart and faith from Jesus Christ is recorded by the fading of the sunshine out of the heart, and the silencing of all the song-birds. Yesterday's faith will not bring joy to-day; you cannot live upon past experience, nor feed your souls with the memory of former exercises of Christian faith. It must be like the manna, gathered fresh every day, else it will rot and smell foul. A present faith, and a present faith only, produces a present joy and peace. Is there, then, any wonder that so much of the ordinary experience of ordinary Christians should present a sadly broken line—a bright point here and there, separated by long stretches of darkness? The gaps in the continuity of their joy are the tell-tale indicators of the interruptions in their faith. If the latter were continuous, the former would be unbroken. Always believe, and you will always be glad and calm.

It is easy to see that this is the natural result of faith. The very act of confident reliance on another for all my safety and well-being has a charm to make me restful, so long as my reliance is not put to shame. There is no more blessed emotion than the tranquil happiness which, in the measure of its trust, fills every trustful soul. Even when its objects are poor, fallible, weak, ignorant dying men and women, trust brings a breath of more than earthly peace into the heart. But when it grasps the omnipotent, all-wise, immortal Christ, there are no bounds but its own capacity to the blessedness which it brings into the soul, because there is none to the all-sufficient grace of which it lays hold.

Observe again how accurately the Apostle defines for us the conditions on which Christian experience will be joyful and tranquil. It is 'in believing,' not in certain other exercises of mind, that these blessings are to be realised. And the forgetfulness of that plain fact leads to many good people's religion being very much more gloomy and disturbed than God meant it to be. For a large part of it consists in sadly testing their spiritual state, and gazing at their failures and imperfections. There is nothing cheerful or tranquillising in grubbing among the evils of your own heart, and it is quite possible to do that too much and too exclusively. If your favourite subject of contemplation in your religious thinking is yourself, no wonder that you do not get much joy and peace out of that. If you do, it will be of a false kind. If you are thinking more about your own imperfections than about Christ's pardon, more about the defects of your own love to Him than about the perfection of His love to you, if instead of practising faith you are absorbed in self-examination, and instead of saying to yourself, 'I know how foul and unworthy I am, but I look away from myself to my Saviour,' you are bewailing your sins and doubting whether you are a Christian, you need not expect God's angels of joy and peace to nestle in your heart. It is 'in believing,' and not in other forms of religious contemplation, however needful these may in their places be, that these fair twin sisters come to us and make their abode with us.

Then, the second step in this tracing of the origin of the hope which has the brighter source is the consideration that the joy and peace which spring from faith, in their turn produce that confident anticipation of future and progressive good.

Herein lies the distinguishing blessedness of the Christian joy and peace, in that they carry in themselves the pledge of their own eternity. Here, and here only, the mad boast which is doomed to be so miserably falsified when applied to earthly gladness is simple truth. Here 'to-morrow *shall* be as this day and much more abundant.' Such joy has nothing in itself which betokens exhaustion, as all the less pure joys of earth have. It is manifestly not born for death, as are they. It is not fated, like all earthly emotions or passions, to expire in the moment of its completeness, or even by sudden revulsion to be succeeded by its opposite. Its sweetness has no after pang of bitterness. It is not true of this gladness, that 'Hereof cometh in the end despondency and madness,' but its destiny is to 'remain' as long as the soul in which it unfolds shall exist, and ' to be full' as long as the source from which it flows does not run dry.

So that the more we experience the present blessedness, which faith in Christ brings us, the more shall we be sure that nothing in the future, either in or beyond time, can put an end to it ; and hence a hope that looks with confident eyes across the gorge of death, to the 'shining tablelands' on the other side, and is as calm as certitude, shall be ours. To the Christian soul, rejoicing in the conscious exercise of faith and the conscious possession of its blessed results, the termination of a communion with Christ, so real and spiritual, by such a trivial accident as death, seems wildly absurd and therefore utterly impossible. Just as Christ's Resurrection seems inevitable as soon as we grasp the truth of His divine nature, and it becomes manifestly impossible that He, being such as He is—

should be holden of death,' being such as it is, so for His children, when once they come to know the realities of fellowship with their Lord, they feel the entire dissimilarity of these to anything in the realm which is subjected to the power of death, and to know it to be as impossible that these purely spiritual experiences should be reduced to inactivity, or meddled with by it, as that a thought should be bound with a cord or a feeling fastened with fetters. They, and death, belong to two different regions. It can work its will on 'this wide world, and all its fading sweets'—but is powerless in the still place where the soul and Jesus hold converse, and all His joy passes into His servant's heart. I saw, not long since, in a wood a mass of blue wild hyacinths, that looked like a little bit of heaven dropped down upon earth. You and I may have such a tiny bit' of heaven itself lying amidst all the tangle of our daily lives, if only we put our trust in Christ, and so get into our hearts some little portion of that joy that is unspeakable, and that peace that passeth understanding.

Thus, then, the sorrows of the earthly experience and the joys of the Christian life will blend together to produce the one blessed result of a hope that is full of certainty, and is the assurance of immortality. There is no rainbow in the sky unless there be both a black cloud and bright sunshine. So, on the blackest, thickest thunder-mass of our sorrows, if smitten into moist light by the sunshine of joy and peace drawn from Jesus Christ by faith, there may be painted the rainbow of hope, the many-coloured, steadfast token of the faithful covenant of the faithful God.

# JOY AND PEACE IN BELIEVING

'The God of hope fill you with all joy and peace in believing, that ye may abound in hope, through the power of the Holy Ghost.'—ROMANS xv. 13.

WITH this comprehensive and lofty petition the Apostle closes his exhortation to the factions in the Roman Church to be at unity. The form of the prayer is moulded by the last words of a quotation which he has just made, which says that in the coming Messiah 'shall the Gentiles hope.' But the prayer itself is not an instance of being led away by a word—in form, indeed, it is shaped by verbal resemblance; in substance it points to the true remedy for religious controversy. Fill the contending parties with a fuller spiritual life, and the ground of their differences will begin to dwindle, and look very contemptible. When the tide rises, the little pools on the rocks are all merged into one.

But we may pass beyond the immediate application of these words, and see in them the wish, which is also a promise, and like the exhibition of every ideal is a command. This is Paul's conception of the Christian life as it might and should be, in one aspect. You notice that there is not a word in it about conduct. It goes far deeper than action. It deals with the springs of action in the individual life. It is the depths of spiritual experience here set forth which will result in actions that become a Christian. And in these days, when all around us we see a shallow conception of Christianity, as if it were concerned principally with conduct and men's relations with one another, it is well to go down into the depths, and to remember that

344

whilst 'Do, do, do!' is very important, 'Be, be, be!' is the primary commandment.  Conduct is a making visible of personality, and the Scripture teaching which says first faith and then works is profoundly philosophical as well as Christian.  So we turn away here from externals altogether, and regard the effect of Christianity on the inward life.

. I. I wish to notice man's faith and God's filling as connected, and as the foundation of everything.

'The God of hope fill you . . .'—let us leave out the intervening words for a moment—'in believing.'  Now, you notice that Paul does not stay to tell us what or whom we are to believe in, or on.  He takes that for granted, and his thought is fastened, for the moment, not on the object but on the act of faith.  And he wishes to drive home to us this, that the attitude of trust is the necessary prerequisite condition of God's being able to fill a man's soul, and that God's being able to fill a man's soul is the necessary consequence of a man's trust.  Ah, brethren, we cannot altogether shut God out from our spirits.  There are loving and gracious gifts that, as our Lord tells us, He makes to 'fall on the unthankful and the evil.'  His rain is not 'like the summer showers that we sometimes see, that fall in one spot and leave another dry; nor like the destructive thunderstorms, that come down bringing ruin upon one cane-brake and leave the plants in the next standing upright.  But the best, the highest, the truly divine gifts which He is yearning to give to us all, cannot be given except there be consent, trust, and desire for them.  You can shut your hearts or you can open them.  And just as the wind will sigh round some hermetically closed chamber in vain search for a cranny, and the man within may be asphyxiated though the atmosphere is surging·up its waves all round his closed domicile, so by lack of our faith, which is at once trust, consent, and desire, we shut out the gift with which God would fain fill our spirits. You can take a porous pottery vessel, wrap it up in waxcloth, pitch it all over, and then drop it into mid-Atlantic, and not a drop will find its way in. And that is what we can do with ourselves, so that although in Him 'we live and move and have our being,' and are like the earthen vessel in the ocean, no drop of the blessed moisture will ever find its way into the heart. There must be man's faith before there can be God's filling.

Further, this relation of the two things suggests to us that a consequence of a Christian man's faith is the direct action of God upon him. Notice how the Apostle puts that truth in a double form here, in order that he may emphasise it, using one form of expression, involving the divine, direct activity, at the beginning of his prayer, and another at the end, and so enclosing, as it were, within a great casket of the divine action, all the blessings, the flashing jewels, which he desires his Roman friends to possess. 'The God of hope fill you . . . through the power of the Holy Ghost.' I wish I could find words by which I could bear in upon the ordinary type of the Evangelical Christianity of this generation anything like the depth and earnestness of my own conviction that, for lack of a proportionate development of that great truth, of the direct action of the giving God on the believing heart, it is weakened and harmed in many ways. Surely He that made my spirit can touch my spirit; surely He who filleth all things according to their capacity can Himself enter into and fill the spirit which is opened for Him by simple faith. We do not need wires for the telegraphy between heaven and the believing soul, but He comes directly to, and speaks in, and moves upon, and moulds and blesses, the waiting heart. And until you know, by your own experience rightly interpreted, that there is such a direct communion between the giving God and the recipient believing spirit, you have yet to learn the deepest depth, and the most blessed blessedness, of Christian faith and experience. For lack of it a hundred evils beset modern Christianity. For lack of it men fix their faith so exclusively as that the faith is itself harmed thereby, on the past act of Christ's death on the Cross. You will not suspect me of minimising that, but I beseech you remember one climax of the Apostle's which, though not bearing the same message as my text, is in harmony with it, 'Christ that died, yea, rather, that is risen again, who is even at the right hand of God, who also maketh intercession for us.' And remember that Christ Himself bestows the gift of His Divine Spirit as the result of the humiliation and the agony of His Cross. Faith brings the direct action of the giving God.

And one more word about this first part of my text: the result of that direct action is complete—'the God of hope fill you' with no shrunken stream, no painful trickle out of a narrow rift in the rock, but a great exuberance which will pass into a man's nature in the measure of his capacity, which is the measure of his trust and desire. There are two limits to God's gifts to men: the one is the limitless limit of God's infinitude, the other is the working limit—our capacity— and that capacity is precisely measured, as the capacity of some built-in vessel might be measured by a little gauge on the outside, by our faith. 'The God of hope' fills you in 'believing,' and 'according to thy faith shall it be unto thee.'

II. Notice the joy and peace which come from the direct action of the God of hope on the believer's soul.

Now, it is not only towards God that we exercise trust, but wherever it is exercised, to some extent, and in the measure in which the object on which it rests is discovered by experience to be worthy, it produces precisely these results. Whoever trusts is at peace, just as much as he trusts. His confidence may be mistaken, and there will come a tremendous awakening if it is, and the peace will be shattered like some crystal vessel dashed upon an iron pavement, but so long as a man's mind and heart are in the attitude of dependence upon another, conceived to be dependable, one knows that there are few phases of tranquillity and blessedness which are sweeter and deeper than that. 'The heart of her husband doth safely trust in her'— that is one illustration, and a hundred more might be given. And if you will take that attitude of trust which, even when it twines round some earthly prop, is upheld for a time, and bears bright flowers—if you take it and twine it round the steadfast foundations of the Throne of God, what can shake that sure repose? 'Joy and peace' will come when the Christian heart closes with its trust, which is God in Christ.

He that believes has found the short, sure road to joy and peace, because his relations are set right with God. For these relations are the disturbing elements in all earthly tranquillity, and like the skeleton at the feast in all earthly joy, and a man can never, down to the roots of his being, be at rest until he is quite sure that there is nothing wrong between him and God. And so believing, we come to that root of all real gladness which is anything better than a crackling of thorns under a pot, and to that beginning of all true tranquillity. Joy in the Lord and peace with God are the parents of all joy and peace that are worthy of the name.

And that same faith will again bring these two bright-winged angels into the most saddened and troubled lives, because that faith brings right relations with ourselves. For our inward strifes stuff thorns into the pillow of our repose, and mingle bitterness with the sweetest, foaming draughts of our earthly joys. If a man's conscience and inclinations pull him two different ways, he is torn asunder as by wild horses. If a man has a hungry heart, for ever yearning after unattained and impossible blessings, then there is no rest there. If a man's little kingdom within him is all anarchical, and each passion and appetite setting up for itself, then there is no tranquillity. But if by faith we let the God of hope come in, then hungry hearts are satisfied, and warring dispositions are harmonised, and the conscience becomes quieted, and fair imaginations fill the chamber of the spirit, and the man is at rest, because he himself is unified by the faith and fear of God.

And the same faith brings joy and peace because it sets right our relations with other people, and with all externals. If I am living in an atmosphere of trust, then sorrow will never be absolute, nor have exclusive monopoly and possession of my spirit. But there will be the paradox, and the blessedness, of Christian experience, 'as sorrowful yet always rejoicing.' For the joy of the Christian life has its source far away beyond the swamps from which the sour drops of sorrow may trickle, and it is possible that, like the

fabled fire that burned under water, the joy of the
Lord may be bright in my heart, even when it is
drenched in floods of calamity and distress.

And so, brethren, the joy and peace that come from
faith will fill the heart which trusts. Only remember
how emphatically the Apostle here puts these two
things together, ' joy and peace in believing.' As long
as, and not a moment longer than, you are exercising
the Christian act of trust, will you be experiencing
the Christian blessedness of ' joy and peace.' Unscrew
the pipe, and in an instant the water ceases to flow.
Touch the button and switch off, and out goes the
light. Some Christian people fancy they can live upon
past faith. You will get no present joy and peace out
of past faith. The rain of this day twelve months will
not moisten the parched ground of to-day. Yesterday's religion was all used up yesterday. And if you
would have a continuous flow of joy and peace
through your lives, keep up a uniform habit and
attitude of trust in God. You will get it then; you
will get it in no other way.

III. Lastly, note the hope which springs from this
experience of joy and peace.

'The God of hope fill you with all joy and peace in
believing, that ye may abound in hope.' Here, again,
the Apostle does not trouble himself to define the
object of the hope. In this, as in the former clause,
his attention is fixed upon the emotion, not upon that
towards which it goes out. And just as there was no
need to say in whom it was that the Christian man
was to believe, so there is no room to define what it is
that the Christian man has a right to hope for. For
his hope is intended to cover all the future, the next
moment, or to-morrow, or the dimmest distance

where time has ceased to be, and eternity stands unmoved. The attitude of the Christian mind ought to
be a cheery optimism, an unconquerable hope. 'The
best has yet to be' is the true Christian thought in
contemplating the future for myself, for my dear ones,
for God's Church, and for God's universe.

And the truest basis on which that hope can rest is
the experience granted to us, on condition of our faith,
of a present, abundant possession of the joy and peace
which God gives. The gladder you are to-day, if the
gladness comes from the right source, the surer you
may be that that gladness will never end. That is not
what befalls men who live by earthly joys. For the
more poignant, precious, and, as we faithlessly think,
indispensable some of these are to us, the more into
their sweetest sweetness creeps the dread thought:
'This is too good to last; this must pass.' We never
need to think that about the peace and joy that come
to us through believing. For they, in their sweetness,
prophesy perpetuity. I need not dwell upon the
thought that the firmest, most personally precious
convictions of an eternity of future blessedness, rise
and fall in a Christian consciousness with the purity
and the depth of its own experience of the peace and
joy of the Gospel. The more you have of Jesus Christ
in your lives and hearts to-day, the surer you will be
that whatever death may do, it cannot touch that, and
the more ludicrously impossible it will seem that anything that befalls this poor body can touch the bond
that knits us to Jesus Christ. Death can separate us
from a great deal. Its sharp scythe cuts through all
other bonds, but its edge is turned when it is tried
against the golden chain that binds the believing soul
to the Christ in whom he has believed.

So, brethren, there is the ladder—begin at the bottom step, with faith in Jesus Christ. That will bring God's direct action into your spirit, through His Holy Spirit, and that one gift will break up into an endless multiplicity of blessings, just as a beam of light spilt upon the surface of the ocean breaks into diamonds in every wave, and that 'joy and peace' will kindle in your hearts a hope fed by the great words of the Lord: 'Peace I leave with you, my peace I give unto you,' 'My joy shall remain in you, and your joy shall be full,' 'He that liveth and believeth in Me shall never die.'

## PHŒBE

'I commend unto you Phœbe our sister, who is a servant of the Church that is at Cenchrea: 2. That ye receive her in the Lord, worthily of the Saints, and that ye assist her in whatsover matter she may have need of you: for she herself hath been a succourer of many, and of mine own self.'—ROMANS xvi. 1, 2 (R.V ).

THIS is an outline picture of an else wholly unknown person. She, like most of the other names mentioned in the salutations in this chapter, has had a singular fate. Every name, shadowy and unreal as it is to us, belonged to a human life filled with hopes and fears, plunged sometimes in the depths of sorrows, struggling with anxieties and difficulties; and all the agitations have sunk into forgetfulness and calm. There is left to the world an immortal remembrance, and scarcely a single fact associated with the undying names.

. Note the person here disclosed.

A little rent is made in the dark curtain through which we see as with an incandescent light concentrated for a moment upon her, one of the many good

woman who helped Paul, as their sisters had helped
Paul's Master, and who thereby have won, little as either
Paul or she thought it, an eternal commemoration.
Her name is a purely idolatrous one, and stamps her as
a Greek, and by birth probably a worshipper of Apollo.
Her Christian associations were with the Church at
Cenchrea, the port of Corinth, of which little Christian
community nothing further is known. But if we take
into account the hideous immoralities of Corinth, we
shall deem it probable that the port, with its shifting
maritime population, was, like most seaports, a soil in
which goodness was hard put to it to grow, and a
church had much against which to struggle. To be a
Christian at Cenchrea can have been no light task.
Travellers in Egypt are told that Port Said is the
wickedest place on the face of the earth; and in
Phœbe's home there would be a like drift of disreput-
ables of both sexes and of all nationalities. It was
fitting that one good woman should be recorded as
redeeming womanhood there. We learn of her that
she was a 'servant,' or, as the margin preferably reads,
a 'deaconess of the Church which is at Cenchrea'; and
in that capacity, by gentle ministrations and the exhibition of purity and patient love, as well as by the
gracious administration of material help, had been
a 'succourer of many.' There is a whole world of un-
mentioned kindnesses and a life of self-devotion hidden
away under these few words. Possibly the succour
which she administered was her own gift. She may
have been rich and influential, or perhaps she but dis-
tributed the Church's bounty; but in any case the gift
was sweetened by the giver's hand, and the succour was
the impartation of a woman's sympathy more than the
bestowment of a donor's gift. Sometime or other, and

z

somehow or other, she had had the honour and joy of
helping Paul, and no doubt that opportunity would be
to her a crown of service.  She was now on the point
of taking the long journey to Rome on her own business,
and the Apostle bespeaks for her help from the Roman
Church 'in whatsoever matter she may have need of
you,' as if she had some difficult affair on hand, and
had no other friends in the city.  Possibly then she was
a widow, and perhaps had had some lawsuit or business
with government authorities, with whom a word from
some of her brethren in Rome might stand her in good
stead.  Apparently she was the bearer of this epistle,
which would give her a standing at once in the Roman
Church, and she came among them with a halo round
her from the whole-hearted commendation of the
Apostle.

Mark the lessons from this little picture.

We note first the remarkable illustration here given
of the power of the new bond of a common faith.
The world was then broken up into sections, which
were sometimes bitterly antagonistic and at others
merely rigidly exclusive.  The only bond of union was
the iron fetter of Rome, which crushed the people, but
did not knit them together.  But here are Paul the
Jew, Phœbe the Greek, and the Roman readers of the
epistle, all fused together by the power of the divine
love that melted their hearts, and the common faith
that unified their lives.  The list of names in this
chapter, comprising as it does men and women of many
nationalities, and some slaves as well as freemen, is
itself a wonderful testimony of the truth of Paul's
triumphant exclamation in another epistle, that in
Christ there is 'neither Jew nor Greek, bond nor free,
male nor female.'

The clefts have closed, and the very line of demarcation is obliterated; and these clefts were deeper than any of which we moderns have had experience. It remains something like a miracle that the members of Paul's churches could ever be brought together, and that their consciousness of oneness could ever overpower the tremendous divisive forces. We sometimes wonder at their bickerings; we ought rather to wonder at their unity, and be ashamed of the importance which we attach to our infinitely slighter mutual disagreements. The bond that was sufficient to make the early Christians all one in Christ Jesus seems to have lost its binding power to-day, and, like an used-up elastic band, to have no clasping grip left in it.

Another thought which we may connect with the name of Phœbe is the characteristic place of women in Christianity.

The place of woman amongst the Jews was indeed free and honourable as compared with her position either in Greece or Rome, but in none of them was she placed on the level of man, nor regarded mainly in the aspect of an equal possessor of the same life of the Spirit. But a religion which admits her to precisely the same position of a supernatural life as is granted to man, necessarily relegates to a subordinate position all differences of sex as it does all other natural distinctions. The women who ministered to Jesus of their substance, the two sisters of Bethany, the mourners at Calvary, the three who went through the morning twilight to the tomb, were but the foremost conspicuous figures in a great company through all the ages who have owed to Jesus their redemption, not only from the slavery of sin, but from the stigma of inferiority as man's drudge or toy. To the world in

which Paul lived it was a strange, new thought that
women could share with man in his loftiest emotions.
Historically the emancipation of one half of the human
race is the direct result of the Christian principle that
all are one in Christ Jesus. In modern life the emancipation has been too often divorced from its one sure
basis, and we have become familiar with the sight of
the 'advanced' women who have advanced so far as to
have lost sight of the Christ to whom they owe their
freedom. The picture of Phœbe in our text might well
be commended to all such as setting forth the most
womanlike ideal. She was 'a succourer of many.' Her
ministry was a ministry of help; and surely such
gentle ministry is that which most befits the woman's
heart and comes most graciously to the woman's
fingers.

Phœbe then may well represent to us the ministry of
succour in this world of woe and need. There is ever a
cry, even in apparently successful lives, for help and a
helper. Man's clumsy hand is but too apt to hurt
where it strives to soothe, and nature itself seems to
devolve on the swifter sympathies and more delicate perceptions of woman the joy of binding up
wounded spirits. In the verses immediately following
our text we read of another woman to whom was
entrusted a more conspicuous and direct form of
service. Priscilla 'taught Apollos the way of God
more perfectly,' and is traditionally represented as
being united with her husband in evangelistic work.
But it is not merely prejudice which takes Phœbe
rather than Priscilla as the characteristic type of
woman's special ministry. We must remember our
Lord's teaching, that the giver of 'a cup of cold water
in the name of a prophet' in some measure shares in the

prophet's work, and will surely share in the prophet's
reward. She who helped Paul must have entered into
the spirit of Paul's labours; and He to whom all service
that is done from the same motive is one in essence,
makes no difference between him whose thirsty lips.
drink and her whose loving hand presents the cup of
cold water. 'Small service is true service while it lasts.'
Paul and Phœbe were one in ministry and one in its
recompense.

We may further see in her a foreshadowing of the
reward of lowly service, though it be only the service
of help. Little did Phœbe dream that her name would
have an eternal commemoration of her unnoticed deeds
of kindness and aid, standing forth to later generations and peoples of whom she knew nothing, as worthy
of eternal remembrance. For those of us who have
to serve unnoticed and unknown, here is an instance
and a prophecy which may stimulate and encourage.
'Surely I will never forget any of their works' is a
gracious promise which the most obscure and humble
of us may take to heart, and sustained by which, we
may patiently pursue a way on which there are 'none to
praise and very few to love.' It matters little whether
our work be noticed or recorded by men, so long as we
know that it is written in the Lamb's book of life and
that He will one day proclaim it 'before the Father in
heaven and His angels.'

### PRISCILLA AND AQUILA

'Greet Priscilla and Aquila my helpers in Christ Jesus; 4. (Who have for my
life laid down their own necks unto whom not only I give thanks, but so all the
churches of the Gentiles :) 5. Likewise greet the church that is in their house.'—
ROMANS XVI. 3-5.

IT has struck me that this wedded couple present, even
in the scanty notices that we have of them, some

interesting points which may be worth while gathering together.

Now, to begin with, we are told that Aquila was a Jew. We are not told whether Priscilla was a Jewess or no. So far as her name is concerned, she may have been, and very probably was, a Roman, and, if so, we have in their case a 'mixed marriage,' such as was not uncommon then, and of which Timothy's parents give another example. She is sometimes called Prisca, which was her proper name, and sometimes Priscilla, an affectionate diminutive. The two had been living in Rome, and had been banished under the decree of the Emperor, just as Jews have been banished from England and from every country in Europe again and again. They came from Rome to Corinth, and were, perhaps, intending to go back to Aquila's native place, Pontus, when Paul met them in the latter city, and changed their whole lives. His association with them began in a purely commercial partnership. But as they abode together and worked at their trade, there would be many earnest talks about the Christ, and these ended in both husband and wife becoming disciples. The bond thus knit was too close to be easily severed, and so, when Paul sailed across the Ægean for Ephesus, his two new friends kept with him, which they would be the more ready to do, as they had no settled home. They remained with him during his somewhat lengthened stay in the great Asiatic city; for we find in the first Epistle to the Corinthians, which was written from Ephesus about that time, that the Apostle sends greetings from 'Priscilla and Aquila and the Church which is in their house.' But when Paul left Ephesus they seem to have stayed behind, and afterwards to have gone their own way.

About a year after the first Epistle to the Corinthians
was sent from Ephesus, the Epistle to the Romans
was written, and we find there the salutation to
Priscilla and Aquila which is my text. So this wandering couple were back again in Rome by that
time, and settled down there for a while. They are
then lost sight of for some time, but probably they
returned to Ephesus. Once more we catch a glimpse
of them in Paul's last letter, written some seven or
eight years after that to the Romans. The Apostle
knows that death is near, and, at that supreme
moment, his heart goes out to these two faithful
companions, and he sends them a parting token of
his undying love. There are only two messages to
friends in the second Epistle to Timothy, and one of
these is to Prisca and Aquila. At the mouth of the
valley of the shadow of death he remembered the old
days in Corinth, and the, to us, unknown instance of
devotion which these two had shown, when, for his life,
they laid down their own necks.

Such is all that we know of Priscilla and Aquila.
Can we gather any lessons from these scattered notices
thus thrown together?

I. Here is an object lesson as to the hallowing effect
of Christianity on domestic life and love.

Did you ever notice that in the majority of the
places where these two are named, if we adopt the
better readings, Priscilla's name comes first? She
seems to have been 'the better man of the two'; and
Aquila drops comparatively into the background.
Now, such a couple, and a couple in which the wife took
the foremost place, was an absolute impossibility in
heathenism. They are a specimen of what Christianity
did in the primitive age, all over the Empire, and is

doing to-day, everywhere—lifting woman to her proper
place. These two, yoked together in ' all exercise of
noble end,' and helping one another in Christian work,
and bracketed together by the Apostle, who puts the
wife first, as his fellow-helpers in Christ Jesus, stands
before us as a living picture of what our sweet and
sacred family life and earthly loves may be glorified
into, if the light from heaven shines down upon them,
and is thankfully received into them.

Such a house as the house of Prisca and Aquila is
the product of Christianity, and such ought to be the
house of every professing Christian. For we should
all make our homes as ' tabernacles of the righteous,'
in which the voice of joy and rejoicing is ever heard.
Not only wedded love, but family love, and all earthly
love, are then most precious, when into them there
flows the ennobling, the calming, the transfiguring
thought of Christ and His love to us.

Again, notice that, even in these scanty references
to our two friends, there twice occurs that remarkable expression ' the church that is in their house.'
Now, I suppose that that gives us a little glimpse into
the rudimentary condition of public worship in the
primitive church. It was centuries after the time of
Priscilla and Aquila before circumstances permitted
Christians to have buildings devoted exclusively to
public worship. Up to a very much later period than
that which is covered by the New Testament, they
gathered together wherever was most convenient.
And, I suppose, that both in Rome and Ephesus, this
husband and wife had some room—perhaps the workshop where they made their tents, spacious enough for
some of the Christians of the city to meet together
in. One would like people who talk so much about

'the Church,' and refuse the name to individual
societies of Christians, and even to an aggregate of
these, unless it has 'bishops,' to explain how the little
gathering of twenty or thirty people in the workshop
attached to Aquila's house, is called by the Apostle
without hesitation 'the church which is in their house.'
It *was* a part of the Holy Catholic Church, but it was
also 'a Church,' complete in itself, though small in
numbers. We have here not only a glimpse into the
manner of public worship in early times, but we may
learn something of far more consequence for us, and
find here a suggestion of what our homes ought to be.
'The Church that is in thy house'—fathers and
mothers that are responsible for your homes and
their religious atmosphere, ask yourselves if any one
would say that about your houses, and if they could
not, why not?

II. We may get here another object lesson as to the
hallowing of common life, trade, and travel.

It does not appear that, after their stay in Ephesus,
Aquila and his wife were closely attached to Paul's
person, and certainly they did not take any part as
members of what we may call his evangelistic staff.
They seem to have gone their own way, and as far as
the scanty notices carry us, they did not meet Paul
again, after the time when they parted in Ephesus.
Their gipsy life was probably occasioned by Aquila's
going about—as was the custom in old days when there
were no trades-unions or organised centres of a special
industry—to look for work where he could find it.
When he had made tents in Ephesus for a while, he
would go on somewhere else, and take temporary
lodgings there. Thus he wandered about as a working
man. Yet Paul calls him his 'fellow worker in Christ

Jesus'; and he had, as we saw, a Church in his house. A roving life of that sort is not generally supposed to be conducive to depth of spiritual life. But their wandering course did not hurt these two. They took their religion with them. It did not depend on locality, as does that of a great many people who are very religious in the town where they live, and, when they go away for a holiday, seem to leave their religion, along with their silver plate, at home. But no matter whether they were in Corinth or Ephesus or Rome, Aquila and Priscilla took their Lord and Master with them, and while working at their camel's-hair tents, they were serving God.

Dear brethren, what we want is not half so much preachers such as my brethren and I, as Christian tradesmen and merchants and travellers, like Aquila and Priscilla.

III. Again, we may see here a suggestion of the unexpected issues of our lives.

Think of that complicated chain of circumstances, one end of which was round Aquila and the other round the young Pharisee in Jerusalem. It steadily drew them together until they met in that lodging at Corinth. Claudius, in the fullness of his absolute power, said, 'Turn all these wretched Jews out of my city. I will not have it polluted with them any more. Get rid of them!' So these two were uprooted, and drifted to Corinth. We do not know why they chose to go thither; perhaps they themselves did not know why; but God knew. And while they were coming thither from the west, Paul was coming thither from the east and north. He was 'prevented by the Spirit from speaking in Asia,' and driven across the sea against his intention to Neapolis, and hounded out

of Philippi and Thessalonica and Beræa; and turned
superciliously away from Athens; and so at last
found himself in Corinth, face to face with the tent-
maker from Rome and his wife. Then one of the two
men said, 'Let us join partnership together, and set
up here as tent-makers for a time.' What came out
of this unintended and apparently chance meeting?

The first thing was the conversion of Aquila and his
wife; and the effects of that are being realised by
them in heaven at this moment, and will go on to all
eternity.

So, in the infinite complexity of events, do not let us
worry ourselves by forecasting, but let us trust, and be
sure that the Hand which is pushing us is pushing us
in the right direction, and that He will bring us, by
a right, though a roundabout way, to the City of
Habitation. It seems to me that we, poor, blind
creatures in this world are somewhat like a man in
a prison, groping with his hand in the dark along the
wall, and all unawares touching a spring which moves
a stone, disclosing an aperture that lets in a breath of
purer air, and opens the way to freedom. So we go on
as if stumbling in the dark, and presently, without
our knowing what we do, by some trivial act we
originate a train of events which influences our whole
future.

Again, when Aquila and Priscilla reached Ephesus
they formed another chance acquaintance in the person of a brilliant young Alexandrian, whose name was
Apollos. They found that he had good intentions and
a good heart, but a head very scantily furnished with
the knowledge of the Gospel. So they took him in hand,
just as Paul had taken them. If I may use such a
phrase, they did not know how large a fish they had

caught. They had no idea what a mighty power for Christ was lying dormant in that young man from Alexandria who knew so much less than they did. They instructed Apollos, and Apollos became second only to Paul in the power of preaching the Gospel. So the circle widens and widens. God's grace fructifies from one man to another, spreading onward and outward. And all Apollos' converts, and *their* converts, and *theirs* again, right away down the ages, we may trace back to Priscilla and Aquila.

So do not let us be anxious about the further end of our deeds—viz. their results; but be careful about the nearer end of them—viz. their motives; and God will look after the other end. Seeing that 'thou knowest not which shall prosper, whether this or that,' or how much any of them will prosper, let us grasp *all* opportunities to do His will and glorify His name.

IV. Further, here we have an instance of the heroic self-devotion which love to Christ kindles.

'For my sake they laid down their own necks.' We do not know to what Paul is referring: perhaps to that tumult in Ephesus, where he certainly was in danger. But the language seems rather more emphatic than such danger would warrant. Probably it was at some perilous juncture of which we know nothing (for we know very little, after all, of the details of the Apostle's life), in which Aquila and Priscilla had said, 'Take us and let him go. He can do a great deal more for God than we can do. We will put our heads on the block, if he may still live.' That magnanimous self-surrender was a wonderful token of the passionate admiration and love which the Apostle inspired, but its deepest motive was love to Christ and not to Paul only.

Faith in Christ and love to Him ought to turn cowards into heroes, to destroy thoughts of self, and to make the utmost self-sacrifice natural, blessed, and easy.  We are not called upon to exercise heroism like Priscilla's and Aquila's, but there is as much heroism needed for persistently Christian life, in our prosaic daily circumstances, as has carried many a martyr to the block, and many a tremulous woman to the pyre. We can all be heroes; and if the love of Christ is in us, as it should be, we shall all be ready to 'yield ourselves living sacrifices, which is our reasonable service.'

Long years after, the Apostle, on the further edge of life, looked back over it all; and, whilst much had become dim, and some trusted friends had dropped away, like Demas, he saw these two, and waved them his last greeting before he turned to the executioner—'Salute Prisca and Aquila.'  Paul's Master is not less mindful of His friends' love, or less eloquent in the praise of their faithfulness, or less sure to reward them with the crown of glory.  'Whoso confesseth Me before men, him will I also confess before the angels in heaven.'


## TWO HOUSEHOLDS

'. . . Salute them which are of Aristobulus' household. 11. . . . Greet them that be of the household of Narcissus, which are in the Lord.'—ROMANS xvi. 10, 11.

THERE does not seem much to be got out of these two sets of salutations to two households in Rome; but if we look at them with eyes in our heads, and some sympathy in our hearts, I think we shall get lessons worth the treasuring.

In the first place, here are two sets of people, members of two different households, and that means mainly, if not exclusively, slaves. In the next place, in each case there was but a section of the household which was Christian. In the third place, in neither household is the master included in the greeting. So in neither case was *he* a Christian.

We do not know anything about these two persons, men of position evidently, who had large households. But the most learned of our living English commentators of the New Testament has advanced a very reasonable conjecture in regard to each of them. As to the first of them, Aristobulus: that wicked old King Herod, in whose life Christ was born, had a grandson of the name, who spent all his life in Rome, and was in close relations with the Emperor of that day. He had died some little time before the writing of this letter. As to the second of them, there is a very notorious Narcissus, who plays a great part in the history of Rome just a little while before Paul's period there, and he, too, was dead. And it is more than probable that the slaves and retainers of these two men were transferred in both cases to the emperor's household and held together in it, being known as Aristobulus' men and Narcissus' men. And so probably the Christians among them are the brethren to whom these salutations are sent.

Be that as it may, I think that if we look at the two groups, we shall get out of them some lessons.

I. The first of them is this: the penetrating power of Christian truth. Think of the sort of man that the master of the first household was, if the identification suggested be accepted. He is one of that foul Herodian

brood, in all of whom the bad Idumæan blood ran cor-
ruptly.   The grandson of the old Herod, the brother of
Agrippa of the Acts of the Apostles, the hanger-on of
the Imperial Court, with Roman vices veneered on his
native wickedness, was not the man to welcome the
entrance of a revolutionary ferment into his household; and yet through his barred doors had crept
quietly, he knowing nothing about it, that great
message of a loving God, and a Master whose service
was freedom.   And in thousands of like cases the
Gospel was finding its way underground, undreamed
of by the great and wise, but steadily pressing onwards,
and undermining all the towering grandeur that was
so contemptuous of it.   So Christ's truth spread at
first; and I believe that is the way it always spreads.
Intellectual revolutions begin at the top and filter
down; religious revolutions begin at the bottom and
rise; and it is always the 'lower orders' that are laid
hold of first.   'Ye see your calling, brethren, how that
not many wise men after the flesh, not many mighty,
not many noble are called,' but a handful of slaves in
Aristobulus' household, with this living truth lodged in
their hearts, were the bearers and the witnesses and
the organs of the power which was going to shatter
all that towered above it and despised it.   And so it
always is.

Do not let us be ashamed of a Gospel that has not
laid hold of the upper and the educated classes, but let
us feel sure of this, that there is no greater sign of
defective education and of superficial culture and of
inborn vulgarity than despising the day of small
things, and estimating truth by the position or the
intellectual attainments of the men that are its wit-

nesses and its lovers. The Gospel penetrated at first,
and penetrates still, in the fashion that is suggested
here.

II. Secondly, these two households teach us very
touchingly and beautifully the uniting power of Christian sympathy.

A considerable proportion of the first of these two
households would probably be Jews—if Aristobulus
were indeed Herod's grandson. The probability that
he was is increased by the greeting interposed between
those to the two households—'Salute Herodion.' The
name suggests some connection with Herod, and
whether we suppose the designation of 'my kinsman,'
which Paul gives him, to mean 'blood relation' or
'fellow countryman,' Herodion, at all events, was a
Jew by birth. As to the other members of these
households, Paul may have met some of them in his
many travels, but he had never been in Rome, and his
greetings are more probably sent to them as conspicuous sections, numerically, of the Roman Church,
and as tokens of his affection, though he had never
seen them. The possession of a common faith has
bridged the gulf between him and them. Slaves in
those days were outside the pale of human sympathy,
and almost outside the pale of human rights. And
here the foremost of Christian teachers, who was a
freeman born, separated from these poor people by a
tremendous chasm, stretches a brother's hand across it
and grasps theirs. The Gospel that came into the
world to rend old associations and to split up society,
and to make a deep cleft between fathers and children
and husband and wife, came also to more than counter-
balance its dividing effects by its uniting power. And
in that old world that was separated into classes by

gulfs deeper than any of which we have any experience, it, and it alone, threw a bridge across the abysses and bound men together. Think of what a revolution it must have been, when a master and his slave could sit down together at the table of the Lord and look each other in the face and say 'Brother,' and for the moment forget the difference of bond and free. Think of what a revolution it must have been when Jew and Gentile could sit down together at the table of the Lord, and forget circumcision and uncircumcision, and feel that they were all one in Jesus Christ. And as for the third of the great clefts—that, alas! which made so much of the tragedy and the wickedness of ancient life—viz. the separation between the sexes—think of what a revolution it was when men and women, in all purity of the new bond of Christian affection, could sit down together at the same table, and feel that they were brethren and sisters in Jesus Christ.

The uniting power of the common faith and the common love to the one Lord marked Christianity as altogether supernatural and new, unique in the world's experience, and obviously requiring something more than a human force to produce it. Will anybody say that the Christianity of this day has preserved and exhibits that primitive demonstration of its superhuman source? Is there anything obviously beyond the power of earthly motives in the unselfish, expansive love of modern Christians? Alas! alas! to ask the question is to answer it, and everybody knows the answer, and nobody sorrows over it. Is any duty more pressingly laid upon Christian churches of this generation than that, forgetting their doctrinal janglings for a while, and putting away their sectarianisms and narrowness, they should show the world that their faith has still

2 A

the power to do what it did in the old times, bridge over the gulf that separates class from class, and bring all men together in the unity of the faith and of the love of Jesus Christ? Depend upon it, unless the modern organisations of Christianity which call themselves 'churches' show themselves, in the next twenty years, a great deal more alive to the necessity, and a great deal more able to cope with the problem, of uniting the classes of our modern complex civilisation, the term of life of these churches is comparatively brief. And the form of Christianity which another century will see will be one which reproduces the old miracle of the early days, and reaches across the deepest clefts that separate modern society, and makes all one in Jesus Christ. It is all very well for us to glorify the ancient love of the early Christians, but there is a vast deal of false sentimentality about our eulogistic talk of it. It were better to praise it less and imitate it more. Translate it into present life, and you will find that to-day it requires what it nineteen hundred years ago was recognised as manifesting, the presence of something more than human motive, and something more than man discovers of truth. The cement must be divine that binds men thus together.

Again, these two households suggest for us the tranquillising power of Christian resignation.

They were mostly slaves, and they continued to be slaves when they were Christians. Paul recognised their continuance in the servile position, and did not say a word to them to induce them to break their bonds. The Epistle to the Corinthians treats the whole subject of slavery in a very remarkable fashion. It says to the slave: 'If you were a slave when you became a Christian, stop where you are. If you have an opportunity of being free, avail yourself of it; if you have not, never mind.' And then it adds this great principle: 'He that is called in the Lord, being a slave, is Christ's freeman. Likewise he that is called, being free, is Christ's slave.' The Apostle applies the very same principle, in the adjoining verses, to the distinction between circumcision and uncircumcision. From all which there comes just the same lesson that is taught us by these two households of slaves left intact by Christianity—viz. that where a man is conscious of a direct, individual relation to Jesus Christ, that makes all outward circumstances infinitely insignificant. Let us get up to the height, and they all become very small. Of course, the principles of Christianity killed slavery, but it took eighteen hundred years to do it. Of course, there is no blinking the fact that slavery was an essentially immoral and unchristian institution. But it is one thing to lay down principles and leave them to be worked in and then to be worked out, and it is another thing to go blindly charging at existing institutions and throwing them down by violence, before men have grown up to feel that they are wicked. And so the New Testament takes the wise course, and leaves the foolish one to foolish people. It makes the tree good, and then its fruit will be good.

But the main point that I want to insist upon is this: what was good for these slaves in Rome is good for you and me. Let us get near to Jesus Christ, and feel that we have got hold of His hand for our own selves, and we shall not mind very much about the possible varieties of human condition. Rich or poor, happy or sad, surrounded by companions or treading a solitary path, failures or successes as the world has it, strong or broken and weak and wearied—all these varieties, important as they are, come to be very small when we can say, 'We are the Lord's.' That amulet makes all things tolerable; and the Christian submission which is the expression of our love to, and confidence in, His infinite sweetness and unerring goodness, raises us to a height from which the varieties of earthly condition seem to blend and melt into one. When we are down amongst the low hills, it seems a long way from the foot of one of them to the top of it; but when we are on the top they all melt into one dead level, and you cannot tell which is top and which is bottom. And so, if we only can rise high enough up the hill, the possible diversities of our condition will seem to be very small variations in the level.

III. Lastly, these two groups suggest to us the conquering power of Christian faithfulness.

The household of Herod's grandson was not a very likely place to find Christian people in, was it? Such flowers do not often grow, or at least do not easily grow, on such dunghills. And in both these cases it was only a handful of the people, a portion of each household, that was Christian. So they had beside them, closely identified with them—working, perhaps, at the same tasks, I might almost say, chained with the same chains —men who had no share in their faith or in their love. It would not be easy to pray and love and trust God and do His will, and keep clear of complicity with idolatry and immorality and sin, in such a pigsty as that; would it? But these men did it. And nobody need ever say, 'I am in such circumstances that I cannot live a Christian life.' There are no such circumstances, at least none of God's appointing. There are often such that we bring upon ourselves, and then the best thing is to get out of them as soon as we can.  But as far as He is concerned, He never puts anybody anywhere where he cannot live a holy life.

There were no difficulties too great for these men to overcome; there are no difficulties too great for us to overcome.  And wherever you and I may be, we cannot be in any place where it is so hard to live a consistent life as these people were.  Young men in warehouses, people in business here in Manchester, some of us with unfortunate domestic or relative associations, and so on—we may all feel as if it would be so much easier for us if this, that, and the other thing were changed. No, it would not be any easier; and perhaps the harder the easier, because the more obviously the atmosphere is poisonous, the more we shall put some cloth over our mouths to prevent it from getting into our lungs. The dangerous place is the place where the vapours that poison are scentless as well as invisible.  But whatever be the difficulties, there is strength waiting for us, and we may all win the praise which the Apostle gives to another of these Roman brethren, whom he salutes as 'Apelles, approved in Christ'—a man that had been 'tried' and had stood his trial.  So in our various spheres of difficulty and of temptation we may feel that the greeting from heaven, like Paul's message to the slaves in Rome, comes to us with good cheer, and that the Master Himself sees us, sympathises with us, salutes us, and stretches out His hand to help and to keep us.

# TRYPHENA AND TRYPHOSA

'Salute Tryphena and Tryphosa, who labour in the Lord.'—ROMANS xvi. 12.

THE number of salutations to members of the Roman Church is remarkable when we take into account that Paul had never visited it. The capital drew all sorts of people to it, and probably there had been personal inter-course between most of the persons here mentioned and the Apostle in some part of his wandering life. He not only displays his intimate knowledge of the persons saluted, but his beautiful delicacy and in-genuity in the varying epithets applied to them shows how in his great heart and tenacious memory individuals had a place. These shadowy saints live for ever by Paul's brief characterisation of them, and stand out to us almost as clearly and as sharply distinguished as they did to him.

These two, Tryphena and Tryphosa, were probably sisters. That is rendered likely by their being coupled together here, as well as by the similarity of their names. These names mean luxurious, or delicate, and no doubt expressed the ideal for their daughters which the parents had had, and possibly indicate the kind of life from which these two women had come. We can scarcely fail to note the contrast between the meaning of their names and the Christian lives they had lived. Two dainty women, probably belonging to a class in which a delicate withdrawal from effort and toil was thought to be the woman's distinctive mark, had fled from luxury, which often tended to be volup-tuous, and was always self-indulgent, and had chosen the better part of 'labour in the Lord.' They had become untrue to their names, because they must be true to their Master and themselves. We may well

take the lesson that lies here, and is eminently needful
to-day amidst the senseless, and often sinful, tide of
luxury which runs so strongly as to threaten the great
and eternal Christian principle of self-denial.

The first thing that strikes us in looking at these
salutations is the illustration which it gives of the
uniting power of a common faith. Tryphena and
Tryphosa were probably Roman ladies of some social
standing, and their names may indicate that they at
least inherited a tendency to exclusiveness; yet here
they occur immediately after the household of Narcissus
and in close connection with that of Aristobulus, both
of which are groups of slaves. Aristobulus was a
grandson of Herod the Great, and Narcissus was a well-
known freedman, whose slaves at his death would
probably become the property of the Emperor. Other
common slave names are those of Ampliatus and
Urbanus; and here in these lists they stand side by
side with persons of some distinction in the Roman
world, and with men and women of widely differing
nationalities. The Church of Rome would have seemed
to any non-Christian observer a motley crowd in which
racial distinctions, sex, and social conditions had all
been swept away by the rising tide of a common
fanaticism. In it was exemplified in actual operation
Paul's great principle that in Christ Jesus 'there is
neither Jew nor Greek, male nor female, bond nor
free, but in Him all are one.' Roman society in that
day, as Juvenal shows us, was familiar with the level-
ling and uniting power of common vice and immorality,
and the few sternly patriotic Romans who were left
lamented that 'the Orontes flowed into the Tiber'; but
such common wallowing in filth led to no real unity,
whereas, in the obscure corner of the great city where

there were members of the infant Church gathered together, there was the beginning of a common life in the one Lord which lifted each participant of it out of the dreary solitude of individuality, and imparted to each heart the tingling consciousness of oneness with all who held the one faith in the one Lord and had received the one baptism in the one Name. That fair dawn has been shadowed by many clouds, and the churches of to-day, however they may have developed doctrine, may look back with reproach and shame to the example of Rome, where Tryphena and Tryphosa, with all their inherited, fastidious delicacy, recognised in the household of Aristobulus and the household of Narcissus 'brethren in the Lord,' and were as glad to welcome Jews, Asiatics, Persians, and Greeks, as Romans of the bluest blood, into the family of Christ. The Romish Church of our day has lost its early grace of welcoming all who love the one Lord into its fellow-ship; and we of the Protestant churches have been but too swift to learn the bad lesson of forbidding all who follow not with us.

Another thought which may be suggested by Tryphena and Tryphosa is the blessed hallowing of natural family relations by common faith. They were probably sisters, or, at all events, as their names indicate, near relatives, and to them that faith must have been doubly precious because they shared it with each other. None of the trials to which the early Christians were exposed was more severe than the necessity which their Christianity so often imposed upon them of breaking the sacred family ties. It saddened even Christ's heart to think that He had come to rend families in sunder, and to make 'a man's foes them of his own household'; and we can little imagine how bitter the pang must have been when family love had to be cast aside at the bidding of allegiance to Him.

But though the stress of that separation between those most nearly related in blood by reason of unshared faith is alleviated in this day, it still remains; and that is but a feeble Christian life which does not feel that it is drawing a heart from closest human embraces and constituting a barrier between it and the dearest of earth. There is still need in these days of relaxed Christian sentiment for the stern austerity of the law, 'He that loveth father or mother more than Me is not worthy of Me'; and there are many Christian souls who would be infinitely stronger and more mature, if they did not yield to the seductions of family affections which are not rooted in Jesus Christ. But still, though our faith ought to be far more than it often is, the determining element in our affections and associations, its noblest work is not to separate but to unite; and whilst it often must divide, it is meant to draw more closely together hearts that are already knit by earthly love. Its legitimate effect is to make all earthly sweetnesses sweeter, all holy bonds more holy and more binding, to infuse a new constraint and preciousness into all earthly relationships, to make brothers tenfold more brotherly and sisters more sisterly. The heart, in which the deepest devotion is yielded to Jesus Christ, has its capacity for devotion infinitely increased, and they who, looking into each other's faces, see reflected there something of the Lord whom they both love, love each other all the more because they love Him most, and in their love to Him, and His to them, have found a new measure for all their affection. They who, looking on their dear ones, can 'trust they live in God,' will there find them ' worthier to be loved,' and will there find a new power of loving them. Tryphena and Tryphosa were more sisterly than ever when they clung to their Elder Brother. 'There is no man that hath left brethren, or sisters, or mother, or father, for My sake, but he shall receive a hundredfold more in this time, brethren, and sisters, and mothers, and in the world to come eternal life.'

The contrast between the names of these two Roman ladies and the characterisation of their 'labour in the Lord' may suggest to us the most formidable foe of Christian earnestness. Their names, as we have already noticed, point to a state of society in which the parents' ideal for their daughters was dainty luxuriousness and a withdrawal from the rough and tumble of common life; but these two women, magnetised by the love of Jesus, had turned their backs on the parental ideal, and had cast themselves earnestly into a life of toil. That ideal was never more formidably antagonistic to the vigour of Christian life than it is to-day. Rome, in Paul's time, was not more completely honeycombed with worldliness than England is to-day; and the English churches are not far behind the English 'world' in their paralysing love of luxury and self-indulgence. In all ages, earnest Christians have had to take up the same vehement remonstrance against the tendency of the average Christian to let his religious life be weakened by the love of the world and the things of the world. The protests against growing luxury have been a commonplace in all ages of the Church; but, surely, there has never been a time when it has reached a more senseless, sinful, and destroying height than in our day. The rapid growth of wealth, with no capacity of using it nobly, which modern commerce has brought, has immensely influenced all our churches for evil. It is so

hard for us, aggregated in great cities, to live our own
lives, and the example of our class has such immense
power over us that it is very hard to pursue the path
of 'plain living and high thinking' in communities,
all classes of which are more and more yielding to
the temptation to ostentation, so-called comfort, and
extravagant expenditure; and that this is a danger—
we are tempted to say *the* danger—to the purity,
loftiness, and vigour of religious life among us, he must
be blind who cannot see, and he must be strangely
ignorant of his own life who cannot feel that it is the
danger for him. I believe that for one professing
Christian whose earnestness is lost by reason of intellectual doubts, or by some grave sin, there are a
hundred from whom it simply oozes away unnoticed,
like wind out of a bladder, so that what was once round
and full becomes limp and flaccid. If Demas begins
with loving the present world, it will not be long before
he finds a reason for departing from Paul.

We may take these two sisters, finally, as pointing
for us the true victory over this formidable enemy.
They had turned resolutely away from the heathen
ideal enshrined in their names to a life of real hard toil,
as is distinctly implied by the word used by the Apostle.
What that toil consisted in we do not know, and need
not inquire; but the main point to be noted is that their
'labour' was 'in the Lord.' That union with Christ
makes labour for Him a necessity, and makes it
possible. 'The labour we delight in physics pain';
and if we are in Him, we shall not only 'live in Him,'
but all our work begun, continued, and ended in Him,
will in Him and by Him be accepted. There is no
victorious antagonist of worldly ease and self-indulgence
comparable to the living consciousness of union with

Jesus and His life in us. To dwell in the swamps at the bottom of the mountain is to live in a region where effort is impossible and malaria weakens vitality; to climb the heights brings bracing to the limbs and a purer air into the expanding lungs, and makes work delightsome that would have been labour down below. If we are 'in the Lord,' He is our atmosphere, and we can draw from Him full draughts of a noble life in which we shall not need the stimulus of self-interest or worldly success to use it to the utmost in acts of service to Him. They who live in the Lord will labour in the Lord, and they who labour in the Lord will rest in the Lord.

## PERSIS

'Salute the beloved Persis, who laboured much in the Lord.'—ROMANS xvi. 12.

THERE are a great number of otherwise unknown Christians who pass for a moment before our view in this chapter. Their characterisations are like the slight outlines in the background of some great artist's canvas: a touch of the brush is all that is spared for each, and yet, if we like to look sympathetically, they live before us. Now, this good woman, about whom we never hear again, and for whom these few words are all her epitaph—was apparently, judging by her name, of Persian descent, and possibly had been brought to Rome as a slave. At all events, finding herself there, she had somehow or other become connected with the Church in that city, and had there distinguished herself by continuous and faithful Christian toil which had won the affection of the Apostle, though he had never seen her, and knew no more about her. That is all. She comes into the

foreground for a moment, and then she vanishes.
What does she say to us?

First of all, like the others named by Paul, she helps us
to understand, by her living example, that wonderful,
new, uniting process that was carried on by means of
Christianity. The simple fact of a Persian woman
getting a loving message from a Jew, the woman being
in Rome and the Jew in Corinth, and the message
being written in Greek, brings before us a whole group
of nationalities all fused together. They had been
hammered together, or, if you like it better, chained
together, by Roman power, but they were melted together by Christ's Gospel. This Eastern woman and
this Jewish man, and the many others whose names and
different nationalities pass in a flash before us in this
chapter, were all brought together in Jesus Christ.

If we run our eye over these salutations, what
strikes one, even at the first sight, is the very small
number of Jewish names; only one certain, and
another doubtful. Four or five names are Latin, and
then all the rest are Greek, but this woman seemingly
came from further east than any of them. There
they all were, forgetting the hostile nationalities to
which they belonged, because they had found One
who had brought them into one great community.
We talk about the uniting influence of Christianity,
but when we see the process going on before us, in a
case like this, we begin to understand it better.

But another point may be noticed in regard to this
uniting process—how it brought into action the purest
and truest love as a bond that linked men. There
are four or five of the people commended in this
chapter of whom the Apostle has nothing to say but
that they are beloved. This is the only woman to

whom he applies that term. And notice his instinctive
delicacy: when he is speaking of men he says, '*My
beloved*'; when he is greeting Persis he says, '*the
beloved*,' that there may be no misunderstanding
about the 'my'—'the beloved Persis which laboured
much in the Lord'—indicating, by one delicate touch,
the loftiness, the purity, and truly Christian character
of the bond that held them together. And that is no
true Church, where anything but that is the bond—
the love that knits us to one another, because we believe that each is knit to the dear Lord and fountain
of all love.

What more does this good woman say to us? She is
an example living and breathing there before us, of
what a woman may be in God's Church. Paul had
never been in Rome; no Apostle, so far as we know,
had had anything to do with the founding of the
Church. The most important Church in the Roman
Empire, and the Church which afterwards became the
curse of Christendom, was founded by some anonymous
Christians, with no commission, with no supervision,
with no officials amongst them, but who just had the
grace of God in their hearts, and found themselves in
Rome, and could not help speaking about Jesus Christ.
God helped them, and a little Church sprang into
being. And the great abundance of salutations here,
and the honourable titles which the Apostle gives to
the Christians of whom he speaks, and many of whom
he signalises as having done great service, are a kind
of certificate on his part to the vigorous life which,
without any apostolic supervision or official direction,
had developed itself there in that Church.

Now, it is to be noticed that this striking form of
eulogium which is attached to our Persis she shares in

common with others in the group. And it is to be
further noticed that all those who are, as it were,
decorated with this medal—on whom Paul bestows
this honour of saying that they had 'laboured,' or
'laboured much in the Lord,' are women that stand
alone in the list. There are several other women in
it, but they are all coupled with men—husbands or
brothers, or some kind of relative. But there are
three sets of women, I do not say single women, but
three sets of women, standing singly in the list, and it
is about them, and them only, that Paul says they
'laboured,' or 'laboured much.' There is a Mary who
stands alone, and she 'bestowed much labour on' Paul
and others. Then there are, in the same verse as my
text, two sisters, Tryphena and Tryphosa, whose names
mean 'the luxurious.' And the Apostle seems to think,
as he writes the two names, that spoke of self-
indulgence: 'Perhaps these rightly described these
two women once, but they do not now. In the bad
old days, before they were Christians, they may have
been rightly named luxurious-living. But here is their
name now, the luxurious is turned into the self-sacrific-
ing worker, and the two sisters "labour in the Lord."'
Then comes our friend Persis, who also stands alone;
and she shares in the honour that only these other
two companies of women share with her. She
'laboured much in the Lord.' In that little community, without any direction from Apostles and
authorised teachers, the brethren and sisters had
every one found their tasks; and these solitary women,
with nobody to say to them, 'Go and do this or that,'
had found out for themselves, or rather had been
taught by the Spirit of Jesus, what they had to do,
and they worked at it with a will. There are many

things that Christian women can do a great deal better than men, and we are not to forget that this modern talk about the emancipation of women has its roots here in the New Testament. We are not to forget either that prerogative means obligation, and that the elevation of woman means the laying upon her of solemn duties to perform. I wonder how many of the women members of our Churches and congregations deserve such a designation as that? We hear a great deal about 'women's rights' nowadays. I wish some of my friends would lay a little more to heart than they do, 'women's duties.'

And now, lastly, the final lesson that I draw from this eulogium of an otherwise altogether unknown woman is that she is a model of Christian service.

First, in regard to its measure. She 'laboured much in the Lord.' Now, both these two words, 'laboured' and 'much,' are extremely emphatic. The word rightly translated 'laboured' will appear in its full force if I recall to you a couple of other places in which it is employed in the New Testament. You remember that touching incident about our Lord when, being *wearied with His journey, He sat thus on the well.' 'Wearied'* is the same word as is here used. Then, you remember how the Apostle, after he had been hauling empty nets all night in the little, wet, dirty fishing-boat, said, perhaps with a yawn, 'Master, we have *toiled* all the night and caught nothing.' He uses the same word as is employed here. Such is the sort of work that these women had done—work carried to the point of exhaustion, work up to the very edge of their powers, work unsparing and continuous, and not done once in some flash of evanescent enthusiasm, but all through a dreary night, in spite of apparent failures.

*There* is the measure of service. Many of us seem to think that if we say 'I am tired,' that is a reason for not doing anything. Sometimes it is, no doubt; and no man has a right so to labour as to impair his capacity for future labour, but subject to that condition I do not know that the plea of fatigue is a sufficient reason for idleness. And I am quite sure that the true example for us is the example of Him who, when He was most wearied, sitting on the well, was so invigorated and refreshed by the opportunity of winning another soul that, when His disciples came back to Him, they looked at His fresh strength with astonishment, and said to themselves, 'Has any man brought Him anything to eat?' Ay, what He had to eat was work that He finished for the Father, and some of us know that the truest refreshment in toil is a change of toil. It is almost as good to shift the load on to the other shoulder, or to take a stick into the other hand, as it is to put away the load altogether. Oh, the careful limits which Christian people nowadays set to their work for Jesus! They are not afraid of being tired in their pursuit of business or pleasure, but in regard to Christ's work they will let anything go to wrack and ruin rather than that they should turn a hair, by persevering efforts to prevent it. Work to the limit of power if you live in the light of blessedness.

She 'laboured much in the Lord,' or, as Jesus Christ said about the other woman who was blamed by the people that did not love enough to understand the blessedness of self-sacrifice, 'she had done what she could.' It was an apology for the form of Mary's service, but it was a stringent demand as to its amount. 'What she could'—not *half* of what she could; not

2 B

what she *conveniently* could. That is the measure of acceptable service.

Then, still further, may we not learn from Persis the spring of all true Christian work? She 'laboured much in the Lord,' because she *was* 'in Him,' and in union with Him there came to her power and desire to do things which, without that close fellowship, she neither would have desired nor been able to do. It is vain to try to whip up Christian people to forms of service by appealing to lower motives. There is only one motive that will last, and bring out from us all that is in us to do, and that is the appeal to our sense of union and communion with Jesus Christ, and the exhortation to live in Him, and then we shall work in Him. If you link the spindles in your mill, or the looms in your weaving-shed, with the engine, they will go. It is of no use to try to turn them by hand. You will only spoil the machinery, and it will be poor work that you will get off them.

So, dear brethren, be 'in the Lord.' That is the secret of service, and the closer we come to Him, and the more continuously, moment by moment, we realise our individual dependence upon Him, and our union with Him, the more will our lives effloresce and blossom into all manner of excellence and joyful service, and nothing else that Christian people are whipped up to do, from lower and more vulgar motives than that, will. It may be of a certain kind of inferior value, but it is far beneath the highest beauty of Christian service, nor will its issues reach the loftiest point of usefulness to which even our poor service may attain.

Persis seems to me to suggest, too, the safeguard of work. Ah, if she had not 'laboured in the Lord,' and

been 'in the Lord' whilst she was labouring, she
would very soon have stopped work.  Our Christian
work, however pure its motive when we begin it, has
in itself the tendency to become mechanical, and to
be done from lower motives than those from which it
was begun.  That is true about a man in my position.
It is true about all of us, in our several ways of trying
to serve our dear Lord and Master.  Unless we make
a conscience of continually renewing our communion
with Him, and getting our feet once more firmly upon
the rock, we shall certainly in our Christian work,
having begun in the spirit, continue in the flesh, and
before we know where we are, we shall be doing work
from habit, because we did it yesterday at this hour,
because people expect it of us, because A, B, or C
does it, or for a hundred other reasons, all of which
are but too familiar to us by experience.  They are
sure to slip in; they change the whole character of the
work, and they harm the workers.  The only way
by which we can keep the garland fresh is by continually dipping it in the fountain.  The only way by
which we can keep our Christian work pure, useful,
worthy of the Master, is by seeing to it that our
work itself does not draw us away from our fellowship
with Him.  And the more we have to do, the more
needful is it that we should listen to Christ's voice
when He says to us, 'Come ye yourselves apart with
Me into a solitary place, and there renew your communion with Me.'

The last lesson about our work which I draw from
Persis is the unexpected immortality of true Christian
service.  How Persis would have opened her eyes if
anybody had told her that nearly 1900 years after
she lived, people in a far-away barbarous island would

be sitting thinking about her, as you and I are doing now! How astonished she would have been if it had been said to her, 'Now, Persis, wheresoever in the whole world the Gospel is preached, your name and your work and your epitaph will go with it, and as long as men know about Jesus Christ, your and their Master, they will know about you, His humble servant.' Well, we shall not have our names in that fashion in men's memories, but Jesus will have your name and mine, if we do His work as this woman did it, in *His* memory. 'I will never forget any of their works.' And if we—self-forgetful to the limit of our power, and as the joyful result of our personal union with that Saviour who has done everything for us—try to live for His praise and glory in any fashion, then be sure of this, that our poor deeds are as immortal as Him for whom they are done, and that we may take to ourselves the great word which He has spoken, when He has declared that at the last He will confess His confessors' names before the angels in heaven. Blessed are the living that 'live in the Lord'; blessed are the workers that work 'in the Lord,' for when they come to be the dead that 'die in the Lord' and rest from their labours, their works shall follow them.

## A CRUSHED SNAKE

'The God of peace shall bruise Satan under your feet shortly.'—ROMANS xvi. 20.

THERE are three other Scriptural sayings which may have been floating in the Apostle's mind when he penned this triumphant assurance. 'Thou shalt bruise

his head'; the great first Evangel—we are to be
endowed with Christ's power; 'The lion and the adder
thou shalt trample under foot'—all the strength that
was given to ancient saints is ours; 'Behold! I give
you power to tread on serpents and scorpions, and
over all the power of the enemy'—the charter of the
seventy is the perennial gift to the Church. Echoing
all these great words, Paul promises the Roman
Christians that 'the God of peace shall bruise Satan
under your feet shortly.' Now, when any special
characteristic is thus ascribed to God, as when He is
called 'the God of patience' or 'the God of hope,' in
the preceding chapter, the characteristic selected has
some bearing on the prayer or promise following. For
example, this same designation, 'the God of peace,'
united with the other, 'that brought again from the
dead the Lord Jesus, that great Shepherd of the sheep,'
is laid as the foundation of the prayer for the perfecting of the readers of the Epistle to the Hebrews in
every good work. It is, then, because of that great
name that the Apostle is sure, and would have his
Roman brethren to be sure, that Satan shall shortly
be bruised under their feet. No doubt there may have
been some reference in Paul's mind to what he had
just said about those who caused divisions in the
Church; but, if there is such reference, it is of secondary
importance. Paul is gazing on all the great things in
God which make Him the God of peace, and in them
all he sees ground for the confident hope that His
power will be exerted to crush all the sin that breaks
His children's peace.

Now the first thought suggested by these words is
the solemn glimpse given of the struggle that goes on
in every Christian soul.

Two antagonists are at hand-grips in every one of us. On the one hand, the 'God of peace,' on the other, 'Satan.' If you believe in the personality of the One, do not part with the belief in the personality of the other. If you believe that a divine power and Spirit is ready to help and strengthen you, do not think so lightly of the enemies that are arrayed against you as to falter in the belief that there *is* a great personal Power, rooted in evil, who is warring against each of us. Ah, brethren! we live far too much on the surface, and we neither go down deep enough to the dark source of the Evil, nor rise high enough to the radiant Fountain of the Good. It is a shallow life that strikes that antagonism of God and Satan out of itself. And though the belief in a personal tempter has got to be very unfashionable nowadays, I am going to venture to say that you may measure accurately the vitality and depth of a man's religion by the emphasis with which he grasps the thought of that great antagonism. There is a star of light, and there is a star of darkness; and they revolve, as it were, round one centre.

But whilst, on the one hand, our Christianity is made shallow in proportion as we ignore this solemn reality, on the other hand, it is sometimes paralysed and perverted by our misunderstanding of it. For, notice, 'the God of peace shall bruise Satan *under your feet.*' Yes, it is God that bruises, but He uses our feet to do it. It is God from whom the power comes, but the power works through us, and we are neither merely the field, nor merely the prize, of the conflict between these two, but we ourselves have to put all our pith into the task of keeping down the flat, speckled head that has the poison gland in it. 'The God of peace'— blessed be His Name—'shall bruise Satan under your feet,' but it will need the tension of your muscles, and the downward force of your heel, if the wriggling reptile is to be kept under.

Turn, now, to the other thought that is here, the promise and pledge of victory in the name, the God of peace. I have already referred to two similar designations of God in the previous chapter, and if we take them in union with this one in our text, what a wonderfully beautiful and strengthening threefold view of that divine nature do we get! 'The God of patience and consolation' is the first of the linked three. It heads the list, and blessed is it that it does, because, after all, sorrow makes up a very large proportion of the experience of us all, and what most men seem to themselves to need most is a God that will bear their sorrows with them and help them to bear, and a God that will comfort them. But, supposing that He has been made known thus as the source of endurance and the God of all consolation, He becomes 'the God of hope,' for a dark background flings up a light foreground, and a comforted sorrow patiently endured is mighty to produce a radiant hope. The rising of the muddy waters of the Nile makes the heavy crops of 'corn in Egypt.'. So the name 'the God of hope' fitly follows the name 'the God of patience and consolation.'

Then we come to the name in my text, built perhaps on the other two, or at least reminiscent of them, and recalling them, 'the God of peace,' who, through patience and consolation, through hope, and through many another gift, breathes the benediction of His own great tranquillity and unruffled calm over our agitated, distracted, sinful hearts. In connection with one of those previous designations to which I have referred, the Apostle has a prayer very different in form from this, but identical in substance, when he says 'the God of hope fill you with all joy and peace in believing.' Is not that closely allied to the promise of my text, 'The God of peace shall bruise Satan under your feet shortly'? Is there any surer way of 'bruising Satan' under a man's feet than filling him 'with joy and peace in believing'? What can the Devil do to that man? If his soul is saturated, and his capacities filled, with that pure honey of divine joy, will he have any taste for the coarse dainties, the leeks and the garlic, that the Devil offers him? Is there any surer way of delivering a man from the temptations of his own baser nature, and the solicitations of this busy intrusive world round about him, than to make him satisfied with the goodness of the Lord, and conscious in his daily experience of 'all joy and peace'? Fill the vessel with wine, and there is no room for baser liquors or for poison. I suppose that the way by which you and I, dear friends, will most effectually conquer any temptations, is by falling back on the superior sweetness of divine joys. When we live upon manna we do not crave onions. So He 'will bruise Satan under your feet' by giving that which will arm your hearts against all his temptations and all his weapons. Blessed be God for the way of conquest, which is the possession of a supremer good!

But then, notice how beautifully too this name, 'the God of peace,' comes in to suggest that even in the strife there may be tranquillity. I remember in an old church in Italy a painting of an Archangel with his foot on the dragon's neck, and his sword thrust through its scaly armour. It is perhaps the feebleness of the artist's hand, but I think rather it is the clearness of his insight, which has led him to represent the victorious angel, in the moment in which he is slaying the dragon, as with a smile on his face, and not the least trace of effort in the arm, which is so easily smiting the fatal blow. Perhaps if the painter could have used his brush better he would have put more expression into the attitude and the face, but I think it is better as it is. We, too, may achieve a conquest over the dragon which, although it requires effort, does not disturb peace. There is a possibility of bruising that slippery head under my foot, and yet not having to strain myself in the process. We may have 'peace subsisting at the heart of endless agitation.' Do you remember how the Apostle, in another place, gives us the same beautiful—though at first sight contradictory—combination when he says, 'The peace of God shall garrison your heart'?

> 'My soul! there is a country
> Far, far beyond the stars,
> Where stands an armed sentry,
> All skilful in the wars.'

And her name is Peace, as the poet goes on to tell us. Ah, brethren! if we lived nearer the Lord, we should find it more possible to 'fight the good fight of faith,' and yet to have 'our feet shod with the preparedness of the gospel of peace.'

'The God of peace shall bruise Satan under your feet'; and in bruising He will give you His peace to do it, and His peace in doing it, and in still greater measure after doing it. For every struggle of the Christian soul adds something to the subsequent depth of its tranquillity. And so the name of the God of peace is our pledge of victory in, and of deepened peace after, our warfare with sin and temptation.

Lastly, note the swiftness with which Paul expects that this process shall be accomplished.

I dare say that he was thinking about the coming of the Lord, when all the fighting and struggle would be over, and that when he said 'God shall bruise him under your feet shortly,' there lay in the back of his mind the thought, 'the Lord is at hand.' But be that as it may, there is another way of looking at the words. They are not in the least like our experience, are they? 'Shortly!'—and here am I, a Christian man for the last half century perhaps; and have I got much further on in my course? Have I brought the sin that used to trouble me much down, and is my character much more noble, Christ-like, than it was long years ago? Would other people say that it is? Instead of 'shortly' we ought to put 'slowly' for the most of us. But, dear friend, the ideal is swift conquest, and it is our fault and our loss, if the reality is sadly different.

There are a great many evils that, unless they are conquered suddenly, have very small chance of ever being conquered at all. You never heard of a man being cured of his love of intoxicating drink, for instance, by a gradual process. The serpent's life is not crushed out of it by gradual pressure, but by one vigorous stamp of a nervous heel.

But if my experience as a Christian man does not enable me to set to my seal that this text is true, the text itself will tell me why. It is 'the God of peace' that is going to 'bruise Satan.' Do you keep yourself in touch with Him, dear friend? And do you let His powers come uninterruptedly and continuously into your spirit and life? It is sheer folly and self-delusion to wonder that the medicine does not work as quickly as was promised, if you do not take the medicine. The

slow process by which, at the best, many Christian
people 'bruise Satan under their feet,' during which
he hurts their heels more than they hurt his head, is
mainly due to their breaking the closeness and the
continuity of their communion with God in Jesus
Christ.

. But, after all, it is Heaven's chronology that we have
to do with here. 'Shortly,' and it will be 'shortly,' if
we reckon by heavenly scales of duration. Weeping
may endure for a night, but joy cometh in the morning.' 'The Lord will help her, and that right early.'
'The Lord is at hand.' When we get yonder, ah! how
all the long years of fighting will have dwindled down,
and we shall say 'the Lord did help me, and that right
early,' and though there may have been more than
threescore years and ten of fighting, that, while we
were in the thick of it, did not seem to come to much,
we shall then look back and say: 'Yes, Lord, it was but
for a moment, and it has brought me to the undying
day of Eternal Peace.'


## TERTIUS

'I, Tertius, who write the epistle, salute you in the Lord.'—ROMANS xvi. 22 (R.V.).

ONE sometimes sees in old religious pictures, in some
obscure corner, a tiny kneeling figure, the portrait of
the artist. So Tertius here gets leave to hold the pen
for a moment on his own account, and from Corinth
sends his greeting to his unknown brethren in Rome.
Apparently he was a stranger to them, and needed to
introduce himself. He is never heard of before or
since. For one brief moment he is visible, like a star
of a low magnitude, shining out for a moment be-

tween two banks of darkness and then swallowed up.
Judging by his name, he was probably a Roman, and
possibly had some connection with Italy, but clearly
was a stranger to the Church in Rome. We do not
know whether he was a resident in Corinth, where he
wrote this epistle, or one of Paul's travelling companions. Probably he was the former, as his name
never recurs in any of Paul's letters. One can understand the impulse which led him for one moment to
come out of obscurity and to take up personal relations with those who had so long enjoyed his pen. He
would fain float across the deep gulf of alienation a
thread of love which looked like gossamer, but has
proved to be stronger than centuries and revolutions.

This humble and modest greeting is an expression of a sentiment which the world may smile at,
but which, being 'in the Lord,' partakes of immortality. No doubt the world's hate drove more closely
together all the disciples in primitive times; but the
yearning of Tertius for some little corner in the love
of his Roman brethren might well influence us to-day.
There ought to be an effort of imagination going out towards unknown brethren. Christian love is not meant
to be kept within the limits of sight and personal
knowledge; it should overleap the narrow bounds of
the communities to which we belong, and expatiate
over the whole wide field. The great Shepherd has
prescribed for us the limits to the very edge of which
our Christian love should consciously go forth; and
has rebuked the narrowness to which we are prone,
when He has said, 'Other sheep I have which are not
of this fold.' We are all too prone to let identities of
opinion and of polity, or even the accident of locality,
set bounds to our consciousness of brotherhood; and

the example of this little gush of affection, that
reaches out a hand across the ocean and grasps the
hands of unknown partakers in the common life of
the one Lord, may well shame us out of our narrowness, and quicken us into a wide perception and
deepened feeling towards all who in every place call
up Jesus Christ as their Lord—'both their Lord and
ours.'

Another lesson which we may learn from Tertius'
characterisation of himself is the dignity of subordinate work towards a great end. His office as amanuensis
was very humble, but it was quite as necessary as
Paul's inspired fervour. It is to him that we owe our
possession of the Epistle; it is to him that Paul owed
it that he was able to record in imperishable words
the thoughts that welled up in his mind, and would
have been lost if Tertius had not been at his side. The
power generated in the boilers does its work through
machines of which each little cog-wheel is as indispensable as the great shafts. Members of the body
which seem to be 'more feeble, are necessary.' Every
note in a great concerted piece of music, and every
instrument, down to the triangle and the little drum
in the great orchestra, is necessary. This lesson of
the dignity of subordinate work needs to be laid to
heart both by those who think themselves to be
capable of more important service, and by those who
have to recognise that the less honourable tasks are
all for which they are fit. To the former it may preach
humility, the latter it may encourage. We are all
very ignorant of what is great and what is small in
the matter of our Christian service, and we have
sometimes to look very closely and to clear away a
great many vulgar misconceptions before we can

clearly discriminate between mites and talents. 'We know not which may prosper, whether this or that'; and in our ignorance of what it may please God to bring out of any service faithfully rendered to Him, we had better not be too sure that true service is ever small, or that the work that attracts attention and is christened by men 'great' is really so in His eyes. It is well to have the noble ambition to 'desire earnestly the greater gifts,' but it is better to 'follow the more excellent way,' and to seek after the love which knows nothing of great or small, and without which prophecy and the knowledge of all mysteries, and all conspicuous and all the shining qualities profit nothing.

We can discern in Tertius' words a little touch of what we may call pride in his work. No doubt he knew it to be subordinate, but he also knew it to be needful; and no doubt he had put all his strength into doing it well. No man will put his best into any task which he does not undertake in such a spirit. It is a very plain piece of homely wisdom that 'what is worth doing at all is worth doing well.' Without a lavish expenditure of the utmost care and effort, our work will tend to be slovenly and unpleasing to God, and man, and to ourselves. We may be sure there were no blots and bits of careless writing in Tertius' manuscript, and that he would not have claimed the friendly feelings of his Roman brethren, if he had not felt that he had put his best into the writing of this epistle. The great word of King David has a very wide application. 'I will not take that which is thine for the Lord, nor offer burnt offerings without cost.'

Tertius' salutation may suggest to us the best thing by which to be remembered. All his life before and after the hours spent at Paul's side has sunk in

oblivion.  He wished to be known only as having
written the Epistle.  Christian souls ought to desire
to live chiefly in the remembrance of those to whom
they have been known as having done some little bit
of work for Jesus Christ.  We may well ask ourselves
whether there is anything in our lives by which we
should thus wish to be remembered.  All our many
activities will sink into silence; but if the stream of
our life, which has borne along down its course so
much mud and sand, has brought some grains of gold
in the form of faithful and loving service to Christ
and men—these will not be lost in the ocean, but
treasured by Him.  What we do for Jesus and to
spread the knowledge of His name is the immortal
part of our mortal lives, and abides in His memory
and in blessed results in our own characters, when all
the rest that made our busy and often stormy days
has passed into oblivion.  All that we know of Tertius
who wrote this Epistle is that he wrote it.  Well will
it be for us if the summary of our lives be something
like that of his!

## QUARTUS A BROTHER

'Quartus a brother.'—ROMANS xvi. 28.

I AM afraid very few of us read often, or with much
interest, those long lists of names at the end of Paul's
letters.  And yet there are plenty of lessons in them,
if anybody will look at them lovingly and carefully.
There does not seem much in these three words; but
I am very much mistaken if they will not prove to be
full of beauty and pathos, and to open out into a

wonderful revelation of what Christianity is and does, as soon as we try to freshen them up into some kind of human interest.

It is easy for us to make a little picture of this brother Quartus. He is evidently an entire stranger to the Church in Rome. They had never heard his name before: none of them knew anything about him. Further, he is evidently a man of no especial reputation or position in the Church at Corinth, from which Paul writes. He contrasts strikingly with the others who send salutations to Rome. 'Timotheus, my workfellow'—the companion and helper of the Apostle, whose name was known everywhere among the Churches, heads the list. Then come other prominent men of his more immediate circle. Then follows a loving greeting from Paul's amanuensis, who, naturally, as the pen is in his own hand, says: '*I*, Tertius, who wrote this epistle, salute you in the Lord.'. Then Paul begins again to dictate, and the list runs on. Next comes a message from 'Gaius mine host, and of the whole Church'—an influential man in the community, apparently rich, and willing, as well as able, to extend to them large and loving hospitality. Erastus, the chamberlain or treasurer of the city, follows—a man of consequence in Corinth. And then, among all these people of mark, comes the modest, quiet Quartus. He has no wealth like Gaius, nor civic position like Erastus, nor wide reputation like Timothy. He is only a good, simple, unknown Christian. He feels a spring of love open in his heart to these brethren far across the sea, whom he never met. He would like them to know that he thought lovingly of them, and to be lovingly thought of by them. So he begs a little corner in Paul's letter, and gets it;

and there, in his little niche, like some statue of a
forgotten saint, scarce seen amidst the glories of a
great cathedral, 'Quartus a brother' stands to all time.

The first thing that strikes me in connection with
these words is, how deep and real they show that new
bond of Christian love to have been.

A little incident of this sort is more impressive than
any amount of mere talk about the uniting influence
of the Gospel. Here we get a glimpse of the power
in actual operation in a man's heart, and if we think
of all that this simple greeting presupposes and implies, and of all that had to be overcome before it
could have been sent, we may well see in it the sign
of the greatest revolution that was ever wrought in
men's relations to one another. Quartus was an in-
habitant of Corinth, from which city this letter was
written. His Roman name may indicate Roman
descent, but of that we cannot be sure. Just as
probably he may have been a Greek by birth, and so
have had to stretch his hand across a deep crevasse
of national antipathy, in order to clasp the hands
of his brethren in the great city. There was little love
lost between Rome, the rough imperious conqueror,
and Corinth, prostrate and yet restive under her
bonds, and nourishing remembrances of a freedom
which Rome had crushed, and of a culture that Rome
haltingly followed.

And how many other deep gulfs of separation had
to be bridged before that Christian sense of oneness
could be felt! It is impossible for us to throw ourselves completely back to the condition of things which
the Gospel found. The world then was like some great
field of cooled lava on the slopes of a volcano, all
broken up by a labyrinth of clefts and cracks, at the

2 c

bottom of which one can see the flicker of sulphurous flames. Great gulfs of national hatred, of fierce enmities of race, language, and religion; wide separations of social condition, far profounder than anything of the sort which we know, split mankind into fragments. On the one side was the freeman, on the other, the slave; on the one side, the Gentile, on the other, the Jew; on the one side, the insolence and hard-handedness of Roman rule, on the other, the impotent, and therefore envenomed, hatred of conquered peoples.

And all this fabric, full of active repulsions and disintegrating forces, was bound together into an artificial and unreal unity by the iron clamp of Rome's power, holding up the bulging walls that were ready to fall—the unity of the slave-gang manacled together for easier driving. Into this hideous condition of things the Gospel comes, and silently flings its clasping tendrils over the wide gaps, and binds the crumbling structure of human society with a new bond, real and living. We know well enough that that was so, but we are helped to apprehend it by seeing, as it were, the very process going on before our eyes, in this message from 'Quartus a brother.'

It reminds us that the very notion of humanity, and of the brotherhood of man, is purely Christian. A world-embracing society, held together by love, was not dreamt of before the Gospel came; and since the Gospel came it is more than a dream. If you wrench away the idea from its foundation, as people do who talk about fraternity, and seek to bring it to pass without Christ, it is a mere piece of Utopian sentiment —a fine dream. But in Christianity it worked. It works imperfectly enough, God knows. Still there is

some reality in it, and some power. The Gospel first
of all produced the thing and the practice, and then
the theory came afterwards. The Church did not talk
much about the brotherhood of man, or the unity of
the race; but simply ignored all distinctions, and
gathered into the fold the slave and his master, the
Roman and his subject, fair-haired Goths and swarthy
Arabians, the worshippers of Odin and of Zeus, the
Jew and the Gentile. That actual unity, utterly irrespective of all distinctions, which came naturally in
the train of the Gospel, was the first attempt to realise
the oneness of the race, and first taught the world
that all men were brethren.

And before this simple word of greeting could have
been sent, and the unknown man in Corinth felt love
to a company of unknown men in Rome, some profound new impulse must have been given to the world;
something altogether unlike any of the forces hitherto
in existence. What was that? What should it be but
the story of One who gave Himself for the whole
world, who binds men into a unity because of His
common relation to them all, and through whom the
great proclamation can be made: 'There is neither
Jew nor Greek, there is neither bond nor free, there
is neither male nor female, for ye are all one in Christ
Jesus.' Brother Quartus' message, like some tiny
flower above-ground which tells of a spreading root
beneath, is a modest witness to that mighty revolution, and presupposes the preaching of a Saviour
in whom he and his unseen friends in Rome are
one.

So let us learn not to confine our sympathy and the
play of our Christian affection within the limits of
our personal knowledge. We must go further a-field

than that. Like this man, let us sometimes send our thoughts across mountains and seas. He knew nobody in the Roman Church, and nobody knew him, but he wished to stretch out his hand to them, and to feel, as it were, the pressure of their fingers in his palm. That is a pattern for us.

Let me suggest another thing. Quartus was a Corinthian. The Corinthian Church was remarkable for its quarrellings and dissensions. One said, 'I am of Paul, and another, I of Apollos, and I of Cephas, and I of Christ.' I wonder if our friend Quartus belonged to any of these parties? There is nothing more likely than that he had a much warmer glow of Christian love to the brethren over there in Rome than to those who sat on the same bench with him in the upper room at Corinth. For you know that sometimes it is true about people, as well as about scenery, that 'distance lends enchantment to the view.' A great many of us have much keener sympathies with 'brethren' who are well out of our reach, and whose peculiarities do not jar against ours, than with those who are nearest. I do not say Quartus was one of these, but he may very well have been one of the wranglers in Corinth who found it much easier to love his brother whom he had not seen than his brother whom he had seen. So take the hint, if you need it. Do not let your Christian love go wandering away abroad only, but keep some for home consumption.

Again, how simply, and with what unconscious beauty, the deep reason for our Christian unity is given in that one word, a 'Brother.' As if he had said, Never mind telling them anything about what I am, what place I hold, or what I do. Tell them I am a brother, that will be enough. It is the only name by which I care to be known; it is the name which explains my love to them.

We are brethren because we are sons of one Father. So that favourite name, by which the early Christians knew each other, rested upon and proclaimed the deep truth that they knew themselves to be all partakers of a common life derived from one Parent. When they said they were brethren, they implied, 'We have been born again by the word of God, which liveth and abideth for ever.' The great Christian truth of regeneration, the communication of a divine life from God the Father, through Christ the Son, by the Holy Spirit, is the foundation of Christian brotherhood. So the name is no mere piece of effusive sentiment, but expresses a profound fact. 'To as many as received Him, to them gave He power to become the sons of God,' and therein to become the brethren of all His sons.

That is the true ground of our unity, and of our obligation to love all who are begotten of Him. You cannot safely put them on any other footing. All else—identity of opinion, similarity of practice and ceremonial, local or national ties, and the like—all else is insufficient. It may be necessary for Christian communities to require in addition a general identity of opinion, and even some uniformity in government and form of worship; but if ever they come to fancy that such subordinate conditions of visible oneness are the grounds of their spiritual unity, and to enforce these as such, they are slipping off the real foundation, and are perilling their character as Churches of Christ. The true ground of the unity of all Christians is here: 'Have we not all one Father?' We possess a kindred life derived from Him. We are a family of brethren because we are sons.

Another remark is, how strangely and unwittingly this good man has got himself an immortality by that passing thought of his. One loving message has won for him the prize for which men have joyfully given life itself,—an eternal place in history. Wheresoever the Gospel is preached there also shall this be told as a memorial of him. How much surprised he would have been if, as he leaned forward to Tertius hurrying to end his task and said, 'Send my love too,' anybody had told him that that one act of his would last as long as the world, and his name be known for ever! And how much ashamed some of the other people in the New Testament would have been if they had known that their passing faults—the quarrel of Euodia and Syntyche for instance—were to be gibbeted for ever in the same fashion! How careful they would have been, and we would be, of our behaviour if we knew that it was to be pounced down upon and made immortal in that style! Suppose you were to be told —Your thoughts and acts to-morrow at twelve o'clock will be recorded for all the world to read—you would be pretty careful how you behaved. When a speaker sees the reporters in front of him, he weighs his words.

Well, Quartus' little message is written down here, and the world knows it. All our words and works are getting put down too, in another Book up there, and it is going to be read out one day. It does seem wonderful that you and I should live as we do, knowing that all the while that God is recording it all. If we are not ashamed to do things, and let Him note them on His tablets that they may be for the time to come, for ever and ever, it is strange that we should be more careful to attitudinise and pose ourselves before one another than before Him. Let us then keep ever in mind 'those pure eyes and perfect witness of the all-judging' God. The eternal record of this little message is only a symbol of the eternal life and eternal record of all our transient and trivial thoughts and deeds before Him. Let us live so that each act, if recorded, would shine with some modest ray of true light like brother Quartus' greeting, and let us seek that, like him,—all else about us being forgotten, position, talents, wealth, buried in the dust, —we may be remembered, if we are remembered at all, by such a biography as is condensed into these three words. Who would not wish to be embalmed, so to speak, in such a record? Who would not wish to have such an epitaph as this? A sweet fate to live for ever in the world's memory by three words which tell his name, his Christianity, and his brotherly love! So far as we are remembered at all, may the like be our life's history and our epitaph!

## Date Due

| | | |
|---|---|---|
| MR 10 '54 | | |
| DE 19 '55 | FEB 2 8 '65 | |
| JA 3 - '56 | JAN 2 3 '56 | |
| MA 17 '56 | | |
| AUG | | |
| NOV 1 0 '60 | | |
| JAN | | |
| FEB 2 3 '62 | | |
| MAR '62 | | |
| APR 4 '62 | | |
| APR 2 3 | | |
| APR '62 | | |
| OCT 2 7 '64 | | |
| '66 | | |
| AUG 4 '66 | | |
| JAN '67 | | |
| AUG 1 8 '67 | | |

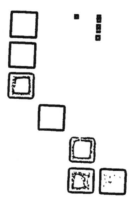

CPSIA information can be obtained
at www.ICGtesting.com
Printed in the USA
LVHW081617020820
662195LV00025B/133

9 781373 368980